ASPECTS OF TOURISM
Series Editors: **Chris Cooper** *(Oxford Brookes University, UK)*, **C. Michael Hall** *(University of Canterbury, New Zealand)* and **Dallen J. Timothy** *(Arizona State University, USA)*

Aspects of Tourism is an innovative, multifaceted series, which comprises authoritative reference handbooks on global tourism regions, research volumes, texts and monographs. It is designed to provide readers with the latest thinking on tourism worldwide and push back the frontiers of tourism knowledge. The volumes are authoritative, readable and user-friendly, providing accessible sources for further research. Books in the series are commissioned to probe the relationship between tourism and cognate subject areas such as strategy, development, retailing, sport and environmental studies.

Full details of all the books in this series and of all our other publications can be found on http://www.channelviewpublications.com, or by writing to Channel View Publications, St Nicholas House, 31–34 High Street, Bristol BS1 2AW, UK.

ASPECTS OF TOURISM
Series Editors: Chris Cooper *(Oxford Brookes University, UK)*, C. Michael Hall *(University of Canterbury, New Zealand)* and Dallen J. Timothy *(Arizona State University, USA)*

Sport Tourism Development
Second Edition

Tom Hinch and James Higham

CHANNEL VIEW PUBLICATIONS
Bristol • Buffalo • Toronto

This book is dedicated to Lorraine Hinch and Linda Buxton and to all of our teachers and mentors who have influenced our careers and lives so profoundly.

Library of Congress Cataloging in Publication Data
A catalog record for this book is available from the Library of Congress.
Hinch, Thomas.
Sport Tourism Development/Tom Hinch and James Higham. – 2nd ed.
Includes bibliographical references and index.
1. Sports and tourism. I. Higham, James E. S. II. Title.
G155.A1H56 2011
338.4'791–dc22 2011015450

British Library Cataloguing in Publication Data
A catalogue entry for this book is available from the British Library.

ISBN-13: 978-1-84541-195-4 (hbk)
ISBN-13: 978-1-84541-194-7 (pbk)

Channel View Publications
UK: St Nicholas House, 31-34 High Street, Bristol BS1 2AW, UK.
USA: UTP, 2250 Military Road, Tonawanda, NY 14150, USA.
Canada: UTP, 5201 Dufferin Street, North York, Ontario M3H 5T8, Canada.

Copyright © 2011 Tom Hinch and James Higham.

The policy of Multilingual Matters/Channel View Publications is to use papers that are natural, renewable and recyclable products, made from wood grown in sustainable forests. In the manufacturing process of our books, and to further support our policy, preference is given to printers that have FSC and PEFC Chain of Custody certification. The FSC and/or PEFC logos will appear on those books where full certification has been granted to the printer concerned.

Typeset by Datapage International Ltd.
Printed and bound by CPI Group (UK) Ltd, Croydon, CR0 4YY

Contents

Illustrations

Figures

Tables

Case Studies

Focus Points

Acknowledgements

This second edition, like the first, has incurred various debts of favour. Elinor Robertson (Channel View Publications) and Aspects of Tourism series editors, Chris Cooper (Oxford Brookes University), Michael Hall (University of Canterbury) and Dallen Timothy (Arizona State University) provided much appreciated support for the development of a second edition. Work on this publication project took place during a period of study leave in June 2010, supported by a research grant from the University of Otago which is gratefully acknowledged, as is the wonderful hospitality that James received during his visit to Edmonton at that time. The research assistance provided by Debbie Hopkins (University of Otago) during the initial preparation for this second edition was of great value, as were the contributions of Stacy-Lynn Sant and Stephanie Qinyan Feng (University of Alberta) during the later stages of this project.

We are particularly appreciative of the case study contributions of Heather Bell, Heather Gibson, Anne-Marie Hede, Debbie Hopkins, Pamm Kellett, Cory Kulczycki, Mike Morgan, Ghazali Musa, Greg Ramshaw, Geoff Wall and Mike Weed whose insights have stimulated our work in the field of sport tourism. We were greatly saddened by the untimely passing of Mike Morgan shortly after he made his contribution to this book. His work on sport and the tourist experience has greatly influenced our writing and teaching on this aspect of the field. Our deliberations on this subject have also been influenced by the contributions of many other researchers who are cited throughout the text. Acknowledgement of contributions from and discussions with Heather Gibson (University of Florida) during her visit to the University of Otago in February/March 2010 is particularly necessary. We have also been influenced by our students, especially those enrolled in the Sport Tourism Development class during the spring of 2010 at the University of Manitoba, who provided direct feedback on this second edition and whose enthusiasm for the topic was a major motivation for us. In the early stages of our collaboration, the Sports Management Association of Australia and New Zealand and the Leisure Studies Association (United Kingdom) hosted conferences that were valuable in developing our thoughts on sport tourism. More recently, the first Commonwealth Conference on Sport Tourism (Kota Kinabalu, Malaysia), which took place in May 2008, served an equally important purpose.

    The administrative support of Suzanne French (University of Alberta), Diana Evans, Helen Dunn and Jo O'Brien (University of Otago) has been crucial. The contributions of Jo O'Brien and Diana Evans in terms of bibliographic and manuscript management (at a time that was unreasonably close to Christmas and summer holidays) have been hugely appreciated. We are also indebted to all of our colleagues with the Faculty of Physical Education and Recreation (University of Alberta) and the Department of Tourism (University of Otago). Thank you for providing a stimulating and enjoyable academic environment. Finally, the support of our immediate families, Lorraine, Lindsay and Gillian, and Linda, Alexandra, Kate and George, has been critical to the completion of this second edition. We both greatly appreciate the continuing and loyal support of our families.

Thomas Hinch
Edmonton, Canada
James Higham
Dunedin, New Zealand

Case Study Contributors

Heather L. Bell, MA, PhD Candidate, Department of Tourism, Recreation and Sport Management, University of Florida, Gainesville, FL, USA. Email: heather.bell@hhp.ufl.edu

Heather J. Gibson, PhD, Associate Professor, Department of Tourism, Recreation and Sport Management and Associate Director, Eric Friedeim Tourism Institute, University of Florida, Gainesville, FL, USA. Email hgibson@hhp.ufl.edu

Anne-Marie Hede, PhD, Associate Professor (Marketing), Victoria University, Melbourne, Australia. Email: anne-marie.hede@vu.edu.au

Debbie Hopkins, MA, PhD Candidate, Department of Tourism, School of Business, University of Otago, Dunedin, New Zealand. Email: debbie.hopkins@otago.ac.nz

Pamm Kellett, PhD, Associate Professor, Deakin University, Melbourne, Australia. Email: pamm.kellett@deakin.edu.au

Cory Kulczycki, MA, PhD Candidate, Faculty of Physical Education and Recreation, University of Alberta, Edmonton, AB, Canada. Email: corykulc@ualberta.ca

Mike Morgan, BA, Bphil, Former Senior Lecturer, Leisure and Tourism Marketing, Bournemouth University, Bournemouth, Poole, Dorset, UK.

Ghazali Musa, PhD, Associate Professor, Faculty of Business and Accountancy, University Malaya, Kuala Lumpur, Malaysia. Email: ghaz8zz@gmail.com

Gregory Ramshaw, PhD, Assistant Professor, Parks, Recreation & Tourism Management, Clemson University, Clemson, SC, USA. Email: gramsha@clemson.edu

Geoffrey Wall, PhD, Professor of Geography and Environmental Management, University of Waterloo, ON, Canada. Email: gwall@uwaterloo.ca

Mike Weed, PhD, Professor of Sport in Society; Director, Centre for Sport, Physical Education & Activity Research (SPEAR), Canterbury Christ Church University, Canterbury, Kent, UK. Email: mike.weed@canterbury.ac.uk

Foreword

The first edition of this book was written in 2002 and published in 2004. At that time, as we noted at the outset of the first edition, the World Tourism Organization and International Olympic Committee had recently hosted a major international conference on sport and tourism in February 2001 in Barcelona, Spain. That conference remains a defining moment in the recognition of the relationship between sport and tourism, a point that has been subsequently addressed by a rapidly expanding group of academic researchers and graduate students, in a growing body of academic literature serving the field.

At that time the field was at a stage of exploration and development. Standeven and De Knop's (1999) book *Sport Tourism* had provided an important platform that offered up a range of avenues for further development of the field. Building upon the earlier works of scholars such as Bale (1989), Glyptis (1991) and Redmond (1991), researchers such as Delpy (1997), Gammon and Robinson (1997), Weed and Bull (1997a, 1997b), Gibson (1998), Chalip (2001) and Green and Chalip (1998) attended directly to the development of the field. To this growing field of scholarship, we sought to make our own theoretical (e.g. Hinch & Higham, 2001) and empirical (e.g. Higham & Hinch, 2002, 2003) contributions. The theoretical framework developed in Hinch and Higham (2001) provided, with minor modification, the structure of the first edition of this book, which is retained for the purposes of this second edition.

This field of academic endeavour has, pleasingly, stimulated a growing range of scholarly contributions. Part of the reason for this is the dynamic and ever-changing sport and tourism landscapes. Most immediately, Weed and Bull's (2003, 2009) thorough treatment of the study of sport tourism policy, participants and providers, as well as Gibson's (2006) edited work addressing sport tourism concepts and theories, have made significant contributions to the academic field. To these discourses we contributed *Sport and Tourism: Globalization, Mobility and Identity* in 2009 (Higham & Hinch, 2009). Equally important has been the transformation of the *Journal of Sport & Tourism* from 2005 into an academic journal of high scholarly aspirations and robust academic standards (see Case study 2.1). This journal has become especially prominent in the development of sport-and-tourism-related research and research agendas over the last five years.

These publications, and others, point to significant changes in the way that sport and tourism are managed (increasingly via genuine collaborative efforts involving multiple stakeholders), in terms of policy and planning settings, the ways in which sports events are staged and the facilitation of sport-related tourist experiences. They point to the changing ways in which sports fans through collective behaviours may burnish place imagery and enhance the visibility of sports places. This relates closely to the concept of co-creating sport experiences through the subjective, spontaneous and unscripted (but facilitated) interplay of hosts and guests.

There is also growing evidence of the power of participation sports and recreational activities in terms of connecting people to place. This aspect of sport and tourism has taken place in association with a distinct blurring of the boundaries that once quite rigidly existed between event, active and nostalgia-based sport tourism experiences. We now see expanding evidence of sports events that accommodate all levels of competitive and recreational participation, cater specifically to wide-ranging spectator and supporter groups and immerse all comers in the historical and/or heritage values associated with sports, sports events and sport places. Simultaneously, over the last decade, we have seen the accelerating pace at which sports resources have become transportable and the opportunities and threats that transportability throws up in terms of the competitiveness of tourism destinations. We have observed with interest the growth of lifestyle/extreme sport and widespread interest in health and active living. The nostalgia and heritage associated with sport and tourism have become an increasingly important part of this mix over the course of the last decade.

Clearly much has changed in the intervening years since the first edition of this book was published. These dynamics have inspired us to revisit the subject of sport and tourism development and to undertake a second edition of this book.

Tom Hinch and James Higham

Publications cited here are listed in the References

Part 1
Introduction

Chapter 1

Sport Tourism in Times of Change

In terms of popular participation, and in some aspects of practice, (sport and tourism) are inextricably linked ... and there are sound reasons for those links to strengthen.

Glyptis, 1989: 165

Introduction

The Football World Cup, hosted most recently by South Africa in June–July 2010, is one of the world's premier team sports events. It is a month-long showcase of football competition, performed in association with (and at times overshadowed by) expressions of high emotion, personal and collective identity, and fervent nationalism. Indeed in a global world, international football is one of the most evident and emotional expressions of national identity (Tomlinson & Young, 2006). The Football World Cup is a stage for Shakespearean-like performances of emotion and drama, glory and despair. Such is the compelling nature of the sport that the stage is inevitably shared by competing actors, including political aspirants, multinational corporate actors, media corporations, spectators and tourists (Cornelissen, 2010).

The Football World Cup is the apex of elite competitive team sport. It stands upon a superstructure of ever-expanding and diversifying participation in sport and recreational activity. Once sport-related international travel was the domain of elite athletes, representing their countries in international competition. With hyper-mobility has come sport-related travel that extends across all spatial scales, levels of competition and competitive–participatory, serious–casual and active–passive dimensions of engagement (Higham & Hinch, 2009). Thus, the Football World Cup has become but one of the manifold diverse forms of sport-related tourism.

Sports, particularly large-scale sporting events dating back to the ancient Olympic Games, have long influenced travel (Keller, 2001). Historically they represent gatherings of athletes, spectators, politicians, royalty and dignitaries, merchants and business people, all seeking an association of some form with sports events that are bounded in space and time. However, the high numbers of travellers currently seeking active and passive involvement in sports is a more recent development (Delpy, 1998). It is increasingly clear that the scale, complexity and potential of sport tourism, as well as the expanding mutual interests of the sport and tourism industries that have developed as a consequence, demand that academic and industry expertise be directed towards this field. This book is about sport tourism and its manifestations in space and time. It seeks to articulate the defining qualities of sport that explain its unique contribution to tourism. It then applies tourism development concepts and themes to the study of sport tourism. Three key questions emerge in the context of sport tourism development: 'What makes sport unique as a tourist attraction or activity?' 'How is sport tourism manifested in space?' and 'How do these manifestations change over time?'.

The book is organised into five parts. Part 1 (Chapter 1) introduces the purpose, structure and goals of the book. It describes the development and growth of sport tourism, and then raises questions that are intended to demonstrate the relevance and challenge the assumptions that the reader may have on this subject. Part 2 (Chapters 2–4) is titled Foundations for Sport Tourism Development. This part is intended to provide the reader with fundamentals in the study of sport tourism, its markets and development processes and the issues relating to sport tourism. Much progress has been made in the study of sport and tourism in recent years (see Chalip, 2006; Chalip & Mcguirty, 2004; Gammon & Ramshaw, 2007; Gibson, 2005; Gratton *et al.*, 2005; Higham & Hinch, 2009; Hinch & Higham, 2005; Hudson, 2003; Jones & Green, 2006; Morgan, 2007; Weed, 2005, 2008a). Chapters 2–4 provide an opportunity to review current insights into sport tourism as a basis for the discussions that follow.

Part 3 (Chapters 5–7) focuses on the spatial elements of sport tourism development. These chapters examine sport tourism development in relation to space, place and the environment. Each of these topics represents important aspects and manifestations of development. Part 4 (Chapters 8–10) examines sport tourism development in relation to time. The short-term, medium-term and long-term time horizons provide a temporal framework that allows the authors to consider the immediate sport tourism experience, sport tourism and seasonality, and the dynamic interrelationship between sport and tourism within evolutionary frameworks. Part 5 (Chapter 11) concludes by reviewing the preceding discussions to serve as a platform from which to consider the future of sport and tourism, and sport tourism research. This structure provides a framework that allows the authors to raise questions relating to sport tourism development in space and time and to address these questions through the application of relevant theory.

Sport Tourism in Times of Change

Democratisation, the process of opening access to previously restricted opportunities, is a term that applies to the development of sport and tourism in the latter half of the 20th century (Standeven & De Knop, 1999). Participation in some sports remains defined by factors such as social class. 'Irrespective of culture or historical period, people use sport to distinguish themselves and to reflect their status and prestige' (Booth & Loy, 1999: 1). The existence of post-class egalitarian consumer cultures in sport is refuted by Booth and Loy (1999), who state that similar-status groups generally share lifestyle and consumption patterns. The links that exist between socio-demographic status, lifestyle and consumption patterns in sport and tourism heighten the value and utility of defining sport tourism markets in practice.

That said, the forces of globalisation (Bernstein, 2000; Milne & Ateljevic, 2004; Thibault, 2009) and democratisation (Standeven & De Knop, 1999) have had significant implications for the consumption of sport and development processes in sport tourism (Chapter 4). The modern development of sport tourism, then, stands at the cross section of contemporary trends that include the following:

(1) the expanding demographic profile of participants in sports (Glyptis, 1989);
(2) heightened interests in health and fitness in Western societies since the 1970s (Collins, 1991);
(3) increasing demand for active engagement in recreational pursuits while on holiday since the 1980s (Priestley, 1995); and
(4) growing interest in the prominent roles played by sports and sports events in urban renewal and urban imagery, and the potential to leverage tourism opportunities associated with sports events (Getz, 1998).

These processes have been driven by economic and political forces (Collins, 1991; Cooper et al., 1993; Gibson, 1998; Giddens, 1993; Hall, 2004; Nauright, 1996) and changing social attitudes and values (Jackson et al., 2001; Kurtzman & Zauhar, 1995; Redmond, 1991). They have also been facilitated by technological advances, such as satellite television broadcasting (Halberstam, 1999), that have influenced the 'sportification of society' (Standeven & De Knop, 1999).

Faulkner et al. (1998: 3) note that 'as a consequence of these developments, the geographical extent and volume of sports related travel has grown exponentially'. Glyptis (1989) provides an early demonstration of these trends. She notes in a study of western European countries that all had experienced strong growth in interest in recreational sport during the 1980s. Furthermore, participation was increasing in all social strata, most sports were receiving participants from an expanding social spectrum and all had recorded significant increases in youth holidays, short breaks and second holidays. The two decades that have followed have served to strengthen these trends (Hall, 1992a; International Olympic

Committee & World Tourism Organization, 2001). Much has continued to change in the study of sport and tourism. Intensifying commercial demands in elite sport, and the continuation apace of globalisation among other things, have changed the relationship between sport and the environment, sport and place, sports fans and their teams, and sports participants and their constructions of identity (Higham & Hinch, 2009).

The Foundations of Sport Tourism Development

The growth of sport tourism demands critical consideration of relevant development issues. This task requires that sport tourism be defined and conceptualised in ways that highlight rather than obscure the diversity of interests in sport and tourism. A number of definitions exist in this field, which afford the opportunity to study sport tourism from various perspectives. For the purposes of this book, sport tourism is conceptualised by considering sport as a tourist attraction, and by highlighting the defining qualities of sport that collectively constitute a unique contribution to tourism (Chapter 2). This approach is intended to give prominence to the dynamic and complex nature of sport and tourism, thereby helping to clarify the parameters and scope of this book.

The diversity of sport tourism markets is explored in Chapter 3, which highlights the rich diversity of motivations, and therefore, the varied approaches to market segmentation that exist in sport tourism. Bale (1989: 9) notes that 'work-play, freedom-constraint, competition-recreation, and process-product are only some of the continua on which sports can be located'. Thus, the experiences of sport tourists are likely to vary considerably with the motivations that travellers hold towards their chosen sports. The motivations associated with sport tourism niche markets raise intriguing questions for sports-event organisers and promoters, sports associations, managers of sporting venues, destination managers and tourism marketers. To what extent, for example, are highly competitive professional athletes interested in tourist experiences at a sport destination, and how may the potential of this market be fully achieved? The promotional opportunities that derive from the association of high-profile athletes with specific tourist destinations are part of this potential. How does tourism based on professional sport differ from the tourism development opportunities associated with recreational sport (Focus point 1.1)? Tourist experiences relating to sport vary within and between niche market segments, which raises questions as to how these markets can be better understood by sport and tourism managers who seek to meet changing sport and travel preferences.

Focus point 1.1
Participation Youth Football in Scandinavia

The largest football tournament in the world, as measured in terms of participation, is the Gothia Cup (Göteborg, Sweden). In 2002, it attracted 25,100 participants (average age 15.5 years), representing 1246 teams from 118 countries who took part in a tournament that included 3420 games played on 72 fields. The opening ceremony was attended by 40,200 people and the finals by 26,700 spectators. The tourist corollary of this event is significant. Direct tourist income of SEK 18 million was spent in the city of Göteborg, generating significant tax income. The Gothia Heden Centre received 295,000 visits in five days during the event. Television broadcasts of Gothia Cup were carried in nine countries, and Swedish newspapers published 1152 articles on the event. International media coverage was provided by 102 accredited journalists from 28 countries (Tourist Authorities of Göteborg, 2002). Similarly, Norway Cup, which was founded in 1972, is also contested annually by more than 1200 teams from around the world. It involves youth teams with players aged 13–19 years in 11- and 7-a-side competitions. The tourism implications of the competition are substantial. It attracts more than 20,000 participants and, because of their age, it also attracts large entourages of team personnel and family support. In a deliberate attempt to encourage secondary trips and leisure activities, all participants are entitled to free travel with the Oslo Transportation System, and are entitled to gratis entrance into museums and outdoor swimming pools in Oslo. Participants also receive a multi-language guide to touring in Norway. The fact that 573 journalists representing print, radio and television outlets from the United States, Mexico, Brazil, Jamaica, Angola, Nigeria, South Africa, China, Thailand and England were accredited in 2001 demonstrates the international significance of this event (Leisure Time, 2002). The growing importance of non-elite sports competitors is underscored by Getz and Andersson (2010). Their study of the Göteborg half marathon draws on theories of serious leisure, social worlds, recreation specialisation and ego involvement to explore the event–tourist profiles of high-involvement amateur distance runners. They present evidence that the careers of amateur distance runners follow a trajectory that can be understood in terms of various dimensions (e.g. travel styles, event participation and destination choice). The implications for destination managers who seek to target non-elite competitive sports participants are significant.

The logical extension of this market analysis is consideration of development processes, sustainability and planning interventions. Development issues that are of particular interest to sport and tourism practitioners include those related to commodification/authenticity, globalisation and industry fragmentation. Hitherto, little consideration has been given to the modification of sports competitions (e.g. through rule changes, length and timing of the competition season, and the televising of live sport) and the implications of perceptions of place and destination imagery associated with sports (Focus point 1.2). The relevance of these processes and issues is introduced to the reader and explored in Chapter 4, thereby providing an important part of the foundation upon which the subsequent chapters are based.

Focus point 1.2
Sport, Heritage and Culture

Heritage and culture contribute to make tourism destinations unique. Sport and sports venues often represent a unique expression of the culture of the destination. UK sports venues such as Lord's (cricket), Wimbledon (lawn tennis), Twickenham (rugby union), St. Andrews (golf), Wembley (football) and Royal Ascot (horse racing) are recognised as the spiritual homes of their sports. Sports' most prestigious tournaments are contested at these venues. With time, they have developed their own aura of tradition. Each represents a significant expression of the heritage and culture of Britain (British Tourist Authority, 2000), and many have developed museums to foster visitor experiences and cement this spiritual status. Other sports, such as baseball (United States), Australian Rules football (Australia) and Thai boxing (Thailand), represent distinctive cultural elements of a destination. These sports allow ready access to the culture of a destination. As an example, and in reference to Maori *haka* (challenge), Laidlaw (2010) notes that since the 1980s the All Blacks performance of *haka* before rugby internationals has been performed with 'genuine cultural meaning'. 'Its evolution mirrors perfectly the cultural renaissance of the Maori in New Zealand' (Laidlaw, 2010: 186). The performance of *haka* on the sports field is available to both New Zealanders and tourists and may form an important and unique part of the visitor experience at a destination (see also Chalip, 2010).

Sport Tourism Development and Space

Chapters 5–8 consider how sport tourism is manifested in space and how these manifestations may be influenced. Chapter 5 explores the interrelationships linking sport tourism–generating areas and destinations, and the travel patterns associated with sport tourism markets. The basic concepts and themes for this chapter have their roots in economic geography. These concepts are drawn from the study of sports geography and the spatial analysis of sports (Bale, 1989, 1993a). Relevant management implications relate, for example, to the allocation of franchise regions within a league or decisions on where to build, develop or enhance sport resources and facilities. The ways in which sports may influence the spatial travel patterns and itineraries of visitors travelling within a destination, whether sport functions as a primary, secondary or tertiary attraction, are also discussed.

The sports played in an area influence the meanings that are attached to this space. Concepts of place and culture are explored in Chapter 6. In many ways, sport infuses tourism spaces with one of the most authentic types of attractions. The link between culture and sport takes many forms: sport and culture, sport as culture and sport subcultures. All of these variations contribute to the meaning attached to sport tourism places. Strategies that incorporate these cultural variations can be used to promote the place to various markets. There are, however, significant challenges associated with the commodification of culture.

The environment is the subject of the third spatial dimension (Chapter 7). This chapter considers the common resource base for sport and tourism facilities and infrastructure. Quite different issues are associated with natural resources and built facilities in sport tourism. Outdoor sports such as downhill skiing, for example, tend to be dependent on specific types of landscape, with the potential for irreversible environmental impacts. Other types of sport are more transportable and feature standard facilities that can be built in locations designed to maximise market access. The development of built resources for sport, and the shift towards artificial, enclosed and controlled sports environments, is one of the most telling and obvious trends of the last decade (Focus point 1.3). The question is, to what extent can nature be removed from sports, and sports from nature, and will there be a backlash?

Focus point 1.3
Doha Going Underground

Increasingly, built sports resources are becoming more removed from nature. Enclosed stadiums simultaneously represent the protection of sports from weather-related interruption, and the removal of sports from unique, place-specific weather conditions. In 2010, Wimbledon revealed the completion of a roof enclosing the historic centre court (departing from the continuing tradition at the US and

French Opens where the Grand Slam tournaments remain outdoors).
While Wimbledon has regularly been subject to weather interruptions,
there are elements of nostalgia associated with weather delays (which
allow for a pint of lager on the hill, or strawberries and cream for some
spectators), the players taking shelter, and the ballboys and ballgirls
bringing the covers onto the centre court. Weather interruptions have
also played a part in swings in the ebb and flow of historic games, and
influenced the outcome of matches and some unforgettable chapters
of this tournament history. The roof may therefore represent a loss
of authenticity for some. While roofed stadiums have become
more common during the last decade, Doha (Qatar) has begun work
on the first underground stadium, which is intended to be complete in
time for the 2011 Asian Cup football tournament and other future
football events. The development of standardised sportscapes extends
to nature-based sports such as golf courses which are manicured to the
point that elements of naturalness are entirely removed. The question
arises as to whether the production of sports in standardised facilities
that represent a complete removal from unique elements of place
actually represents a threat to tourism. Will there be a backlash? Does
standardisation ultimately result in a complete loss of local uniqueness? Does it lead to a loss of place differentiation, uniqueness and
recognisability? If it does, the visibility and status of unique destinations that seek to host sports events will be compromised as the
venues for sport become more standardised, and less distinctive and
recognisable (see also Case study 6.1; Focus point 7.2).

Sport Tourism Development and Time

Part 4 (Chapters 8–10) considers the manifestations of sport tourism in
time. Chapter 8 explores the short-term temporal horizon of sport
tourism. The visitor experience is concerned with the timing and
duration of visits, engagement in sports, tourist and leisure activities at
the destination and visitor expenditures. It is also associated with
recollections of the tourist experience and, therefore, visitor satisfaction
and repeat visitation. Different forms of sport tourism manifest themselves in contrasting tourist experiences. Chapter 8 explores manifestations of sport tourist experience employing the classic framework
developed by Clawson and Knetsch (1966), which has been applied
widely in the study of the tourist experience. This framework lends itself
to consideration of the co-creation of sports experiences at a destination
(Morgan, 2007) but situates the sport activities experience, people and
places within the wider temporal time frame of pre-trip anticipation and
post-visit reflection. Chapter 8 also examines the relevance of the sport

and tourism systems that mediate the sport tourist experience at a destination. This approach is intended to provide insights into strategies that may influence and enhance sport tourism visitor experiences.

The medium term or seasonal dimension of sport tourism is the subject of Chapter 9. Few tourism destinations are unaffected by systematic seasonal fluctuations in the tourism phenomenon. Strategies designed to extend shoulder seasons or create all-season destinations are commonplace. Therefore, the manner in which sports moderate, or may be engineered to alter seasonal patterns of visitation, is worthy of careful consideration. The reverse also applies, whereby tourism may influence patterns of seasonal participation in sport. It is not enough to know that there are seasonal patterns of sport and tourism, but to understand the reasons for these patterns is also important. Leisure constraints theory provides insights into such patterns. Consideration can then be given to strategies, such as facility design, pricing and promotions and event production, that may moderate or alter patterns of seasonality in sport and tourism (Focus point 1.4).

Focus point 1.4
Sport and Seasonality

The technology of modern stadiums and arenas allows many sports to be performed without interference or interruption caused by the natural elements. The extent to which sports may become detached from the influences of the weather is, in many cases, so complete that sports managers may moderate the seasonal context of sports. The retractable stadium roof has significant implications for sport and tourism seasonality. Indeed, the first international rugby and cricket fixtures contested indoors took place out of season at Millennium Stadium, Cardiff (Wales), in October 1999, and Colonial Stadium, Melbourne (Australia), in July 2001, respectively. The former features a playing surface that rests on pallets which can be removed and replaced when necessary. Following these vanguard examples, the cases of enclosed stadiums have proliferated worldwide. For example, Sapporo, situated in Hokkaido, Japan's northern-most island, features a futuristic dome, where World Cup matches were played in 2002. The Sapporo Dome is an all-weather covered stadium designed with a view to the local climate conditions, particularly heavy snow in winter. This hi-tech facility, which combines indoor and outdoor arenas and an unprecedented hovering football stage, makes it possible to play at any time of the year regardless of the weather. The natural grass playing surface can be moved in and out of the stadium, being kept outside the dome to allow the grass to grow when the field is not in use and to provide a natural playing surface inside when needed. The entire lower section of the field is rolled into the Dome on a cushion of air. As it does so, a rotating seat system moves aside before the pitch turns sideways on its axis and the seating areas automatically slide back into place. The entire manoeuvre takes two hours to complete. The air inside is moderated by an air-conditioning unit and a natural ventilation system in summer, while in winter spectators are kept comfortable by a heating system applied directly to the seats (http://fifaworldcup.yahoo.com/en/da/c/sapporo.html).

Chapter 10 examines the interrelationship between sport and tourism within an evolutionary or long-term context. Tourism development processes, as conceptualised in the evolution in tourism destinations through a life cycle (Butler, 1980), may be influenced by the powerful dynamics of sport. For example, evolving spatial patterns of sport may have a direct bearing on tourism development. The reverse is also true, as tourism may impact upon the types of sports practiced in destination areas. Golf serves as a good illustration of this process given its introduction into the 'new world' by Scottish migrants, and diffusion into new regions throughout the world in response to tourist demand. Nostalgia sport tourism is a unique form of tourism in which tourists search for sporting experiences associated with earlier periods.

The last decade has been characterised by a surge in demand for nostalgia and heritage in sport (Gammon & Ramshaw, 2007). Perhaps this is a response to the growing dominance of commercial interest in sport, reigning over the personal interests of fans and participants (Laidlaw, 2010). Clearly, sport is a dynamic field of study in terms of its manifestations in space and time and the interplay between sport and tourism. For example, the challenges associated with commodification, finding a balance between progress and tradition, and the accelerated nature of globalisation in sport need to be systematically explored with direct reference to the study of tourism. Figure 1.1 presents the framework that provides the structure for the chapters that follow. The chapters following this introductory chapter (Chapters 2–4) address the development, planning and market contexts that serve as a platform for the discussions presented in Chapters 5–10: the spatial and temporal dimensions of sport and tourism.

These spatial (space, place and environment) and temporal (experience, seasons and evolution) themes form the structure of Chapters 5–7 (Part 3) and Chapters 8–10 (Part 4), respectively. The foundations of the book, then, lie in the geographical principles of space, place and environment. The application of these themes to sport tourism presents the challenges of a multi-disciplinary approach. This book draws from

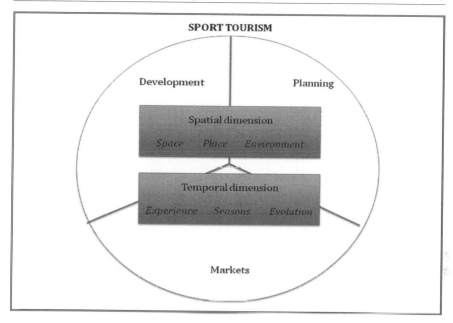

Figure 1.1 Conceptual framework providing the book structure

the fields of sport management, the sociology of sport, consumer behaviour, sports marketing, economic, urban and sports geography, and tourism studies in discussing the manifestations of sport tourism development in space and time.

To illustrate points of discussion, Chapters 2–10 include case studies provided by leading and emerging scholars in the study of sport and tourism from a range of disciplines. 'Focus points' are also integrated into each of these chapters in an attempt to illustrate key points with real-world examples. The overarching goal is to advance theoretical thinking on the subject of sport tourism development generally and critical thinking on the localisation of the discussions that follow.

Part 2

Foundations of Sport Tourism Development

Chapter 2
The Study of Sport Tourism

> *From the standpoint of theory, it is necessary to understand what sport tourism*
> *shares with, and what distinguishes it from other touristic activities.*
> Green and Chalip, 1998: 276

Introduction

The tourism and sport industries cater to travellers seeking sport and tourism experiences. This reality and the significant implications of these activities justify targeted scholarly attention to the sport tourism phenomenon. While it is not being suggested that the study of sport tourism should become the sole domain of specialists, new insights can be gained by an increased focus on the confluence of sport and tourism. Such an approach offers the opportunity to examine untested assumptions, to develop an understanding of complex relationships and processes and to influence the outcomes resulting from the interaction of sport and tourism. A focused approach to sport tourism will capture synergies leading to new insights into this phenomenon that would not otherwise emerge. Chapter 2 is an articulation of this argument. It examines the conceptual foundations of the study of sport and tourism, arguing in support of directed scholarly attention to this area and consideration of sport within a tourist attraction framework. Mike Weed's case study of the evolution of the *Journal of Sport & Tourism* is included in this chapter to highlight the advances made in sport tourism as a field of academic endeavour (Case study 2.1).

Conceptual Foundations

The logical starting point to understanding the confluence of sport and tourism is to articulate the essence of each of the parent fields of study. This is not a simple task, as there are multiple perspectives of each realm (Hinch & Higham, 2001). A range of definitions for sport and tourism can be justified in different contexts. In revisiting the concept of sport, Hsu (2005) categorised attempts to define sport as narrow (closed) or broad (open). In the first instance, sport is seen as something that can be demarcated from non-sport activities while the latter suggests that this distinction is not possible at least at a universal level. Commentators such as Andrews (2006) fall into the latter group with their warnings that definitions that try to delineate socially constructed phenomena are bound to be futile as social constructions vary across time and space.

While agreement on a single universal definition is unlikely and perhaps undesirable, it is helpful for the readers of this text to understand the perspectives that have been adopted for this book. The basic parameters that follow are not meant to deny or diminish other perspectives but rather to position our discussions.

Domain of sport

The popular perception of sport is best reflected by the adage that sport is what is written about on the sport pages of daily newspapers (Bale, 1989). However, a cursory comparison of the sport pages of newspapers from various countries demonstrates that sporting activities vary substantially between places, thereby supporting the contention that such definitions are socially constructed. While attractive in terms of simplicity, this definitional approach fails to capture the essence of sport in terms of the commonalities found in diverse sporting activities.

Classic definitions found in the realm of sport sociology have been useful to us as we considered the basic parameters of sport. This is particularly true of the strong influence of Loy *et al.*'s (1978a, 1978b) game occurrence approach which conceptualises sport as a subset of games, which, in turn, is a subset of play. They describe sport in terms of institutionalised games that require physical prowess. In a similar fashion, McPherson *et al.* (1989: 15) defined sport as 'a structured, goal-oriented, competitive, contest-based, ludic physical activity'.

Basic parameters that emerge from this perspective include rules, competition, play and physical activity. Sport is governed by rules that relate to space and time. These rules are observable in various ways, including the dimensions of the playing area and the duration and pacing of the game or contest. They tend to be more specific in formal variations of a sport, especially as the level of competition increases. Complex codes of rules normally govern international competition at an elite level while the rules may be very general for informal activities such as the unwritten etiquette of surfing (Law, 2001) or the simple rules agreed to during a spontaneous game of football during a grade-school recess.

Sport is also characterised by being goal-oriented, competitive and contest-based. All these three characteristics are closely related. Sport is goal-oriented in the sense that sporting situations usually involve an objective for achievement in relation to ability, competence, effort, degree of difficulty, required skill set and mastery or performance. In most instances, this goal orientation is extended to some degree of competition. At one extreme, competition is expressed in terms of winning or losing. Alternatively, competition can be interpreted much less rigidly in terms of competing against standards, inanimate objects, forces of nature or oneself. In the context of sport tourism, the latter interpretation of competition offers a much more inclusive approach that covers recreational sports such as those commonly associated with outdoor pursuits. It is also inclusive of the 'sport-for-all' concept of participation (e.g. Nogawa *et al.*, 1996) and contemporary urban sports such as Parkour (the art of physical movement in the urban environment) (Lawrence, 2010). Competition is probably best conceptualised as a continuum that ranges from recreational to elite. Closely associated with competition is the contest-based nature of sport in which outcomes are determined by a combination of physical prowess, game strategy and, to a greater or lesser degree, chance.

The third parameter of sport abstracted from the McPherson *et al.* (1989) definition is its 'ludic' or playful nature, a term which is derived from the Latin word *ludus*. This component of the definition states that sport is rooted in, although not exclusive to, the concept of play. Those activities that are seen as pure work would not normally be considered sport, but the presence of some degree of work, in and of itself, does not rule out an activity as sport. Professional sport therefore fits this definition, as does recreational sport. The presence of play in sport is accompanied by uncertain outcome and sanctioned display. Uncertain outcomes help to maintain suspense throughout a sporting engagement and, by doing so, they present unique advantages in terms of tourism authenticity (Chapter 4). Sanctioned display tends to emphasise the exhibition of athletic skills, and, as such, it broadens the scope of involvement to spectators as well as participating athletes.

Finally, underlying all of these parameters of sport is its physical and kinaesthetic nature. While different sports require different configurations of fine and gross motor movement, this is the most universally recognised characteristic of sport. Physical prowess consists of physical speed, stamina, strength, accuracy and coordination (Gibson, 1998) and is the most widely accepted parameter of the concept.

Domain of tourism

Typically, tourism definitions include those that are associated with the popular usage of the term (e.g. Simpson & Weiner, 1989), those that are used to facilitate statistical measurement (e.g. World Tourism Organization, 1981) and those that are used to articulate its conceptual domain (e.g. Murphy, 1985). Definitions arising from all of these perspectives tend to share three key dimensions. The most prevalent of these is a spatial dimension (Dietvorst & Ashworth, 1995; Murphy, 1985). To be considered a tourist, individuals must leave and then eventually return to their home. While the travel of an individual does not in itself constitute tourism, it is one of the necessary conditions. Various qualifiers have been placed on this dimension, including a range of minimum travel distances, but the fundamental concept of travel is universal.

A second common dimension involves the temporal characteristics associated with tourism. Tourist trips are characterised by a 'temporary stay away from home of at least one night' (Leiper, 1981: 74). Definitions developed for statistical purposes often distinguish tourists from excursionists. The difference between the two is that the former visit a destination for at least one night, while the latter visit for less than 24 hours (World Tourism Organization, 1981). Often in popular literature and the media, however, the term tourist is used to refer to both groups.

A third common dimension of tourism definitions concerns the purpose or the activities engaged in during travel, and it is within this dimension that many subfields of tourism research find their genesis (e.g. ecotourism and adventure tourism). Of the three dimensions, this is perhaps the one characterised by the broadest range of views. For example, popular dictionary interpretations of tourists tend to focus on pleasure as the primary travel activity (e.g. Simpson & Weiner, 1989), while definitions developed for statistical and academic purposes tend to include business activities (Murphy, 1985). Specific reference is made to sport in the tourism definition of the World Tourism Organization (1981), which lists it as a subset of leisure activities.

Confluence of sport and tourism

These parameters imply a significant convergence of interests in tourism and sport (Figure 2.1). Sport is an important activity within tourism while tourism and travel are fundamentally associated with many types of sport. The specific confluence of the two concepts varies according to the perspectives of stakeholders and their particular

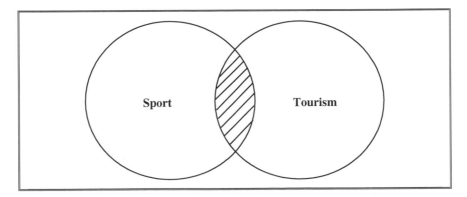

Figure 2.1 The confluence of sport and tourism

interests in sport tourism. A diversity of interests in sport tourism gives rise to the question of whether the study of sport tourism is supported by a strong theoretical foundation and dedicated academic literature.

Conceptualising sport tourism

Attempts to articulate the domain of sport tourism have resulted in a proliferation of definitions (Table 2.1). These definitions tend to parallel the spatial, temporal and activity dimensions of key definitions for tourism (Gibson, 1998). Sport is often positioned as the primary travel activity although Gammon and Robinson (2003) make a distinction between sport tourists and tourism sports. The latter recognises sport as a secondary and sometimes even an incidental travel activity. These various levels of involvement in sport are assumed under the term 'sport tourism' in this book. Most definitions encompass spectators as well as athletes and recreational as well as elite competitors (Standeven & De Knop, 1999; Weed, 1999, 2009a, 2009b). They also tend to include explicit requirements for travel away from the home environment along with at least an implicit temporal dimension that suggests that the trip is temporary and that the traveller will return home within a designated time. Somewhat surprisingly, the major limitation of existing definitions is that the concept of sport is rather vague. This may reflect the differing social constructions of this concept, but this vagueness is problematic as sport is a central focus of the sport tourism development.

Weed and Bull (2003, 2009) consciously break the pattern of conceptualising 'sports tourism' based on the existing parameters of sport or tourism with the rationale that sports tourism is a unique phenomenon. They see it as more than simply the sum of the separate entities of sport and tourism. Instead, they define it as a 'social, economic and cultural phenomenon arising from the unique interaction of activity, people and place' (2003: 258). While it is agreed that sport tourism is more than the sum of its parts (e.g. see the underlying framework used in Higham & Hinch, 2009), the conceptualisation of sport tourism in this book has consciously combined the dominant parameters of sport and tourism. This approach is part of the authors' 'social construction' of the term, reflecting backgrounds in tourism and a conscious attempt to understand sport. Similarly, the term 'sport tourism' rather than 'sports tourism' is adopted not because the unique characteristics of individual sports are not appreciated but rather to reflect an emphasis on the common elements of sport as a social institution and the characteristics that distinguish it from other types of tourism activity (see Gibson, 2002).

For the purposes of this book, sport tourism is conceptualised as sport-based travel away from the home environment for a limited time where

Table 2.1 Selected definitions relating to the study of sport tourism

Dimension	Definition and source
Sport tourism	Travel for non-commercial reasons to participate or observe sporting activities away from the home range (Hall, 1992a: 194) An expression of a pattern of behaviour of people during certain periods of leisure time – such as vacation time, which is done partly in specially attractive natural settings and partly in artificial sports and physical recreation facilities in the outdoors (Ruskin, 1987: 26) Holidays involving sporting activity either as a spectator or as a participant (Weed & Bull, 1997b: 5) Leisure-based travel that takes individuals temporarily outside of their home communities to participate in physical activities, to watch physical activities or to venerate attractions associated with physical activity (Gibson, 1998: 49) All forms of active and passive involvement in sporting activity, participation in a casual or an organised way for non-commercial or business/commercial reasons, that necessitate travel away from home and work locality (Standeven & De Knop, 1999: 12)
Sports tourism	Sports tourism is a social, economic and cultural phenomena arising from the unique integration of activity, people and place (Weed & Bull, 2003: 37; see also Weed & Bull, 2009)
Sport tourist	Individuals and/or groups of people who actively or passively participate in competitive or recreational sport, whilst travelling to and/or staying in places outside their usual environment (sport as the primary motivation of travel) (Gammon & Robinson, 2003: 23) A temporary visitor staying at least 24 hours in the event area and whose primary purpose is to participate in a sports event with the area being a secondary attraction (Nogawa *et al.*, 1996: 46)
Tourism sport	Persons travelling to and/or staying in places outside their usual environment and participating in, actively or passively, a competitive or recreational sport as a secondary activity (Gammon & Robinson, 2003: 24)

sport is characterised by unique rule sets, competition related to physical prowess and play (Hinch & Higham, 2001). Sport is recognised as a significant travel activity whether it is a primary, a secondary or even a tertiary feature of the trip. It is seen to be an important factor in many decisions to travel and one that may feature prominently in the travel experience and its assessment. This perspective enables the adoption of an attractions approach to the discussion of sport tourism development.

Scholarship in Sport Tourism

Sport studies and tourism studies share many of the same institutional characteristics. Both are relatively new areas of academia in which scholars have worked hard to establish respected fields of scholarship. Both disciplines have developed systematic interests in sport tourism, which have manifested themselves in a growing body of literature (e.g. Gibson, 1998, 2005; Glyptis, 1991; Higham, 2005b; Higham & Hinch, 2009; Keller, 2001; Standeven & De Knop, 1999; Weed, 2006, 2008a, 2008b).

Perhaps the most frequently used argument for focused study in the realm of sport tourism is the significance of the practice of sport tourism throughout the world. For example, a July 2010 post on Travel News reported that 3 million sport enthusiasts accounted for 14% of all international tourist arrivals to the United Kingdom in 2008. These visitors spent £2.3 billion and were estimated to support 50,000 jobs (Travel News, July 15, 2010).

In Canada, the economic impact of sport tourism is similarly significant. An analysis of travel data from 2007 determined that tourism receipts related to sport tourism totalled $2.05 billion Canadian dollars and were credited with creating more than 28,000 jobs in the country (The Outspan Group Inc., 2009). Specific events, such as the 2009 Canada Summer Games hosted in Prince Edward Island, have also been shown to have a significant economic impact on their host destinations. In this instance, the combined capital, operations and visitor expenditures totalled $37.7 million and created 778 jobs in Canada's smallest province (Canadian Sport Tourism Alliance, 2010).

It has also been demonstrated that other benefits accrue as a result of sport tourism. Weed (1999) has highlighted a number of these, including the increased supply of urban-based sport facilities and developments that can be used for locally based sport. In recognising the mutual interests of sport and tourism, it is possible to capture the synergies of joint funding, research and strategic initiatives. Notwithstanding these benefits, there are also potentially negative aspects of the sport tourism link (Weed, 1999). For example, the introduction of 'nuisance activities' to the countryside, particularly mechanised sports such as trail biking, jet skiing and 'skidooing', has the potential to cause significant social and environmental impacts. Adventure and extreme sports, such as BASE jumping, practiced in places such as the Lysefjord and Trollveggen regions of Norway, are characterised by safety and liability issues (Mykletun & Vedø, 2002). In such cases, the advantages of developing a better understanding of the dynamics of sport tourism are that these impacts can be recognised, understood and managed in the development process.

Scholarly justification

The study of tourism and the study of sport are both characterised by numerous hyphenated subfields. In an age of competitive funding in academic institutions, the danger of splintering existing fields of study is a real as well as a perceived threat. At the 2001 meeting of the Leisure Studies Association in the United Kingdom, critics of sport tourism argued that insight into this phenomenon is most likely to emerge from within the respective realms of tourism studies and sport studies. This implies that collaborative approaches can be adopted using interdisciplinary and multidisciplinary approaches on an *ad hoc* basis. Resistance to any fundamental shift towards a subfield in this area is perhaps due to the relatively early stage of theoretical development for sport tourism. However, as theoretical foundations continued to be developed (Gibson, 2006), this argument has lost its potency.

Hall's (1992a, 1992b) early work in this area not only identified sport as a major special interest of tourism but also articulated three related tourism domains: hallmark events, outdoor recreation (adventure tourism) and tourism associated with health and fitness (Figure 2.2). Of these three related domains, the area of hallmark events is probably the most direct link to sport as epitomised by national championship competition finals such as American football's Superbowl and international sport mega events such as the Olympic Games. The profile and scale of these sport events attract the attention of tourists, media and tourism researchers. This attention is reflected in the prominence of sport-event–based articles published in journals such as *Event Management*, and increasingly published in journals such as the *Journal of Vacation Marketing, Current Issues in Tourism* and *Tourism Management.* Similarly, tourism-related articles are increasingly appearing in sport-based journals such as the *Journal of Sport Management, the European Sport Management Quarterly* and *Sport in Society.*

Ritchie's (1984) classification of hallmark events identifies sport as just one of seven event categories, although others have argued that it is one of the most significant of these categories (Getz, 1997; Ryan *et al.*, 1996). While providing substantial insight into sport tourism, these publications have not highlighted the distinguishing features of sporting events relative to other types of events. Even if they did, events only comprise one aspect, albeit a high profile one, of sport tourism.

Outdoor recreation represents a second related area that is inextricably linked to sport tourism. The essence of this contextual domain lies in recreational activities that occur within natural settings, many of which are

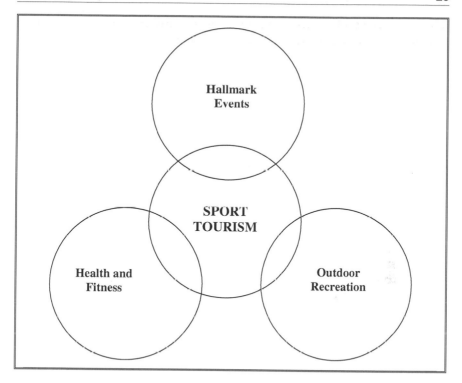

Figure 2.2 Sport tourism and related contextual domains

commonly classified as sports, such as canoeing, skiing and surfing. One of the most dynamic components of outdoor recreation is adventure tourism. Hall (1992a) identifies adventure tourism as a rapidly growing segment of the special interest tourism market. For example, Kane and Zink's (2004) work on package adventure tours, while not explicitly positioned in terms of active sport tourism, provides relevant and significant insight into this dimension of the field. Once again, there is a clear overlap between outdoor recreation and sport tourism both conceptually and in terms of research activity. However, these domains are not synonymous. A substantial amount of sport activity occurs outside the realm of the natural environment, while conversely, many tourism activities that occur in natural settings are inconsistent with the conceptualisation of sport used in this book (e.g. camping and picnicking).

Health and fitness activities provide a third related domain of relevance to sport tourism. The essence of this domain is evident from both historical and contemporary perspectives. The former is most commonly illustrated by the tourist activity associated with the therapeutic spas of Eastern and Mediterranean Europe in Roman times

(Hall, 1992a). In a contemporary context, travel to partake in therapeutic spas continues, but a health focus is also found in resorts featuring activities such as tennis and golf (Nahrstedt, 2004; Redmond, 1991; Spivack, 1998). While the realm of health and fitness can be defined in ubiquitous terms, it has generally been treated much more narrowly in the literature.

Research in all three of these areas has contributed to the understanding of sport tourism, yet the essence of sport extends beyond the collective parameters of these related domains. The defining parameters of sport and their relevance to tourism are not the central interest of research related to hallmark events, outdoor recreation or health tourism. Focused study on sport tourism can, therefore, provide new and challenging insights into this field of expanding academic and industry interest.

A maturing body of literature

Just as the marketplace has responded to the consumer demand for sport tourism products and services, the academic community has started to consciously respond to a gap in the literature related to sport tourism. Initially, this response was relatively isolated and *ad hoc* (Garmise, 1987), but over the past 25 years, a growing flow of scientific publications has contributed to a maturing body of literature.

Evidence of academic activity related to the study of sport tourism includes conferences focused on the subject, seminal articles in tourism and sport management journals (e.g. Gibson, 1998; Green & Chalip, 1998), special themed issues of tourism and sport journals (e.g. *Journal of Vacation Marketing*, 1997; *Journal of Sport Management*, 2003), the establishment of a series titled the *Journal of Sport & Tourism* (see Case study 2.1 by Mike Weed at the end of this section) as well as a trade journal titled *Sports Travel*, the publication of introductory texts (e.g. Hinch & Higham, 2004; Standeven & De Knop, 1999; Turco *et al.*, 2002; Weed & Bull, 2003, 2009) and edited collections (e.g. Gammon & Kurtzman, 2002; Gibson, 2006; Higham, 2005b; Weed, 2008a) and in-depth explorations of selected dimensions of sport tourism (Higham & Hinch, 2009). Consequently, synergies that are inherent in a well-established body of literature are beginning to emerge as new sport tourism research initiatives are consciously positioned relative to earlier studies.

Gibson (1998) provided a thorough review of the sport tourism literature as it stood more than 10 years ago. Her critical analysis suggested a maturing body of relevant literature that was still in want of better coordination among agencies at a policy level, multi-disciplinary research approaches and greater cooperation between tourism- and sport-centred units in academic settings. Seven years later, Weed (2005) acknowledged the growth of publications in this area but used the analogy of a 'brickyard' in arguing that these studies were being grouped randomly in piles rather than being constructed into 'edifices' in which new publications are consciously positioned in terms of proceeding work. Both Weed (2006, 2009b) and Gibson (2005) have continued to track the development of the sport tourism body of literature, and while noting impressive progress, have called for additional focus on explanation over description. Weed's (2009b) meta-analysis of the sport tourism literature confirmed the dominance of event-related articles, a shift from research on impacts to leveraging, and concerns about the quality of behavioural research in the field. He concludes that the field has shown signs of increasing maturity as reflected in

> a strong conceptualization of the field; the underpinning of empirical work by appropriate theory; the robust, appropriate and transparent application of methods and methodology; and a clear community of scholars with a sustained interest in the area, served by a credible academic journal and wider body of knowledge. (p. 625)

He continues by arguing that the field must become comfortable with the existence of 'contested ideas' and that it must be 'reflexive, self-critical and responsive to external challenges' (p. 626).

Case study 2.1

The *Journal of Sport & Tourism:* A Maturing Literature

Mike Weed, Canterbury Christ Church University

The *Journal of Sport & Tourism* (JS&T), owned and published by Routledge, was relaunched in its current form in 2006. It was the result of major and extensive changes to the purpose, direction, style and format of a predecessor publication, the *Journal of Sport Tourism* (JST). JST, which had run online for seven years before being launched in hard copy in 2003, was owned by the Sport Tourism International Council (STIC). As befits a publication of a body such as STIC, JST attempted to serve a trade/professional audience as well as the academic community. However, while such a dual role was laudable, in practice it proved difficult to fulfil, with the result that the content of JST sometimes disappointed the academic community, and this, albeit inadvertently, perhaps contributed to some negative perceptions of the quality of research in sport and tourism. To address these concerns, in 2006 STIC relinquished its ownership of the journal (thus

releasing it from its obligations to its trade/professional audience), and the journal was relaunched, re-positioned and renamed as the *JS&T* with myself as the Editor, alongside a new editorial team, and new aims and scope which emphasised its new academic direction:

> ... the standard for publication in the *Journal of Sport & Tourism* is that manuscripts must make a clear contribution substantively, theoretically, or methodologically to the body of knowledge relating to the relationship between sport and tourism.

I have noted elsewhere that any field of academic study requires various markers to establish its legitimacy (Weed, 2009b), and undoubtedly *JS&T* has helped contribute to strengthening such markers for the study of the relationship between sport and tourism in the last five years. The journal provides not only an important outlet for a 'cadre' of researchers working in sport and tourism to debate key issues but also an opportunity for authors in related fields to contribute to discussions about sport and tourism, and it helps demonstrate how research in sport and tourism can contribute to wider debates, such as those on climate change and international terrorism.

There are a range of indicators that suggest that since its relaunch in 2006, *JS&T*'s contribution to debates both within and outside the field of sport and tourism has increased and, indeed, that this contribution is valued. Subscription rates have almost doubled in the five years since the relaunch, while there has been an exponential increase in the number of articles downloaded from the journal's web pages. Furthermore, the contribution that the journal makes to wider debates is evidenced by increased citations in other outlets, not only those in sport, tourism and leisure but also those in broader fields such as international relations and development studies.

However, this does not mean that *JS&T* is resting on its laurels. In 2009, I conducted a meta-review of the development of sports tourism knowledge (Weed, 2009b) in which I identified two continuing issues for research in the field as it continues to mature, and there is a clear role for *JS&T* in helping to address these issues.

Firstly, it is important to recognise that a unified view of the relationship between sport and tourism may be unattainable. Researchers in a mature field of study will recognise that even foundational ideas are contested. Inevitably, as *JS&T* contributes to the development of a greater volume of work in the area, further competing perspectives will emerge. However, as McFee (2007) notes, researchers in a mature field of social science will recognise that the existence of contested ideas is a healthy state of affairs, because it brings a range of alternative perspectives to bear on the issues researchers in the field face, none of which will be dominant or hegemonic. As such, *JS&T* is committed to encouraging debates between scholars holding different perspectives, and welcomes the open discussion of contested ideas.

Secondly, research into the relationship between sport and tourism needs to be reflexive, self-critical and responsive to wider external issues and perspectives that may interact with the study of sport and tourism. *JS&T* has sought to develop an extended advisory board of scholars from a wide range of subjects and disciplines, and actively encourages perspectives from scholars working in other fields. In this respect, *JS&T* is committed to ensuring that it does not fall into the *paradigm-trap* of becoming 'self-referential' (Bailey, 2006), because this would significantly affect the increasing relevance that the research it publishes has been shown to have for wider debates on major social science issues such as global warming and economic development. As such, in making a contribution to the increasing maturation of the field of sport and tourism, *JS&T* seeks to encourage a 'comfortableness' among researchers with the existence of contested perspectives and ideas, and to promote a reflexive appreciation of the strengths and weaknesses of research in the field, particularly in response to wider external issues in society.

In conclusion, I would suggest that the maturation of *JS&T* into a publication recognised as providing a high-quality forum for the discussion of both contested issues and issues of wider relevance mirrors the increasing maturation of the field of sport and tourism itself, which increasingly draws on a wide range of disciplinary perspectives and theories. In the last five years, papers published in *JS&T* have utilised perspectives from sociology (e.g. Harris, 2006; Mansfield, 2007), social psychology (e.g. Gillett & Kelly, 2006; Kaplanidou, 2009), geography (e.g. Higham & Hinch, 2006), anthropology (e.g. a special issue of *JS&T* edited by Chalip, 2010), marketing (e.g. Page *et al.*, 2006), economics (e.g. Allen *et al.*, 2007; Preuss, 2007), narrative theory (e.g. Berger & Greenspan, 2008; Smith & Weed, 2007), management (e.g. Chalip, 2006; Snelgrove *et al.*, 2008) and sustainable development (e.g. a special issue of *JS&T* edited by Fyall & Jago, 2009). I fully expect to see the range and scope of discussions expand further as *JS&T*, and the study of sport and tourism, develops further in the future.

Literature cited in this case study is included in the list of references at the end of this book.

Conceptualising Sport as a Tourist Attraction

Green and Chalip (1998: 276) have noted that 'from the standpoint of theory, it is necessary to understand what sport shares with, and what distinguishes it from other touristic activities'. We have adopted tourist attraction theory as a useful framework for gaining insight into these unique aspects of sport tourism. While the idea of sport as a tourist attraction is not new (e.g. Rooney, 1988), the theoretical basis for this claim is more recent (Higham & Hinch, 2003; Hinch & Higham, 2001). Leiper's (1990: 371) systems approach to tourist attractions provides a useful foundation for this exercise. He defined a tourist attraction as 'a system comprising three elements: a tourist or human element, a nucleus or central element, and a marker or informative element. A tourist attraction comes into existence when the three elements are connected'.

The first component of Leiper's (1990) attraction system is the human element. The tourist or human element consists of persons who are travelling away from home to the extent that their behaviour is motivated by leisure-related factors. Leiper (1990) makes five assertions about the nature of this behaviour.

> First, the essence of touristic behaviour involves a search for satisfying leisure away from home. Second, touristic leisure means a search for suitable attractions or, to be more precise, a search for personal (*in situ*) experience of attraction systems' nuclear elements. Third, the process depends ultimately on each individual's mental and non-mental attributes such as needs and ability to travel. Fourth, the markers or informative elements have a key role in the links between each tourist and the nuclear elements being sought for personal experience. Fifth, the process is not automatically productive, because tourists' needs are not always satisfied (these systems may be functional or dysfunctional, to varying degrees). (Leiper, 1990: 371–372)

The second major element of Leiper's (1990) tourist attraction system is the nucleus, which refers to the site where the tourist experience is produced and consumed. More specifically, in the context of sporting attractions, it is the attributes of the sporting activity and the conditions for its conduct that make up the nucleus of the attraction (Lew, 1987). Leiper (1990) recognises that attractions may play various roles in a tourist's experience, which he describes in terms of a nuclear mix and hierarchy. A nuclear mix refers to the combination of nuclei that a tourist wishes to experience while the hierarchy suggests that some of these nuclei are more important in influencing a visitor decisions than others. This aspect of the attraction system reflects established sport tourism typologies associated with multiple sport trips and categories of sport tourists' motivations (Gammon & Robinson, 2003; Standeven & De Knop, 1999).

Primary attractions are those that have the power to influence a visitor's decision to travel to a destination based solely on that attraction. Secondary attractions are known to a person prior to the visit but are not instrumental in and of themselves in the determination of travel itineraries. Tertiary attractions are unknown to the traveller prior to the visit but may serve as centres for entertainment, activity or experience once the visitor is at the destination (Leiper, 1990). This hierarchy is evident in sport tourism, with many travellers primarily motivated by a particular sporting opportunity, others whose travel decisions depend on a combination of sporting and non-sporting attractions and still others whose original travel decision may not have been driven by sporting opportunities in the destination but whose destination experiences are based on sport. The attraction system, therefore, recognises that sport may function as a tourist attraction in various ways for various people. Appreciating the place of sport within a destination's nuclear mix and hierarchy of attractions, as it relates to different tourist market segments, has significant management implications (e.g. attendance, participation, travel flows, visitor behaviour and timing of visit).

The third element of the attraction system consists of markers, which are items of information about any phenomenon that is a potential nucleus element in a tourist attraction (Leiper, 1990). Markers may be detached or removed from the nucleus, contiguous or on-site. In each case, the markers may be positioned consciously or unconsciously to function as part of the attraction system. Examples of conscious attraction markers featuring sport are common. Typically, they take the form of advertisements showing visitors involved in destination-specific sport activities and events. Unconscious detached markers are even more pervasive. At the forefront of these are televised broadcasts of elite sport competitions and advertisements featuring sports in recognisable destinations (Chapter 6). Broadcast listeners and viewers have the location marked for them as a tourist attraction, which may influence future travel decisions.

It is our contention that sport-based attractions are unique. The human element of attractions is distinctive in its breadth, which includes forms as varied as event-based sports, team and individual sports, active involvement in competitive or recreational sports and spectatorship. Similarly, the significance of the popular media as sport tourism markers is arguably matched by few, if any, other types of tourist activity. While these two differences are important, the unique features of sport as the nucleus of the attraction present the strongest justification for focused study on sport tourism.

The conceptualisation of sport tourism used in this book highlights these components of the nucleus. Firstly, each sport has its own set of rules that provide characteristic spatial and temporal structures such as the dimensions of a playing surface or the duration of a match (Bale, 1989). Secondly, competition relating to physical prowess encompasses the goal orientation, competition and contest-based aspects of sport (McPherson *et al.*, 1989). Thirdly, sport is characterised by its playful nature. This last element includes the notions of uncertainty of outcome and sanctioned display.

Rules, competition relating to physical prowess and the playfulness inherent in sport make it a unique type of tourism attraction. Specific types of sport, such as football, skiing or BASE jumping, possess their own distinctive traits as tourist attractions, but, as a whole, they are distinct from other broad categories of tourist attractions. By analysing sports in the context of these three components, insight can be gained into the way that sport functions as a tourist attraction. The impact of changes to the sport attraction can then be considered within the broader context of the spatial and temporal dimensions of sport tourism development (Focus point 2.1).

Focus point 2.1

The Tour de France as a Tourist Attraction

Initiated in 1903 by Géo Lefèvre, a journalist with *L'Auto* magazine, with the support of his editor Henri Desgrange, the Tour de France has grown from a fringe bike touring race to not only the world's highest profile bike race but one of the most significant sporting events on the annual calendar. An indication of the popularity of the Tour de France is the fact that the Google search engine identified more than 23 million websites when prompted by the race name.

One does not have to do an intensive investigation to appreciate that the Tour de France is a major tourist attraction. Applying Leiper's (1990) tourism attraction framework to the Tour de France illustrates the utility of his framework. The nucleus of the Tour de France as an attraction is the cycling race that lies at its core. In 2011, the 98th race is scheduled to last from 2 July to 24 July. It will consist of 21 stages and a 3471-km route throughout some of the most scenic countryside in France with the final stage ending in Paris along the Champs-Élysées. Performance is measured by an aggregation of the times of individuals on each team for each stage.

In terms of the human element, centre stage is held by the cyclists themselves. These competitors are supported by a retinue of coaches, managers and medical staff. Race officials and media personnel represent two other significant groups. However, all of these partici-pants combined represent but a small fraction of the 12–15 million spectators who have typically lined the route in recent history. It is estimated that approximately 85% of these spectators are French nationals and that, on average, spectators have travelled 130 km to see the tour.

Markers for the tour are many and varied. One of the most unique is the publicity caravan that precedes each segment of the race featuring floats of the various sponsors. It has been an integral part of the race since 1930 and exemplifies the on-site or contiguous marker under Leiper's framework. The official Tour de France website cited below is a formal off-site marker, but it is joined by some 23 million other websites, some of which market the event specifically as a tourism attraction (e.g. Tourism France and tour companies) but most of which refer to it much more subtly as, perhaps, a reference in a personal blog by a visitor to France. Numerous variations of these markers exist given the tour's place in global culture. The newsworthiness of the competition is particularly noteworthy and ranges from excited commentaries on the competition itself through to investigative reporting on doping scandals that first emerged in the 1960s. Of particular relevance from a tourism perspective are the visual images that are broadcast through television coverage in more than 180 countries. These images make for good television not only because of the drama of the race but also because of the beauty of the landscapes and the uniqueness of the French rural lifestyle as evident in the places that the racers pass through.

Source: http://www.letour.fr/us/homepage_horscourseTDF.html. Accessed 26 November 2010.

Conclusion

Sport and tourism are closely related in terms of practice. Tourists participate in sports while on their travels, and spectators and athletes travel in search for competition or in pursuit of their sporting passions. Despite the obvious overlap between sport and tourism, little is known about the dynamics of this relationship. Systematic advances in this realm will be greatly aided by focused study in the area of sport tourism rather than the *ad hoc* treatment of the subject prior to 2000. While the study of sport tourism is still relatively young, it has made significant strides towards maturity over the past decade. A coherent and insightful body of literature is emerging. However, coherence does not imply a single perspective. In fact, a mature area of study embraces multiple perspectives that challenge underlying assumptions and accept and even celebrate the tensions that naturally accompany these perspectives. This depends in a large part on the articulation and clarification of these perspectives as attempted in this chapter. Especially important is our conceptualisation of sport tourism as sport-based travel away from the home environment for a limited time where sport is characterised by unique rule sets, competition related to physical prowess and play (Hinch & Higham, 2001). Similarly, we have situated sport as a unique type of tourist attraction using Leiper's (1990) tourist attraction framework. This allows for the unique aspects of sport to be articulated in terms of the human element, nucleus and markers of a tourist attraction. By using this attraction framework and our conceptualisation of sport tourism, it is possible to demonstrate 'what sport tourism shares with, and what distinguishes it from other touristic activities' (Green & Chalip, 1998: 276).

Chapter 3
Sport Tourism Markets

> *Research into who is a sport tourist, and why sport tourists engage in this sort of tourism may prove to be more complex than is first apparent.*
> Gibson, 1998: 57

Introduction

Delpy (1997: 4) states that a 'travel market focussed entirely on participating or watching sport is a unique and exciting concept'. Sport tourism is widely viewed as a niche sector for the tourism industry (Commonwealth Department of Industry, Science and Resources, 2000) that may be targeted to broaden the suite of visitor markets that are attracted to a destination (Bull & Weed, 1999). It is also a market that may be approached generically, as demonstrated by the mass tourism promotion of major sporting events. The reality, however, is that sport tourism comprises a diverse range of niche markets (Collins & Jackson, 2001; Maier & Weber, 1993). Chalip (2001) observes that many Australian cities targeted specific market segments during the lead up to the 2000 Olympic Games. Indeed, Bull and Weed (1999: 143) explain that sport tourism is really a collection of separate niches, but while tourism associated with mega sporting events in major urban locations is clearly evident, the potential of sport as a tourism niche elsewhere is perhaps less well appreciated.

Understanding sport tourist markets is an important aspect of the foundation for sport tourism development. Important questions include 'who are sport tourists?' 'what factors motivate sport tourists?' 'to what extent do motivations differ between distinct groups of sport tourists?' and 'what travel experiences do sport tourists seek in association with the sports that they pursue at a given destination?' Addressing these questions provides valuable insights into niche market segments and the basis for making market segmentation decisions. Market analysis, then, is critical to the effective development of sport tourism within the context of regional, national or international tourism destinations. The first part of this chapter discusses conceptual approaches to the classification of sport tourist types. This is followed by an examination of sport tourism niche markets and the means by which these markets are effectively segmented.

Conceptualising Demand for Sport Tourism

Conceptualising sport tourism is a useful starting point in the study of sport tourism markets. The distinction between spectatorship and physical participation, for example, is a fundamental difference that merits consideration. Glyptis (1989, 1991) introduced the terms 'general dabbler' and 'specialist' to describe different levels of tourist engagement in participant and spectator sports. Hall (1992b) also identified two types of active sport tourists: 'activity participants', who regard their participation as a medium of self-expression, and 'players', who are competitive in their participation. The distinction between 'sport-orientated holidays' and 'less sport-orientated holidays' is the conceptual basis for the study of sports activities during the outbound holidays of German, Dutch and French conducted by the World Tourism Organization and the International Olympic Committee (2001).

Tourists who engage in sports at a destination do so with varying degrees of commitment, competitiveness and active/passive engagement. The sport tourism market may be segmented on these grounds into niche markets or 'demand groups' which differ in many aspects of the visitor experience (Chapter 8). Maier and Weber (1993) identify four demand groups based on the intensity of the sports activities pursued at the destination (Table 3.1). They also describe the unique resource development requirements of each demand group. The resource requirements that top-performance athletes seek at a tourism destination relate specifically to the enhancement of performance in sport (e.g. training, sports science and sports medicine facilities).

Much less is known about the importance of opportunities for leisure and unique tourism experiences at places of training or competition in terms of how they may serve the achievement of 'tour balance' (Higham & Hinch, 2009; Hodge *et al.*, 2009). This term describes the need for elite athletes to occasionally escape from routine (e.g. training schedules), experience the stimulation of new and unique places and achieve periodic relief from the pressures of competition (Hodge & Hermansson, 2007). Hodge *et al.* (2009) consider 'tour balance' in professional sport to be critical to achieving high performance while on tour, as well as countering the prospects of 'burnout' in the longer (career) temporal dimension. Occasional sports (wo)men and passive sport tourists stand in significant contrast, given the priority that they are likely to place in the experience of place and tourist experiences that a destination may offer.

Reeves (2000) identifies six 'types' of sport tourists and explains the distinctions between them in terms of decision making, motivations, lifestyle and spending profiles (Table 3.2). The diversity that exists within the sport tourism market is, once again, highlighted. However, it should be noted that Reeves's (2000) typology is illustrative rather than

Table 3.1 Sport tourism demand groups and requisite visitor facilities

Demand groups	Visitor demands and required facilities
Top-performance athletes	Efficiency is the main aim during holidays. Access to competition and suitable training conditions and facilities are the priority for these travellers. When meeting the priorities of this group, tour organisers and destination managers need to give consideration to specific accommodation and dining demands (e.g. dietary requirements) as well as access to physicians, injury rehabilitation facilities and other performance-related services.
Mass sports	Preserving health and maintaining fitness is the aim of this demand group. Performance targets are individually fixed. The accessibility of holiday regions and the quality of sports facilities are the key considerations for this market segment.
Occasional sports (wo)men	Compensation and prestige play greater roles than sporting ambition in the pursuit of occasional sports. This demand group gives preference to less demanding sports such as recreational skiing and bowling. Sporting activities receive no greater priority over cultural sightseeing and other interests within this market group.
Passive sports tourists	No individual sports activities are pursued. The focus of this group lies with mega sports events and distinguished sports sites. Includes coaches and attendants to high-performance athletes as well as media reporters. Requires high-volume infrastructures to accommodate the needs of large numbers of event sport attendees.

Source: Maier and Weber (1993: 38)

definitive. It contains generalisations relating, for instance, to visitor expenditures that require the support of rigorous quantitative market research. Furthermore, autonomy in destination choice may exist for 'driven' athletes based on alternative training philosophies (Focus point 3.1). Despite these limitations, the value of this typology lies in its clear conceptualisation of sport tourist types. It provides marketing professionals with important insights into a range of tourist types that are represented within the sport tourism market.

Table 3.2 Sport tourism types and visitor profiles

Type	Decision making	Participation	Non-participation	Group profile	Lifestyle	Spending
Incidental	Unimportant	Out of duty	Not relaxing, holiday-like	Family	Sport is significant	Minimal
Sporadic	Relatively important	If convenient	Easily contained / put off	Friends and family	Non-essential	Minimal except for 'one-offs'
Occasional	Sometimes determining	Welcome addition to tourist experience	Other commitments	Often individual, especially business tourists	Conspicuous consumption	High on occasions
Regular	Important	Significant part of enjoyment	Money or time become prohibitive	Group or individual	Important	Considerable
Dedicated	Very important	Central to experience	Because of unforeseen barriers	Individuals and groups of like-minded	Defining element	Extremely high and consistent
Driven	Very important but little autonomy	Sole reason	Through injury or fear of it	Elite groups or solitary	The profession	Extremely high but funded by others

Source: Reeves (2000)

Focus point 3.1
International Football Camp Styria

International Football Camp Styria is located in the Alps region of Steiemark (Austria). It provides integrated high-altitude football training venues that target elite football clubs and international football teams to prepare for domestic competitions (summer camps) and international events (Fédération Internationale de Football Association [FIFA] World Cup camps). These elite sports markets have high discretion in terms of selected training and preparation locations, and the high-altitude environments of Steiemark (Austria) provide a desirable setting for the physical conditioning and preparation of sports teams. The development of world-class training facilities has allowed Football Camp Styria to increasingly attract international football squads and clubs from beyond Europe. With Graz serving as the regional air transport gateway, international teams from England, New Zealand and Spain engaged in pre-FIFA World Cup training camps during the early summer of 2010. In addition, summer camps include a wide range of elite European and Asian football clubs engaging in pre-season training. In 2010, they numbered 24 teams from 12 nations, including FC Copenhagen (Holland), Blackburn Rovers, Stoke City and Arsenal (England), FK Jablone (Czech Republic), Rapid Vienna (Austria), Werder Bremen and Borussia Dortmund (Germany), Urawa Red Diamonds and Sanfrecce Hiroshima (Japan), Bursaspor and Genclerbirligi Ankara (Turkey), Kazma Kuwait (Kuwait) and Team Bahrain (United Arab Emirates). A programme of warm-up games involving clubs from various national premier competitions runs through June and July, often on consecutive days and with upward of two to three matches on some days.

Source: www.footballcampstyria.com. Accessed 22 November 2010.

Robinson and Gammon (2004) advance the conceptualisation of sport tourists based on the motivations held by tourists vis-à-vis their involvement in sport (Table 3.3). Their contribution lies in the distinction between two forms of sport tourism. They use the term 'sport tourism' where sport is the primary travel motivation with other tourist activities an important but secondary element of the tourist experience. In the case of 'tourism sport', sport is the secondary or incidental component of the tourist experience. Gammon and Robinson (1997) also distinguish between active and passive involvement in competitive and non-competitive sports. Therefore, both 'sport tourism' and 'tourism sport' may be defined in terms of hard and soft participation. The distinction between the two lies in the seriousness with which travellers engage in

Table 3.3 Conceptualisation of sport tourists based on sport and travel motivations

Sport tourism	Individuals and/or groups of people who actively or passively participate in competitive or recreational sport while travelling. Sport is the prime motivation to travel although the tourist element may reinforce the overall experience.
Hard definition	Active or passive participation in a competitive sporting event. Sport is the prime motivational reason for travel (e.g. Olympic Games, Wimbledon and the London Marathon).
Soft definition	Active recreational participation in a sporting/leisure interest (e.g. skiing, walking, hiking and kayaking).
Tourism sport	Active or passive participation in competitive or recreational sport as a secondary activity. The holiday or visit, rather than the sport, is the prime travel motivation.
Hard definition	Competitive or non-competitive sport acts as an important secondary motivation that enriches the travel experience (e.g. sports cruises, health and fitness clubs).
Soft definition	Competitive or non-competitive sport or leisure as a purely incidental element of the holiday experience (e.g. mini golf, indoor bowls, ice skating and squash).

Source: Gammon and Robinson (1997: 10–11)

their chosen sports. This conceptual framework captures the diversity of the sport tourism travel market, which varies along scales of participation and competitiveness, and where sport may function as a primary, secondary or purely incidental travel motivation. It also complements the discussion of the tourism attraction hierarchy presented in Chapter 2.

Gammon and Robinson (1997), therefore, identify three dimensions that highlight the variation that exists within the demand side of sport tourism. They include the status of the sport activity in the motivational profile of the tourist (primary, secondary or incidental), the type of involvement in the sport activity (active or passive) and the competitive or non-competitive nature of the sport activity. In doing so, they contribute to a better understanding of sport tourism consumer markets, which provides insights into the distinct sport- and tourism-related services and experiences required by each. However, the criticism of this typology is that it fails to capture the interplay of 'activity, people and place' and as such simplifies our understanding of sport tourism phenomena (Weed, 2005). 'The primacy of the sport or the tourism element in many sports tourism experiences cannot be established and, in fact, for many experiences separate and distinguishable sport and tourism elements may not be present' (Weed, 2009b: 619). Rather, it is the unique cultures of different places, which extend to the cultures – values, beliefs, behaviours (including styles of play and interpretations of rules) and traditions – of sport (Chalip, 2010), that contribute to a complexity in the study of sport tourism that challenges typological classification.

It is the extent to which sporting activities are pursued by tourists that forms the basis of Standeven and De Knop's (1999) conceptual classification (Table 3.4). The sport activity holiday segment of Standeven and De Knop's classification illustrates the diversity of the sport tourism market. Single-sport activity holidays comprise those who seek to engage in specific sports, such as downhill skiing, cross-country skiing or snowboarding. The wider tourist element of the destination may hold little sway in the travel decision process in these instances. This market stands in contrast to the multiple-sport activity holidays market in which opportunities to engage in sporting pursuits are more broad ranging, casual and less likely to be the sole focus of visitor activity.

Table 3.4 Sport tourism activities classification

Classification	*Examples*

Sport activity holidays:
  Single-sport activity holidays
  Multiple-sport activity holidays
	Skiing, cycling, trekking
	Sports camps, holiday clubs (e.g. Club Méditerranée; see also Focus point 3.2)

Holiday sport activities:
  Organised holiday sport activities
  Independent holiday sport activities
	Golf, rafting, cruise ship sport activities
	Adventure activities (e.g. bungee jumping)

Passive sports on holidays: Connoisseur observer Casual observers	Olympic Games, Masters Golf, Wimbledon Tennis Championship, Kentucky Derby, Museums, Halls of Fame, Stadium tours Hurling (Ireland), Thai Boxing (Thailand), Bull Fighting (Spain)
Active sports during non-holiday time	Training camps, recreational sport during business and conference travel
Passive sports during non-holiday time	Dragon boat racing spectatorship while in Hong Kong on business

Source: Adapted from Standeven and De Knop (1999)

These and other segments within this classification are associated with distinct market characteristics. The terms active and passive are used in this classification in reference to sport participation and non-participation, respectively. This should not be confused with other forms of active involvement in sport tourism such as team management and officiating. Furthermore, in some sports, spectators are encouraged to be active in the support of a competitor or team (e.g. banner competitions and inter-session spectator competitions) as a means of generating atmosphere at stadiums and other sports venues. In other cases, spectators need no such encouragement in their expressions of contemporary culture, which may relegate the sports display to secondary importance behind the performance of fan identification.

Redmond's (1990) tripartite sport tourism classification includes sport vacations, multi-sport festivals and world championships, and sports halls of fame and museums. Gibson's (1998) literature-based analysis of sport tourism adopts a similar approach in a general analysis of sport tourism markets. Her classification includes active, event and nostalgia sport tourism. This schema serves as the framework for the following discussion.

Active Sport Tourism Markets

The active sport tourism market is constituted of individuals who pursue physical involvement in competitive or non-competitive sports while travelling. A number of published articles examine the active sport tourism market (Green & Chalip, 1998; World Tourism Organization & International Olympic Committee, 2001; Yusof & Douvis, 2001). However, Gibson (1998: 53) notes that active sport tourism market research is generally 'scarce, usually descriptive and typically atheoretical'. In 1992, Gibson and Yiannakis introduced the term 'sportlover' to describe the growing travel market represented by individuals who are physically active, and prefer to remain so while travelling for business and/or leisure. More significant, perhaps, are those who are motivated to travel to specific locations to actively engage in their sporting passions (Focus point 3.2). These active participants may seek to develop their sporting abilities, seek competition, experience first-hand unique or famous sports places, develop a sense of personal identity and/or develop their standing within a sport subculture (Higham & Hinch, 2009).

Focus point 3.2

Club Med: Repositioning for Sport Tourism

While Club Med has had a long history of promoting active vacations, it has recently taken it to a new level. For example, Club

Med's Sandpiper Bay property in Florida is going beyond the mainstays of beach activities, upscale dining and accommodation, Kids Clubs and the like, to an offering that features sport – front and centre. Premium sport choices include tennis, golf, fitness, sailing and team sports. 'The pinnacles of this new dimension are specialised Club Med Academies offering group and *à la carte* private instruction programs led by some of America's biggest names in coaching, including tennis gurus Gave Jaramillo and Scott Del Mastro, PGA instructors Brad Brewer and Don Law and five-time Ironman champion Heather Gollnick.' Club Med North America CEO Xavier Mufraggi states that these coaches 'enable us to offer an unparalleled approach to elite training within a resort setting'. Elite training for serious sport enthusiasts is complemented by a 'Le Petit Sport' programme with customised mini versions of golf, hockey, soccer and tennis designed for 4 to 10-year-olds. While moms and dads are refining their sport skills under the watchful eyes of elite coaches, their children are being introduced to these games in an age-appropriate manner. Aimed at an upper middle class clientele who can afford the costs of admission, this Club Med strategy is a great example of an entrepreneurial response to the growing demand for sport experiences in tourism settings.

Source: Randall Anthony Communications (2010) Take your active family vacation to a new level (A special information feature). *The Globe and Mail*, 4 December, 2010.

Subsequently, Delpy (1998) profiled the active sport tourist as physically active, college educated, relatively affluent and 18–44 year old. Such a generalised approach fails to capture the diversity of the market segments that exist in active sport tourism. In fact, numerous approaches to segmenting the active sport tourism market are evident, but not clearly stated, in the empirical research literature. These studies may be organised under the approaches to market segmentation identified by Swarbrooke and Horner (1999) as geographic, socio-economic, demographic and psychographic.

Geographic market segmentation

Geographic segmentation of the active sport tourism market, based on visitor origins or market location, is a popular approach to the practice of sport tourism. The geography of sport establishes the link between place of residence and opportunities to engage in certain sports in specified locations (Bale, 1989; Rooney & Pillsbury, 1992). Proximity to sports resources, be they natural (e.g. surf beaches), built (e.g. sports stadia) or a combination of the two (e.g. ski resorts), bears upon the propensity to consume certain sports, as competitors, participants and/or spectators. Location of residence also exposes individuals and communities to the sport cultures of a place, which although challenged by the relentless progress of global forces in sport and tourism (Higham & Hinch, 2009) continue to exist at a range of spatial scales of analysis (Focus point 3.3).

Focus point 3.3
Sport and Space

More than a game, sport is 'a social phenomenon in its own right' (Laidlaw, 2010: 49). Indeed, Laidlaw (2010) explains that sport matters so much to national identity that it can alter the course of social and political history. Sport functions as a social phenomenon at a range of spatial scales. Laidlaw (2010) notes the important role of sports in forging national identity in countries such as New Zealand (rugby union) and Australia (rugby league) just as in the cases of India (cricket), Brazil (football), Canada (ice hockey) and Ireland (Gaelic football). Similarly at a regional level, the north of England developed as a stronghold of rugby league in response to the exclusivity of rugby union in the English Home Counties (Laidlaw, 2010). Rugby union in North America demonstrates equally entrenched patterns of participation; both in the United States and Canada, the sport prevails on the west coast. The same even applies at urban and suburban levels of analysis. Despite attempts to globalise sports, Melbourne (Victoria) remains an Australian Rules stronghold as Sydney (New South Wales) remains the Australian home of rugby union and Brisbane (Queensland) rugby league. The same sociological patterns can even be discerned in suburbia. Sydney working class suburbs, such as Balmain and Paramatta, are loyal rugby league communities. In Wellington (New Zealand), the suburb of Wainouiamata is defined by rugby league as Petone is by rugby union (Laidlaw, 2010). As such, identification with sports clearly takes place at national, regional, local, and even suburban scales of analysis.

Understandably then, the link between nationality and patterns of sport participation is well established. For instance, considerable differences exist in the sport activities engaged by outbound tourists from Germany, the Netherlands and France (World Tourism Organization & International Olympic Committee, 2001). Sport-related trips account for more than 50% of all outbound travel undertaken by German and Dutch nationals, compared with 23% in the case of French outbound travellers. These markets also support segmentation on the basis of 'sport-orientated' and 'less sport-oriented' holiday preferences. The former is the general preference of Dutch travellers. The latter, which involves holidays where active involvement in sport is a secondary rather than the primary point of the holiday, is the preference of 85% of French travellers. Geographic segmentation is based on important differences in the preferred destinations, tourist activities, spending patterns and travel seasons of the study groups (World Tourism Organization & International Olympic Committee, 2001: 4).

> Three types of sport-orientated holidays – summer sport holidays, winter sport holidays, mountain holidays – enjoyed similar popularity among French and Dutch travellers. Germans preferred mountain holidays (43%) to summer holidays (19%). Skiing and hiking/walking were most popular activities among winter sport holidaymakers and mountain sport travellers, respectively. In the case of summer sport holidays, French travellers favoured diving/snorkelling, whereas Dutch and German travellers were keen on walking/hiking.

Patterns of active sport tourism participation can also be generalised at a national level. The largest single segment of the New Zealand domestic travel market identified by Lawson et al. (1997) was labelled 'sports devotees'. This segment represents 21% of the New Zealand domestic travel market, and its members are generally motivated by participation in sports at the tourist destination. The value of studies such as this is enhanced when positioned alongside the results of national sport and physical activity surveys (Walker, 2001), which report current patterns of participation and trends in the popularity of sports. Such exercises provide sport and tourism managers with rich veins of information relating to the increasing intersection between, and changing patterns of, sport participation and travel preferences.

Socio-economic market segmentation

Socio-economic market segmentation is based upon variables such as occupation and income. Participation in inexpensive, team-based contact sports such as street basketball and baseball is typical of lower socio-economic urban youth in North America and Cuba (Thomson, 2000). So too is participation in low-barrier, low-cost individual sports such as boxing, which has paved the way for elite athletes such as Manny Pacquiao (Kibawe, Philippines), and many others before him, to escape poverty. By contrast, expensive, individual and non-contact sports are favoured by the upper social classes (Yiannakis, 1975). Booth and Loy (1999: 10) argue that 'sports such as golf, tennis, sailing, show jumping and skiing … reflect the upper class's unique aesthetic and ethical dimensions, temporal/spatial orientations, material and symbolic status signs ...'. These consumers of sport are '... free to play sport at midday, mid-week or out of season [by travelling to the opposite hemisphere], and ... have the resources to play in exclusive and secluded places: cloisters, country clubs and lodges, and private game reserves' (Booth & Loy, 1999: 11).

The links between sport and socio-economic status, while also subject to the forces of social and economic globalisation, are inescapable, in terms of both participation and spectatorship. Many sports in England – croquet, polo, tennis and rugby union – according to Laidlaw (2010: 49) have 'served to divide for a very long time. The exclusive preserve of the English public schools ... unimaginable to those beneath the upper middle class'. The masses, Laidlaw points out, no doubt attracted by the simplicity and accessibility of the sport, took to football instead, both in England and around the world. Rugby union remains, in terms of spectatorship, the domain of the gentile in contrast to the local tribal hordes of the fandoms associated with football clubs across all continents. While democratisation has been the dominant trend in recent decades, these sports demonstrate and reaffirm socio-economic standing.

Demographic market segmentation

Swarbrooke and Horner (1999: 95) confirm that 'segmentation based on subdividing the population on the basis of demographic factors has proved particularly popular in tourism'. The demographic profiling of sport tourism markets in North America shows, for instance, that active participation in sports varies on the basis of age (Loverseed, 2001). The most popular participation sports in the United States in 2000 included recreational swimming (94%), recreational walking (83%) and bowling (74%). Activities such as fitness walking, treadmill exercises and stretching, and sports such as golf and fishing, are the preference of the seniors market (55 years and older), while basketball, soccer and baseball are favoured by the youth market (6–17 years). Participation in golf is influenced by demographic variables such as income, senior citizenry and 'empty nest' status (Tassiopoulos & Haydam, 2008).

Socio-demographic variables often serve as a second step in sport tourism market segmentation. Tokarski's (1993) study of holiday clubs in Caldetas and Fuerteventura (Spain) and Korfu (Greece) highlights significant differences within the German sport tourism market that exist on the basis of age. Young German travellers (15–21 years) identified good weather, relaxation and sports activities as important factors in a successful holiday. Water sports such as swimming, surfing, water skiing and diving held strong appeal for the youth market. The married and family travel markets were less inclined to actively engage in sports while on vacation, but the German senior market demonstrates a propensity to rediscover their interests in actively engaging in sporting activities (Tokarski, 1993). Hudson *et al.* (2010) demonstrate that the perceptions of constraints acting upon participants in downhill skiing vary on the basis of cultural or ethnic background (distinguishing in their study between Chinese and Anglo-Canadians) in Canada.

Gibson *et al.* (1998) provide one of the more detailed demographic analyses of the active sport tourism market from a lifespan perspective. They profile the active sport tourist market in the early adulthood (17–39 years), middle adulthood (40–59 years) and late adulthood (60–91) life stages. While active sport tourism proved to be pursued particularly by those in early adulthood, 'a sizeable number of both men and women choose sport orientated vacations in middle and late adulthood as well' (Gibson *et al.*, 1998: 52). They, like Tokarski (1993) and Harahousou (1999), identify physical activity among people in late adulthood as an increasingly apparent trend. The active sport tourism market is also influenced by changes in societal conventions regarding female participation in sports.

Gibson *et al.* (1998: 54) state that 'the subject of gender and sport is full of examples showing how gender-typed social expectations affect women's participation in sport and physical activity'. This situation is emerging from historical male domination of participation, particularly in professional sports, due to the changing societal ideologies about the gender-appropriateness of many activities (Wiley *et al.*, 2000). Women's rugby union and football have become major growth markets, which, in turn, has stimulated the study of the differentiated sport participation experiences on the basis of gender. Specific sport niche markets may also be defined by the survival of gender-specific medical conditions such as breast cancer (see Case study 3.1 by Heather Bell and Heather Gibson). Funk *et al.* (2007) demonstrate the gender-specific experiences of females competing in running events, which give priority to socialisation, relaxation and cultural learning. Similarly, in terms of sexuality, Pitts (1997: 32) profiles the gay and lesbian sport tourism niche market describing it as a clearly differentiated and '... viable, potentially lucrative, chic and high brand loyal market'.

Case study 3.1

Dragon Boat Festivals – Creating a Demand for Active Sport Tourism

Heather L. Bell & Heather J. Gibson (University of Florida)

Dragon boat festivals originated in China over 2000 years ago as important community cultural occasions. Traditionally, dragon boat festivals were held simultaneously in various locations on the fifth day of the fifth month in the lunar calendar. This day commemorated the suicide by drowning of the beloved poet Qu Yuan and his attempted rescue by villagers using dragon boats. Teams of paddlers used long slim boats colourfully decorated as dragons to race each other while spectators cheered. In a dragon boat, paddlers paddle in unison, have a steersperson at the back of the boat and a seated drummer at the front beating a rhythm for the paddlers to follow. In the 1970s, the Hong Kong Tourist Association revitalised the event and ushered in the era of the modern dragon boat festival by recognising its potential as a tourist attraction.

Growth of the Dragon Boat Festival

Dragon boat racing was introduced to Canada in 1986 in conjunction with Vancouver's Expo'86 World Fair. In recent years, Vancouver's annual dragon boat festival has drawn 180 teams and 100,000 spectators. In 1996, Dr Don McKenzie brought a group of breast cancer survivors (BCS) together as a dragon boat team as part of a study on vigorous upper body exercise and survivors' health. This team came to be known as Abreast in a Boat, and their success has spawned a worldwide movement of more than 100 BCS dragon boat paddling teams.

Dragon boating's popularity has spread across Canada and the United States, both as a spectator and as a participatory event. Dragon boat festivals now occupy various weekends throughout the summer months, planned strategically to fit into the existing event portfolio of the host community as well as the regional dragon boat event calendar. Part of the appeal is that dragon boating is social, with up to 22 participants per team. The races are sprint distances, usually between 200 and 500 m, making the activity accessible to people of average fitness levels. Teams consist of people of all age groups, from teens to adults in their 70s.

In North America, the number of people involved in dragon boat paddling continues to grow, evidenced by the addition of new festivals every year and the increase in people attending existing festivals. As dragon boating has developed in North America, dragon boat festivals are now hosted by such diverse organisations as dragon boat festival organising committees, service clubs, Chinese cultural associations, not-for-profit organisations and private companies.

Dragon Boat Festivals as Active Sport Tourism

Dragon boat paddling provides several opportunities for the active sport tourist. Paddlers may travel to attend dragon boat training camps or may add to an existing trip by contacting a local team and attending practices with it while in town. The most common form of active sport tourism is participation through dragon boat festivals. Typically, in many parts of Canada and the United States, the paddling season ends with the onset of colder weather, the last festivals occurring in early October. Warm weather destinations such as Florida are appealing for keen sport tourists wishing to extend their paddling seasons.

Orlando, FL, is a world-renowned tourism destination because of its theme parks. Since the late 1990s one theme park has been hosting a diverse range of amateur sports events as a way of attracting additional tourists. In 2008, it partnered with a Canadian event management company specialising in dragon boat festivals to coordinate the inaugural Orlando Dragon Boat Festival (ODBF). Individuals participated by attending with their regular team or by joining as a spare on a team needing an extra paddler or as a member of a team made up of other individual registrants.

Semi-structured interviews were conducted with participants from out-of-town teams at the second annual ODBF in October 2009. Participants were asked why and how they chose to attend this particular festival. Some wanted to come to the ODBF specifically and did whatever was needed to ensure that they were able to attend, such as finding a team to join. However, most participants expressed a strong link to their regular teams, and went wherever the team decided to go. For example, one paddler said:

> I try and attend every festival that our team is going to, unless there's some really major reason I can't go. Like this festival, I can't even paddle, I have a bad back, but I came anyway just because my team's coming, so I came. Yeah, so wherever the team decides where we're going to go, that's where I go.

Among the teams, several models of team decision making were evident. For example, having a coordinator make the choices for the team or having a race committee research opportunities followed by a team vote. Democratic team decision making was common, as described by one participant:

> We sort of come to a consensus. We look at all the races that are out there, and we have team meetings. . . . we pass a sheet around. We sign up for all the different races and whatever gets the most votes . . .

Many of the individuals from BCS teams expressed other layers of consideration that their teams negotiated, such as choosing to attend only those events that had BCS-specific divisions or that tried to support the efforts of other BCS teams, for example, 'If a breast cancer team is having their 10th anniversary and we can make it, we try to do it. Like London it was their 10 year, so we were in London (Ontario, Canada)'. Factors specific to the ODBF included prize money for the winning team, discounted theme park tickets, or as one participant said, 'It was a great way to end the season, and we wanted to extend our season, because we're done, we're from where it's cold. We did our last practice last Saturday'. As the popularity of dragon boating continues to grow and more destinations realise the tourism potential of hosting such festivals, this sport will likely become a popular opportunity for active sport tourists.

Further reading

McCartney, G. & Osti, L. (2007) From cultural events to sport events: A case study of cultural authenticity in the dragon boat races. *Journal of Sport & Tourism* 12 (1), 25–40.
McKenzie, D. (1998) Abreast in a boat – The race against breast cancer. *Canadian Medical Association Journal* 159 (4), 376–378.
Sofield, T.H.B & Sivan, A. (2003) From cultural festival to international sport – The Hong Kong Dragon Boat Races. *Journal of Sport Tourism* 8 (1), 9–20.

Psychographic market segmentation

Psychographic markets are targeted on the premise that 'the lifestyle, attitudes, opinions and personality of people determine their behaviour as consumers' (Swarbrooke & Horner, 1999: 96). For example, the psychographic profile of *sports-for-all* participants differs from that of those who pursue technical challenge or competition through active involvement in sports. The defining criteria of sport-for-all include the absence of entry qualifications, championship prizes and competition between participants (Nogawa *et al.*, 1996). Instead 'sport-for-all ... emphasises the joy of sport participation and health-related fitness while de-emphasising excessive competition. The concept of a sport-for-all event is that every participant is a winner' (Nogawa *et al.*, 1996: 47). The active sport tourism market can be effectively segmented based on the differences between sport-for-all participants and their more competitive counterparts.

Active participation in some sports may also be associated with distinctive subcultures that are an expression of identity (Green & Chalip, 1998). Wheaton (2000, 2004) examined one such subculture in her ethnographic study of windsurfing. She observed that the emergence of new and individualised leisure sports, such as windsurfing, snowboarding and mountain biking, represents 'much more than ... intermittent recreation; participants are involved in a multi-layered leisure subculture' (Wheaton, 2000: 256). Subcultures are expressed in various ways, including life choices such as career, work time, place of residence and tourist destination preferences. Similar conclusions have been made in the case of snowboarding (Heino, 2000). Both studies suggest that the values associated with individual sports can be instrumental in shaping the attitudes and personalities of participants (Chapter 6). Less organised and regulated sports, such as beach volleyball, street basketball, touch rugby and skateboarding 'emphasise values such as excitement, spontaneity, rebellion, non-conformity, sociability and creativity, and these are assuming considerable importance within the context of youth culture' (Thomson, 2000: 34).

The psychographic profile of sport tourists also evolves over time. Donnelly and Young (1988) identify career stages that characterise subcultural identities. Such studies 'highlight the utility of leveraging event consumers' identification with a sport's subculture when promoting sports events' (Green & Chalip, 1998: 288). Indeed Green and Chalip (1998) propose that active sport tourists may give priority to sharing and affirming their identities over the competitive element of their participation in sport. An understanding of the psychographic profile of these niche markets, then, is of great managerial as well as academic relevance.

Behaviouristic market segmentation

This avenue of segmentation classifies consumers according to their behavioural relationship with a product (Swarbrooke & Horner, 1999), with implications for the visitor experience (Chapter 8). Millington *et al.* (2001), for example, profile the growing number of participants in adventure tourism dividing the market based on soft (e.g. cycling, canoeing and horse riding) and hard (e.g. rafting, kayaking, climbing and caving) adventure activities. These adventure sports can be further differentiated based on the behaviours of participants. Downhill mountain bike racing and white water kayaking are extreme versions of sport that appeal to segments of the sport tourism market. They can be segmented based on the motivations and behaviours of participants, and then profiled demographically (Millington *et al.*, 2001). The link between motivation and behaviour, which is well established in the sport and recreation literature (Jackson, 1989), is of high relevance to sport tourism. It is important for destination marketers to understand the motivational and behavioural profiles of sport tourism market segments. They determine the desired visitor experience and the secondary activity sets that are associated with members of specific tourism market segments (Nogawa *et al.*, 1996).

The sport of skiing provides an illustration of the varied motivations and behaviours that exist within the tourist market (Klenosky *et al.*, 1993). Richards (1996), for instance, analysed the extent to which British skiers are motivated by technical challenge and the enhancement of skiing ability. This research identified a market segment that pursued and was stimulated by challenging skiing experiences. The quality of ski conditions and varied terrain were found to be fundamental to the experiences sought by this market segment (Richards, 1996). By contrast, the decision-making process of less experienced skiers was influenced more by price and accommodation. Participants in scuba diving (Tabata, 1992) and sport fishing (Roehl *et al.*, 1993) give increasing priority to the quality of the sport experience over other aspects of the visitor experience as they become more experienced in their sports. Davies and Williment's (2008b) study of New Zealand and British rugby fans confirms the relevance of various forms of segmentation, including demographic (e.g. age and income), psychographic and behavioural. These studies confirm that the motivational and behavioural profiles of sport tourist may be of greater relevance to sport and tourism managers than other approaches to market analysis.

Event Sport Tourism Markets

Event sport tourism, in its most prominent guise, involves travel to experience sporting events, where the body of spectators usually outweighs a small number of typically elite competitors (Getz, 1998). The most widely researched examples of event sport tourism include the Olympic Games, FIFA World Cup, Rugby World Cup and Formula One Grand Prix (Burgan & Mules, 1992; Ritchie, 1984; Webb, 2005; Weed, 2008b). However, sports competition may or may not be the primary attraction of a sports event. The Wimbledon Lawn Tennis Championship may be attended for its heritage and traditional value, Americas Cup for reasons of fashion and exclusivity and the Superbowl for commercial and business purposes. Large-scale spectator sports events may, then, attract tourists for whom the sporting competition is a coincidental or a secondary factor in their attendance. This suggests that the approaches to market segmentation to which reference has been made (Swarbrooke & Horner, 1999) are also applicable to the event sport tourism market, an exercise that requires further empirical research than that currently exists. Getz (1998: 8) correctly points out that a 'more comprehensive, systematic research effort is needed to answer key questions such as who is the sport-event tourist'.

Much research in this field focuses on large-scale spectator events. However, this is only a partial picture of the relationship between spectators and participants in event sport tourism (Bull & Weed, 1999).

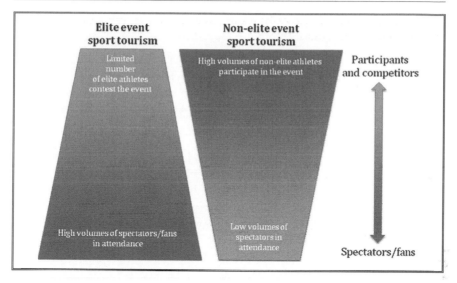

Figure 3.1 Conceptualisation of the relative engagement of spectators and participants in elite and non-elite sport events

Event sport tourism includes non-elite competitor events, where the number of competitors may be large, and the number of spectators negligible or non-existent (Figure 3.1). Exceptions to this general rule exist where non-elite events attract large numbers of family and friends as spectators (Carmichael & Murphy, 1996). In some instances, elite and non-elite competitors are accommodated in a single event, which creates a broad catchment range of elite athletes, spectators and non-elite competitors. The London, New York and Boston marathons provide evidence of the success of such events. The relationship between participation and spectatorship in event sport tourism deserves more academic attention as the markets, promotional possibilities, infrastructure requirements, tourist behaviours, travel patterns and associated tourist experiences of each may stand in significant contrast.

Elite sports events and tourism

Numerous avenues of tourism development may be associated with elite sports events. Faulkner *et al.* (1998: 1) emphasise the need for sport and tourism authorities to establish a set of conditions to ensure that this potential is captured. In a study of the 2000 Olympic Games, they state that

> ... in reality, there are both tourism opportunities that can be derived from hosting the games and offsetting negative effects, and the degree to which the former are accentuated and the latter ameliorated ultimately depends on the extent to which the leveraging

strategies adopted by the industry and relevant public agencies are effectively integrated.

The build-up to the Sydney 2000 Olympic Games involved a coordinated leveraging programme to which both sport and tourism administrators actively contributed, much more so than the subsequent Olympic Games held in Athens (Greece) and Beijing (China). The outcome was effective destination promotion, successful pre-games training and acclimatisation camps, the stimulation of convention and incentive travel, the promotion of pre- and post-games travel itineraries and the minimisation of diversion and aversion effects (Faulkner *et al.*, 1998). Leveraging elite sports events requires a clear understanding of the tourism development opportunities that exist beyond games-induced travel. Indeed, recent Olympic Games have been studied to forecast and/ or measure games-induced travel (Kang & Purdue, 1994; Pyo *et al.*, 1991). Such studies have generally overestimated levels of visitation and, as Faulkner *et al.* (1998: 10) observe, 'once the normal level of travel to the host city is factored into estimates the net effect of games induced travel is much reduced'.

It is important to acknowledge the complex flows of visitors into and out of a spatial unit of analysis (which varies with the defined scale of the event destination) (Preuss, 2007; Weed, 2008a). The diversion effects (real or perceived) may be encouraged by the media attention paid to capacity constraints at the destination (e.g. traffic congestion, over-demand for accommodation, resulting in inconvenience, inflated costs and security issues), which may be placed under strain when events take place. Pyo *et al.* (1991) identify a range of factors that may discourage attendance at summer Olympic Games, including political boycotting, price gouging, crowding and congestion. Ticket distribution may also bear upon the propensity of sport tourists to attend events such as the Olympic Games (Thamnopoulos & Gargalianos, 2002). Chalip *et al.* (1998) present an analysis of sources of interest in travel to attend the Olympic Games. Such analyses provide valuable insights into the relative importance of the event itself, and the destination hosting the event, in terms of the travel decision-making process. These studies offer information that is critical to the successful leveraging of sports events.

Sport tourism markets vary from one event to another. However, useful generalisations are possible. For example, Faulkner *et al.* (1998) employ the term 'sport junkies' to describe tourists who visit a destination specifically to attend a sporting event, but demonstrate little propensity to engage in pre- and post-event itineraries. This term describes a sport tourism market that is single-mindedly focused on the sports event itself. The Formula One Grand Prix Racing Champion-ship is considered to generally attract this type of tourist. Not only are the tourists who come to this type of event likely to displace other types of tourists at a destination, but they may also be associated with specific negative impacts that are unique to this market segment (Faulkner *et al.*, 1998).

Alternatively, sport spectators may engage in a more casual relationship with the sports that they follow. In these cases 'general interest and match attendance can shift in response to wins and losses, the state of the venue, the appearance of star players and a change in the weather' (Stewart, 2001: 17). Casual consumers of sport present sport markets with unique challenges associated with accessing this element of sport tourism demand. The importance of studying and understanding the travel motivations and wider pre- and post-event itineraries of sports tourists emerges clearly from these studies. The leveraging of sport tourism events require consideration of the sport and tourism product at the destination, supply and demand for sports facilities and services, and tourism experiences before, during and after the event (Faulkner *et al.*, 1998). Much less is known about the tourism experiences of elite athletes. Conceiving elite athletes as tourists who visit destinations, albeit for different reasons to those who travel to destinations to experience their sporting performances, is an interesting proposition. Some destinations now seek to actively attract and cater to elite athletes and sports teams (Chalip, 2005). There is increasing evidence that the behaviours of travelling fans may be influenced by the location (e.g. training bases) of teams in advance of and during competition.

Non-elite event sport tourism

Bale (1989: 114) observes that 'even quite small sporting events can generate substantial amounts of revenue for the communities within which they are located'. Destinations that are unable to host large-scale sporting events because of capacity constraints may compete to attract competitive but non-elite sport tourism events (Higham, 1999). Chogahara and Yamaguchi (1998), for example, report on the National Sports Festival for the Elderly (Japan). This study identifies that participants tend to engage in a wide range of tourist activities, particularly sightseeing and visiting hot spas both during and following the completion of the event. This study confirms that those who participate in lesser or non-competitive sports events are more likely to take advantage of opportunities to engage in tourist activities at a destination. Little is known about the travel preferences of participants who form the less competitive element of the event sport tourism market. This niche market is characterised by travel motivations that are distinct from those of elite and competitive event participants. It is a market that presents unique opportunities to generate business opportunities for other tourist attractions and services within a destination.

The distinction between elite and non-elite event sport tourism is important (Figure 3.1). Carmichael and Murphy (1996) suggest that event sport tourists should be differentiated on the basis of spectatorship and participation; the latter includes athletes, officials and coaches. Their study provides insights into visitor origin, length of stay, expenditure patterns, numbers of friends and relatives accompanying participants, and their intentions to return to the town hosting the event. This points towards the tourist motivations that distinguish those who attend elite sports events from those who travel to participate in non-elite sports competitions (Chapter 8).

In response to this point, some attention has been usefully paid to 'second-order' (subelite) sports events which have been pursued by marginal or provincial cities seeking to 'shine on the global stage' (Whitson, 2004: 1221). Gratton *et al.* (2005) highlight the sharply contrasting tourism contexts associated with second-tier sports events which serve as a warning to guard against the overselling of the tourism and economic benefits of hosting such events. Black (2008: 467) notes in reference to 'second-order' sports events that 'their benefits continue to be chronically oversold and their opportunity costs minimized or overlooked'. Similarly, Whitson and Macintosh (1996: 288) observe that in the absence of an established tourism trade '... it is a mirage to think that a substantial tourist economy can be constructed on the back of such events alone. The imaging effect is too small and the competition is too great'. While Higham (1999) notes the potential for small-scale events to generate the same positive impacts as larger events (within their own geographical scales of analysis), it is critical that they are realistically considered within the infrastructural and 'tourist economy' limitations of smaller communities. So, too, are means by which to foster 'flow on' tourism to maximise the benefits that sports events may generate for regional economies (Focus point 3.4).

Focus point 3.4
Edmonton 2005 World Masters Games (WMG)

The Edmonton 2005 World Masters Games (WMG) was held in Edmonton, AB, Canada, from 22 to 31 July 2005. It attracted 21,600 registered competitors, with 14,267 of these coming from Canada, 1973 from the United States and a further 5360 from 87 other countries. There were an additional 3000 registered companions, coaches and managers as well as 1000 officials. One of its distinguishing features was that it was sport-for-all participation type of event rather than one restricted to elite athletes. While WMG's athletes were serious about their personal performance, they actively sought social, cultural and travel opportunities associated with the games. A post-games study estimated that they generated $36.4 million for the City of Edmonton and $70.3 million for the Canadian economy against event expenditures of $13.9 million. A significant portion of this benefit accrued as a result of the tourist behaviour of visiting athletes while they were in Edmonton competing during the event, along with pre-games and post-games vacations. While staying in Edmonton for their competitions, 63% of the athletes shopped, 39% visited a bar or nightclub and 32% attended a non-WMG sporting event (e.g. Canadian Football League). Of all athletes, 22% incorporated a vacation into their travel to Edmonton, with 34% taking a vacation after the competition while on their way home. For the pre-games vacationers, the average length of the vacation was 8.9 days, with 28% having primary destinations in Alberta, 28% in British Columbia and a further 24% in Edmonton. The most popular activities of these vacationers included visiting national or provincial parks (69%), shopping (68%) and active participation in sports or outdoor recreation (52%). Post-games vacationers travelled for an average of 9.4 days, with 44% identifying Alberta as their primary destination, 28% the United States and 14% Edmonton. The top three tourist activities that they participated in were similar to those identified by pre-games vacationers: shopping (64%), visiting a national or provincial park (59%) and actively engaging in sport or outdoor recreation (37%). While it is impossible to make direct empirical comparisons to other sporting events because of data limitations, anecdotal evidence suggests that the actual tourist engagement of athletes and spectators for the WMG was much more substantial than for the athletes and spectators who attended the higher profile Edmonton 2001 World Championships in Athletics. Given its significant media profile, the latter event likely had a greater impact on destination awareness than did the WMG. However, the sport-for-all approach of the WMG appears to have resulted in a much higher level of tourist engagement prior to, during and immediately surrounding this event. Sport event planners would do well to consider these distinctions in their bidding strategies.

Source: Hinch, T. & Walker, G. (2006). Motivations, *Travel Behaviours and Socio-Demographic Profiles of Registered Athletes at the 2005 Edmonton World Masters Games*. Research Report prepared at the University of Alberta, for the City of Edmonton, Edmonton, Alberta (see http://www.imga.ch/ for supplemental information. Accessed 31 May 2010)

Nostalgia Sport Tourism

Within Gibson's (1998) classification framework, nostalgia sport tourism is the least researched and understood. This form of sport tourism includes tourist visitation to sport museums, halls of fame, themed bars and restaurants, heritage events and sports reunions. Nostalgia sport tourism is a rapidly developing sector of the sport tourism industry but one that has hitherto been developed almost exclusively in North America. Stevens (2001: 68–69) notes that in the United Kingdom sports-based visitor attractions 'are limited to museums at Manchester United, Chelsea, Liverpool, Bolton, Aston Villa and Arsenal football clubs, the recently opened National Football Museum in Preston, the Wimbledon Tennis Museum, the Newmarket Horse Racing Museum and British Golf Museum that opened at St. Andrews in 1990'. This short list pales alongside Redmond's (1990) extensive listing of sports museums in North America.

Gammon (2002) discusses the commercialisation of the past in tourism and relates this to sport tourism. He documents the growth of nostalgia sport tourism with reference to the mature sport nostalgia industry in North America (Gibson, 2002; Redmond, 1990). The resource base for nostalgia sport tourism focuses particularly on halls of fame and sport museums. While the former venerate the famous, the gifted or the exceptional, the latter contain collections of artefacts and memorabilia that celebrate a sport, rather than high-performing individuals or teams within a sport (Gammon, 2002). The growth in demand for nostalgia sport tourism is not yet reflected in a published body of research on this topic.

Nostalgia represents an avenue of sport tourism that demonstrates parallels with heritage tourism (Redmond, 1990). Bale (1989) notes that sport edifices may develop such a mystique that they become subjects of visitor attention in their own right. Examples of sports venues that are the subject of interest among nostalgia sport tourists include Wembley Stadium and the Wimbledon Lawn Tennis Club (London), the Athens (1896) and Berlin (1936) Olympic stadiums and (prior to its dismantling and redevelopment in 2009) the Holmenkollen ski jump (Oslo) (Bale, 1989). Numerous questions relating to the nostalgia sport tourism market currently remain unanswered. The need exists to understand why people engage in this form of tourism and how nostalgia relates to other forms of tourism and sport tourism at a destination.

The focus of research in this field has hitherto examined resources for nostalgia sport tourism (Redmond, 1990) rather than the people who actually engage in this form of sport tourism (Gammon, 2002), although this has started to change (Morgan, 2007). How nostalgia sport tourism relates to the demand for active and event sport tourism experience is also poorly understood. It is likely that this form of sport tourism has indistinct boundaries with active and event sport tourism. Travel packages that follow the tour matches of an international sports team, and which are often led by former star players, illustrate the overlap between event and nostalgia sport tourism. Similarly, cruise ship packages that offer passengers the opportunity to meet, or be coached by sports personalities (Gibson, 1998), hold elements of both active sport tourism and nostalgia. An increasingly apparent trend over the last decade has, in fact, been the development of sports events that embrace the widest possible spectrum of niche markets, incorporating elements of competition (elite and non-elite), active participation, spectatorship and nostalgia. This points to a blurring of the events, active and nostalgia tripartite in many forms of contemporary sport tourism.

Conclusion

This chapter confirms that sport tourism may be accurately conceptualised as a specialised market in itself while also being characterised by numerous niche markets (Bull & Weed, 1999; Chalip, 2001). These niche markets can be differentiated through geographic, socio-economic, demographic, psychographic and behaviouristic segmentation techniques. The managerial relevance of sport tourism market research lies in the diversity of the constituent segments that collectively comprise the sport tourism market. The travel profiles (e.g. length of stay, modes of transport and accommodation preferences) and secondary tourism motivations (e.g. attractions and activities) that these travellers bring to the tourism destination are the subject of tourism market research. Sport and tourism market information pertaining to different niche markets is a prerequisite to the effective development of sport tourism at a destination.

More market research is needed in the realm of sport tourism. The travel motivations and preferences of distinct sport tourism markets, and the tourism development opportunities that they offer, have become subjects of a developing academic literature. Glyptis (1991: 181) observes that sport tourism development necessitates that 'sport and tourism authorities talk to one another and forge real working partnerships'. Detailed insights into sport tourism markets, and the development opportunities associated with these markets, will help to facilitate the establishment of such partnerships.

Chapter 4
Development Processes and Issues

*Management of the process of renewal and the redesigning of products and services is
a field where sport and tourism can exchange valuable experiences.*
de Villers, 2001: 12

Introduction

Change is one of the few constants in contemporary society. By understanding the nature and process of development, trends can be predicted and potentially influenced. This chapter discusses the concept of development as it exists in relation to sport tourism. It is argued that if sport tourism development is to comply with the dominant paradigm of sustainability, then planned and informed intervention into the development process is required. The latter part of this chapter highlights three key issues facing sport tourism development: commodification/ authenticity, globalisation and organisational fragmentation. Failure to understand these issues compromises the development potential of sport tourism. Wall's case study on the Beijing Olympics provides a unique perspective of the way China positioned this event in the context of global and local interests (Case study 4.1).

The Concept of Development

Development is an elusive term as its meaning differs with the context in which it is used. Members of a broad range of disciplines and professions interpret development in ways that make sense to themselves, perhaps more so than others. Even in the context of popular usage, fundamentally different meanings of the term exist. Common interpretations include development as philosophy, process, plan and product.

> As a philosophy, development refers to broad perspectives concerning appropriate future states and means of achieving them. As a process it emphasizes the methods, which might be employed to expand or bring about the potentials or capabilities of a phenomenon. A development plan sets out specific steps through which desirable future states are to be achieved and development as a product indicates the level of achievement of an individual or society, as in developing and underdeveloped countries. (Wall, 1997: 35)

Of these perspectives, the most common are development as a product and development as a process. In the case of the former, development is treated as a state. This approach is being used when reference is made to levels of development. Such levels are often assessed in terms of economic measures such as income and employment but increasingly include non-economic measures such as the social conditions found in a region. In the latter case, development is seen as an evolutionary process. Freidmann (1986) described development as a process of change or as a complex of such processes. He suggested that these changes were predictable enough that intelligent statements could be made about them. Development, as used in the title of this book, refers to the process of development, and the issues and challenges associated with change in the way that sport tourism is manifested in space and time.

Sport tourism exists within social, cultural, political, economic and environmental contexts that are in constant flux. This is true of the factors that affect demand as well as those that affect supply. Change in sport tourism is, therefore, inevitable. Given its inevitability, Pigram and Wahab (1997) have argued that [sport] tourism managers should be prepared to

> welcome change and take up the opportunities that change offers. Change is a powerful and positive force which, when harnessed constructively, challenges individuals, groups and organizations to perform to their optimum capability. (p. 28)

Planners and policymakers seek change that is accompanied by positive impacts and implications. Growth in its various forms, including the number of sport-related visitors to a destination, the amount that these visitors spend and the physical development of sport tourism sites, may be the foremost objectives. Nevertheless, it is inappropriate to simply equate growth with development, especially when a long-term perspective is taken that incorporates the various interests of all stakeholders (Atkisson, 2000; Binns, 1995). Development is not just change in terms of growth, but it is change that has a positive overall impact. It should, therefore, be assessed in the context of a full range of stakeholders and their often competing and sometimes contradictory goals, including social, cultural, ethical and environmental goals.

While there is general agreement that development as a planned process should be aimed at positive change over time, there has been less agreement as to what should be used to measure change. Typically, economic measures have been used as indicators. This is consistent with the dominant political–economic system operating throughout the developed world in '... which maintaining or increasing levels of economic growth has been a virtually unassailable policy goal' (Hall, 2000a: 6). Notwithstanding this entrenched perspective, definitions of development 'have tended to be broadened over time and development has gradually come to be viewed as a social as well as an economic process which involves the progressive improvement of conditions and the fulfilment of potential' (Wall, 1997: 34). For example, poverty reduction has increasingly been recognised by agencies such as the World Bank as a key development objective (Hawkins & Mann, 2007).

Other indicators of development that have emerged over the past three decades include modernisation, distributive justice and spatial reorganisation (Pearce, 1989). The last of these – development as spatial reorganisation – is particularly relevant to this book. From this perspective, spatial form represents the physical manifestation of changing patterns of social relations. The appeal of this approach lies in its tangible expression in terms of space, place and physical impacts. While it is recognised that there are various valid approaches to considering development, it is not possible to do them all justice in one book. The balance of this book focuses on development in its spatial and temporal dimensions.

Sustainable Development

Sustainable development is a contested concept. While few people would claim that they do not support the principle of sustainable development, the meaning of the concept is not universally shared (Hall & Lew, 1998; Hopwood *et al.*, 2005; Pesqueux, 2009). Business advocates tend to emphasise 'development' while environmentalists tend to focus on 'sustainability'. As a result, the phrase can sometimes seem like a contradiction of terms. Yet behind the rhetoric of the various stakeholders and scholars who debate its merits, it is a concept that holds widespread appeal. Tourism proponents have argued that '... conditions can be created (in tourism) so that real development, in terms of human betterment and enhanced life opportunities, is nurtured to be handed on to future generations for their growth and prosperity' (Pigram & Wahab, 1997: 3, 4).

The World Commission on Environment and Development's (WCED, 1987: 4) definition of sustainable development is '... development that meets the needs of the present without compromising the ability of future generations to meet their own needs'. While there are many other definitions, most tend to focus on the sustainability of natural ecosystems. The WCED definition is, however, robust enough to include the sustainability of cultural resources. Mowforth and Munt (1998: 109) describe this type of sustainability as 'the ability of people or a people to retain or adapt elements of their culture which distinguish them from other peoples'. In the case of sport tourism, this aspect of the definition encompasses sport as an expression of culture (Chapter 6) as well as the impacts that sport tourism has on the physical environment in which it occurs (Chapter 7).

There is a difference between sustainable tourism and sustainable development (Liu, 2003; Saarinen, 2006; Wall, 1997; Zhu, 2009). Sustainable tourism is '... tourism which is in a form which can maintain its viability in an area for an indefinite period of time' (Butler, 1993: 29). In contrast, tourism in the context of sustainable development is tourism which is developed and maintained in an area (community, environment) in such a manner and at such a scale that it remains viable over an indefinite period and does not degrade or alter the environment (human and physical) in which it exists to such a degree that it prohibits the successful development and well-being of other activities and processes (Butler, 1993: 29).

Clearly, the latter goal is of a higher order. Maintaining sport tourism at the expense of the cultural and physical environments in which it exists contradicts the fundamental principles of sustainable development.

Accounting for this broader development context is challenging but necessary. The achievement of sustainable sport tourism requires a balance between social, economic and environment goals. This approach has become known as the 'triple bottom line' (Smith, 2009). Authors such as Pawlowski (2008) argue that there are even more dimensions that should be considered such as the moral, legal, technical and political realms.

While sustainable sport tourism is the essence of Figure 4.1, the broader concept of sport tourism in the context of sustainable development is embodied in the spheres adjoining the centre. A healthy sport tourism economy should ideally support and enhance the social/cultural dimension of the community. It should also play a similar role in the context of the natural environment, which features prominently in many types of sport tourism activity. In addition, sport tourism social/cultural practices should serve as positive forces in relation to the natural environment. There is, however, no guarantee that the interaction between sport and tourism will necessarily be positive. To achieve positive outcomes, those with management and planning interests in sport tourism must be conscious of the impacts of their decisions throughout the full range of these realms rather than just at the centre. This awareness needs to be accompanied by a constructive integrated approach to development.

The sport and tourism industries have vested interests as well as a moral obligation to meet the goal of sustainability. At a micro level, sustainable development has a direct impact on the return on investment for sport tourism businesses and the communities in which it functions. At the macro level, sustainable development has global implications across an intricate web of social, economic and environmental domains. The natural tendency of developers is to focus on economic goals, but if environmental and social cultural resources are viewed as a form of capital, a strong business argument exists for sustainable practices

Figure 4.1 Sustainable sport tourism
Source: Hall (1995)

(Hall, 2000a: 6). Beyond the business rationale, a moral responsibility exists for the pursuit of sustainable development at both the micro and macro levels (Pawlowski, 2008).

Planning

Planning is a means of managing change. Given that sport tourism exists in a dynamic environment and given that these dynamics do not necessarily lead to sustainable outcomes, some sort of intervention into the development process is required to foster the type of change that helps stakeholders to achieve their objectives. Essentially, 'planning is a process of human thought and action based upon that thought ...'

(Chadwick, 1971: 24). Planning is 'concerned with anticipating and regulating change in a system, to promote orderly development as to increase the social, economic, and environmental benefits of the development process' (Murphy, 1985: 156). It is based on the assumption that even a partial understanding of the dynamics of sport tourism and the world in which it exists provides the basis to influence change. By consciously initiating this type of process, developers of sport tourism not only act in their best self-interests, but they make positive contributions to the sustainability of the social, cultural, economic and environmental systems in which they function.

The underlying process for planning is consistent across a broad range of fields and disciplines. It is based on an assessment of the current situation, likely changes that will occur in the environment in which the plan is being conducted, decisions on the desired end state, formulation of some sort of action plan, its implementation, followed by monitoring, assessment and adjustment as required (Esfahani *et al.*, 2009; Inskeep, 1991; World Tourism Organization, 1994). Bagheri and Hjorth (2007) emphasise that 'process-oriented' planning is more important than 'goal-oriented' planning because sustainable development is an ideal not an absolute end point. From this perspective, the true benefit lies in the social learning process of engaged stakeholders. Yang and Wall (2009) illustrate this with their study of sustainable planning for ethnic tourism in Xishuangbanna, China. They make the point that planners must deal with dynamic issues which require ongoing resolution rather than one-time attention. While Young and Wall drew their conclusions in the context of ethnic tourism, parallel issues that require continuous attention exist in the realm of sport tourism.

Development Issues

If planning interventions into the development process are to be successful, then informed consideration of the many issues that exist within the field of sport tourism is necessary. A number of specific issues are introduced and discussed in the chapters that follow, but three issues have particular significance to sport tourism development. These issues include commodification/authenticity, globalisation and organisational fragmentation.

Commodification and authenticity

One of the most fundamental issues of sport tourism development is the process of commodification and its implications in terms of authenticity. The importance of this issue is predicated on the belief that the search for authenticity is one of the main driving forces for tourism (MacCannell, 1976; Urry, 1990). It is also predicated on the fact that sport represents a dynamic and increasingly prominent stage for the expression of culture. Plog's (1972: 4) warning that '[d]estination areas carry with them potential seeds of their own destruction, as they allow themselves to become more commercialized and lose their qualities which originally attracted tourists' needs to be carefully considered. Selling sport culture as a tourism product can have major negative as well as positive impacts on sport within the destination community.

In a tourism context, Cohen (1988: 380) has defined commoditisation, a term synonymous with commodification, as a

> process by which things (and activities) come to be evaluated primarily in terms of their exchange value, in a context of trade, thereby becoming goods (and services); developed exchange systems in which the exchange value of things (and activities) is stated in terms of prices form a market.

Similarly, in the context of sport, McKay and Kirk (1992: 10) defined commodification as

> the process by which objects and people become organized as things to be exchanged in a market. Whereas cultural activities such as ... sport once were based primarily on intrinsic worth, they are now increasingly constituted by market values.

These definitions feature the same fundamental characteristics, a process of commercialisation that superimposes economic values on things or activities that were not previously valued in this way. One important point of difference is that commodification is almost an axiom of tourism given its commercial nature. Sport, on the other hand, has a rich non-commercial history although there are certainly heightened levels of commercialisation associated with modern sport. Tourism is one agent of commercialisation as it 'packages' and 'sells' sport to travellers.

Tourism critics argue that the commercialisation of culture introduces economic relations into an area where they previously played no part. In the process of commercialisation, real authenticity is destroyed and a covert 'staged authenticity' emerges. As the fact that this staged authenticity is not real dawns on tourists, it thwarts their genuine search for authenticity (MacCannell, 1973; Yang & Wall, 2009). Cohen (1988: 383), however, counters by observing that

> Commoditization does not necessarily destroy the meaning of cultural products, neither for the locals nor for the tourists, although it may do so under certain conditions. Tourist-oriented products frequently acquire new meanings for the locals, as they become a diacritical mark of their ethnic or cultural identity, a vehicle of self-representation before an external public.

Critics of the commodification of sport suggest that the professionalisation of various competitions and the broader commercialisation of sport through the media and the interests of large manufacturing/retail corporations have had a detrimental effect. Stewart (1987: 172) articulates this position by arguing that the

> social hegemony of the commodity form is apparent as the practice of sport is shaped and dominated by the values and instrumentalities of a market. . . . the idealized model of sport, along with its traditional ritualized meanings, metaphysical aura, and skill democracy, is destroyed as sport becomes just another item to be trafficked as a commodity.

A particularly good illustration of this line of argument is the commodification of the Olympic Rings logo (Van Wynsberghe & Ritchie, 1998). The blatant commercialisation of this logo by way of licensing agreements presents a stark contrast to the altruistic tone of the Olympic Charter. Clearly, the commodification of sport is not always viewed as a problem. Williams (1994) points out that the commodification of sport has brought about several benefits, including new funds, better performances, improved stadia, professionalism in performance and staging, and some new sources of support and opportunities for grassroots development. He tempers this rosy picture, however, by noting that in the process of capturing these benefits, the traditional power brokers of sport have abdicated significant influence to media, sponsors and corporate clients. For example, corporate interests in sport have influenced the relocation of sporting events such as the Belgian Grand Prix (Formula One) to avoid locations where government legislation prevents tobacco company sponsorship.

Authenticity is closely related to commodification. It can be viewed in a number of ways. Cole (2007), for example, distinguishes between the perspectives of government, tourist and villager in eastern Indonesia. While governments and tourists found authenticity to be problematic, villagers did not. They saw the commodification of their culture as being empowering.

In a tourism context, authenticity has traditionally been viewed in relation to the object of interest, the originals or the thing or activity that the tourists have come to see (Wang, 1999). This can be thought of as comparable to a museum curator's perspective where experts in such matters test whether objects of art are what they appear to be or are claimed to be (Cohen, 1988). The sporting parallel is manifested in popular criticism of any break from tradition, especially in relation to rule changes. From this perspective, a thing or activity is judged to be authentic or not in a relatively objective manner. Reisinger and Steiner (2005) take issue with this view, arguing that it is not possible to judge object authenticity. In the face of such criticism, the pursuit of objective authenticity has gradually given away to more flexible interpretations of authenticity where it is appreciated that there is seldom an absolute authenticity, but that it is more often negotiated in some fashion. Wang (1999) has termed this constructive authenticity. As part of the commodification process, the tourism industry has continued to present 'staged authenticity', albeit increasingly in an overt form. Rather than taking tourists to the backstage of a destination to experience real culture, tourism operators use the front stage where a destination's culture is presented in a controlled way via museums, heritage centres, cultural performances and other similar forums. A dedicated stage for tourism allows for greater influence over impacts and addresses the operational constraints associated with tourist activity such as the restricted scheduling that typically characterises tourists. Cohen (1988) also discussed the concept of 'emergent authenticity', which reflects the gradual emergence of authenticity in the eyes of visitors. A classic example is Disneyland, which initially was viewed as being inauthentic but which has 'emerged' as an authentic representation of American culture. Many of the new extreme sports would fit into this category.

Timothy and Boyd's (2002) review of the authenticity debate in the context of heritage tourism highlights several important issues that are especially relevant in relationship to nostalgia sport tourism. They suggest five types of common distortions of the past: invented places or reconstructed pasts, relative authenticity that recognises the subjective nature of interpreting the past, ethnic intruders in the form of non-local interpreters, sanitised and idealised pasts and, finally, the unknown past in which it is recognised that interpretations of the past can only be partial. Sport tourism examples in these categories include fantasy sport camps, contradictory views of historic sporting matches, great geographic diversity reflected in the playing and coaching rosters, highly nostalgic interpretations of past sporting glory and hero worship, and memories of the past built on selected statistical summaries associated with elite competition (Gammon & Ramshaw, 2007). All of these distortions compromise objective authenticity, but they do not necessarily detract from the experience of the visitor.

While many academics have criticised the tourism industry's failure to provide 'objective authenticity' (e.g. Boorstin, 1975; Greenwood, 1989), others recognised that tourists often seek contrived experiences as part of their desire to have fun (Moscardo, 2000; Urry, 1990). Butler (1996: 93) captures this notion in his view that

> most tourist destinations, and certainly those aimed at the mass market, are not intended, and never were intended to be examples of the real world. A holiday destination to most visitors is not the real

world, it is generally an imaginary world, a wishful world, or a Shangri-La … In the case of the present day tourists, it would appear that what most wish to take back home with them, most importantly, are themselves, intact, refreshed, happy, and with good feelings and memories.

Notwithstanding this perspective, it is acknowledged that many tourists are searching for authentic experiences rather than authentic objects (McIntosh & Prentice, 1999) (Focus point 4.1). This is consistent with the more general consumer search for authenticity in products, services and experiences (Gilmore & Pine, 2007; Yeoman *et al.*, 2007). Wang (1999: 352) has articulated this 'rethinking' of authenticity describing an activity-related authenticity which he refers to as existential authenticity:

> Existential authenticity refers to a potential existential state of Being that is to be activated by tourist activities. Correspondingly, authentic experiences in tourism are to achieve this activated existential state of Being within the liminal process of tourism. Existential authenticity can have nothing to do with the authenticity of toured objects.

This type of authenticity would seem to hold considerable relevance for sport tourism with its focus on experience. It also represents an interesting dynamic in relation to the blurring of sport and entertainment. The key is engagement. If tourists are actively engaged as spectators or as active participants in a sport, they are likely to view their experience as being authentic regardless of how others may assess the situation. Sport is unique compared with other types of tourist attractions in this regard. Key characteristics of sport that promote experiential authenticity include uncertain outcomes, display as part of performance, its physical basis and all-sensory nature, self-making and the construction of identity, and its propensity to develop community. To a large extent, authenticity is what makes sport so compelling (Hinch & Higham, 2005).

Wang (1999) expands on his interpretation of existential authenticity by introducing four subcategories. The first of these is intrapersonal authenticity as manifested in bodily feelings – a major dimension of active sport tourism. Intrapersonal authenticity as manifested in self-identity is the second subcategory. This category is described as 'self-making' and is often found in sports such as rock climbing in which participants can reaffirm and develop their sense of identity. A third type is interpersonal authenticity that enhances family ties. In a sporting context, family ties are closely related to the concept of a team. Finally, interpersonal authenticity can be found in the vibrant communities associated with various sports. In many instances, the emergence of these new types of authenticity is closely tied to changing external conditions such as the process of globalisation.

Focus point 4.1

Chasing Authenticity

Not only is authenticity hard to define, it is also hard to achieve even if an experiential perspective is adopted. The very nature of tourism – especially mass tourism – tends to constrain one's ability to connect with places in anything more than a superficial way. Short visits and tourism infrastructure designed to capture cost economies and to facilitate mass transport, accommodation and affiliated services also tend to separate the tourists from the locals and the places in which the locals live. This is true of most forms of travel. Strategies to achieve a more authentic experience are varied, with most being positioned as 'alternatives' to mass tourism. But how does a mass tourist chase authenticity? In Italy, a visitor is welcome to view the authentic work of Italian masters found in places such as Florence but what of authentic experiences. Vagnoli (2010) offers several travel tips for visitors to Italy who are looking for this type of authenticity. These include visiting smaller towns, staying in accommodations catering to locals, eating where the locals eat, walking rather than driving, learning Italian and patronising local fairs and festivals. All of these strategies have the potential of facilitating authentic tourist experiences. It is the last of these strategies that is particularly attractive in a sport tourism context. Attending an Italian premier league football game, the Formula 1 Italian Grand Prix or the Giro d'Italia cycling race will all immerse a visitor in genuine Italian culture. Participating in smaller scale local sporting events will heighten this experience even further.

Based in part on Vagnoli, G. (2010) Travel tips to Italy: How to have a more authentic experience. On WWW at http://www.suite101.com/content/travel-tips-to-italy-how-to-have-a-more-authentic-experience-a230582. Accessed 2 December 2010.

Globalisation

The term 'globalisation' can bring forth various reactions, as exemplified by the positive response to the concept of a 'global village' through to the passionate protests decrying economic inequities and cultural imperialism that have become a predictable part of world economic summits. Simply put, globalisation is the process that leads to an ever-tightening network of connections which cut across national boundaries. It is characterised by the worldwide compression of time and space (Mowforth & Munt, 1998). Sport is increasingly being used as a way to position destinations within this global world (Case study 4.1 by Geoff Wall).

Case study 4.1
Beijing Olympics: Positioning China in a Global World

Geoffrey Wall, University of Waterloo, Canada

China's entry into the World Trade Organization in 2001 and its selection over Toronto in the same year as the site for the 29th Summer Olympic Games in 2008 were both met with euphoria in China: people celebrated in the streets. China has had a long and complex political history, with many invasions and much political infighting and, under Chairman Mao during the Cultural Revolution, it turned its back on the rest of the world. Since 1978 and the introduction of the 'open door' policy, China has engaged increasingly with the outside world and its economy has grown by leaps and bounds. At many levels, the Beijing Olympics represent a critical juncture in the strategic positioning of China in the context of globalisation processes occurring throughout the world. The decisions to allocate such international opportunities to China, including the 2010 Shanghai World Fair, can be interpreted as tangible evidence that China is now taking a prominent place in world affairs. The Olympic Games, which were shown on television in homes throughout the world, clearly indicated that China was able to host a major event effectively and put on an impressive spectacle. Certainly, no expense was spared by the government to ensure that the event would take place smoothly but the enormous financial commitment could have scarcely been contemplated by a democratic government that would be held accountable for its expenditures by a probing media and a public electoral system. For example, Toronto's bids for this and similar events have been undermined, in part, by a pressure group called 'Bread not Circuses' that believes that there are better ways of spending large amounts of money.

The hosting of such an event is fraught with planning and development challenges. Certainly, major plans were made and these plans, given the role of the International Olympic Committee, were more accessible for scrutiny than many such plans made in top–down political systems in which decision-making is made behind closed doors. Many issues had to be addressed. For example, environmentally, Beijing's frequently putrid air was a potential threat to the event and, fearing for their health, renowned athletes in long-distance events threatened not to participate. A massive planting scheme was undertaken in Beijing to give the appearance of a clean and green city, some polluting industries were closed or relocated, cars were allowed to enter the centre of the city only on alternative days according to their license plate (a policy that is still in place) and pollution recorders were relocated to ensure that declining pollution levels would be recorded. The subway was extended (although several people died in the construction) and linked to an expanded airport. Thus, various environmental initiatives were undertaken that have become a positive legacy. However, iconic buildings, such as the 'Bird's Nest' stadium that housed the opening and closing ceremonies and the athletic events, have become tourist attractions that run at a loss and could end up being 'white elephants' as has been the case with Olympic venues in some other cities.

The Beijing Olympics was not really about tourism, although there were many visitors during the event, and it was hoped that the fostering of a positive image might encourage return visits and prompt those who had not yet been to eventually come for the first time. International tourism was down in the Olympic year. High prices for accommodation meant that many hotels were not full. International visitation began to decline from the start of the year as many not specifically interested in the event put off their visits. In fact, to enforce tight security, entry visas were difficult to acquire and even those from elsewhere who had been working in China had their visa renewals turned down. Thus, it became more rather than less difficult for visitors to go to Beijing during the Olympic year. Furthermore, media coverage in North America focused very much on the Olympic events, with little coverage of tourism attractions, even in Beijing. The coverage that did occur was often fleeting and puerile, directed at amusing the audience rather than truly informing them, such as reporting of the unusual contents of some Beijing snack foods rather than discussion of the varied regional cuisines of which the Chinese people are so proud.

Thus, the argument can be made that although China was pleased to be able to present a modern, well-organised and welcoming face to the world, the Olympics were very much about national unity and pride and even though few local people (let alone those from the Chinese periphery) could afford to attend the events, they were pleased to celebrate the successful staging of the extravaganza. Although the circumstances were very different, somewhat similar arguments might be made with regard to the subsequent Vancouver Winter Olympics in Canada, when proud Canadians danced in the streets of the city clad in clothes decorated with emblematic maple leaves.

Problems in Beijing identified by the Western media (such as the replacement of a child singer by a more photogenic counterpart for the opening ceremony, the use of military personnel in ethnic clothing to represent minority people, the doctoring of 'live' shots of fireworks for the consumption of television viewers and the arresting of individuals who dared to present their views in an area designated for the purpose) were not apparent to the Chinese people and, when mentioned to students in Beijing, were met with surprise and essentially dismissed as unimportant. However, the publicity given to disabled athletes and the opportunity provided for them to perform on a public stage may turn out to be one of the more important outcomes of the Paralympics, hopefully with lasting implications for the well-being of people with disabilities in China.

Thus, international sporting events may have both global and local meanings that may not always be congruent, and consequences of many kinds that extend well beyond the event itself, both spatially and temporally.

Further reading

Burbank, M.J., Andranovich, G. and Heying, C.H. (2002) Mega-events, urban development and public policy. *Review of Policy Research* 19 (3), 179–202.

De Groote, P. (2005) Economic and tourism aspects of the Olympic Games. *Tourism Review* 60 (1), 12–19.

European Tour Operators Association (No date) *Olympic Report*. London: ETOA. On WWW at http://www.etva.org/Pdf/ETOA%20Report%20Olympic.pdf.

Owen, J. G. (2005) Estimating the cost and benefit of hosting Olympic Games: What can Beijing expect from its 2008 games? *The Industrial Geographer* 3 (1), 1–18.

Tian, J. and Johnston, C. (2008) The 2008 Olympic Games leveraging a 'best ever' games to benefit Beijing. *Asian Social Science* 4 (4), 22–47.

Wang, X., Westerdahl, D., Chen, L.C., Wu, Y., Hao, J., Pan, X., Huo, X. and Zhang, K. (2009) Evaluating the air quality impacts of the 2008 Beijing Olympic Games: On-road emission factors and black carbon profiles. *Atmospheric Environment* 43 (30), 4535–4543.

In many ways, globalisation is a new way of looking at development. Globalisation is manifested in a web of political, economic, cultural and social interconnections (Go, 2004; Harvey *et al.*, 1996; Milne & Ateljevic, 2004). It is no longer possible for communities to function in isolation from other parts of the globe. Globalisation is a complex process and various interpretations and perspectives have emerged (Silk & Jackson, 2000). The cultural imperialist interpretation sees local culture as being displaced by a foreign one, causing a homogenising trend and the creation of a common global culture. This form of imperialism is often equated with Americanisation, as the US economy and culture are viewed as the dominant forces in the global system. A cultural hegemony interpretation sees globalisation as a two-way process. Local communities receive global images, goods and services but interpret them on their own terms. In this two-way relationship, local groups play a key role in the way global trends are manifested in their locale (Whitson & Macintosh, 1996). Finally, the figuration perspective advocates a view of globalisation as a process. This perspective emphasises a long-term historical approach that involves the examination of cases of domination and resistance over time. Maguire's (1999: 3) definition of globalisation fits this interpretation:

> Globalization processes are viewed here as being long-term processes that have occurred unevenly across all areas of the planet. These processes – involving an increasing intensification of global interconnectedness – appear to be gathering momentum and despite their 'unevenness', it is more difficult to understand local or national experiences without reference to these global flows. Every aspect of social reality – people's living conditions, beliefs, knowledge and actions – is intertwined with unfolding globalization processes. These processes include the emergence of a global economy, a transnational cosmopolitan culture and a range of international social movements.

One of the dominant interdependencies that characterises globalisation is the relationship between economics and culture. On the one hand, globalisation can be described as a culture of consumption inclusive of sport and tourism. On the other hand, it can be characterised as the consumption of culture (Higham & Hinch, 2009). For example, media conglomerates and major sporting goods manufacturer/retailers such as Nike have been identified as the most powerful forces influencing the globalisation of sport (Harvey *et al.*, 1996; Thibault, 2009). While Maguire (1994) has argued that the influence of developments such as the Internet demonstrate that the globalisation process is not necessarily guided or planned, others (e.g. Goldman & Papson, 1998) have demonstrated that major international corporations (e.g. Nike) have consciously developed promotional strategies aimed at global markets. The actions of these players in globalisation are driven by self-interest through the commodification of sport.

Mowforth and Munt (1998) have suggested a similar dynamic in the case of tourism. There is a constant process of commodification driven by the tourism industry's relentless search for 'new destinations'. As these places are increasingly connected to tourism-generating regions, globalisation through tourism is manifested in a very tangible fashion. One example of this is the increasing fragmentation of production through practices such as 'outsourcing' in the production of tourist experiences (Nowak *et al.*, 2009). Other characteristics of globalisation that have been identified in a tourism context include transnational ownership, labour mobility, cross-border marketing and the sale of intellectual know-how (Hjalager, 2007).

Tourism is, in fact, a significant force in the globalisation of sport. Jackson and Andrews (1999) have pointed out the influence of tourism-savvy Disney Corporation on the business model adopted by David Stern during his tenure as the Commissioner of the National Basketball League. In her critique of globalisation in sport, Thibault (2009) describes its 'inconvenient truths'. These include the emerging division of labour such as the use of cheap workers from developing countries to manufacture sporting goods, increased mobility of elite athletes from poor to wealthy countries, increased influence by the global media and increased environmental impacts which are in part due to sport-based travel.

One of the most interesting aspects of these debates from a tourism perspective is whether globalisation is leading towards a homogenisation of sport culture or whether local resistance will retain or even foster greater differences between places (Go, 2004; Maguire, 2002). This is especially significant because in a world where there are growing similarities between many places, there really is little need to travel. Homogenisation is seen as a significant concern in tourism (Wahab & Cooper, 2001) but has also been raised in the context of sport. For example, Silk and Andrews (2001) suggest that electronic spaces or the 'space of flows' may supersede the 'space of places'. In the context of sport tourism, if sporting culture were to evolve into a homogeneous global culture, much of the existing incentive to travel for sport would be lost. This debate is, therefore, an important one for sport tourism development.

The essence of the homogenisation/heterogenisation debate in sport is nicely summarised by Silk and Jackson (2000. 102).

[h]omogenization heralds the advent of an era dominated by creeping global standardization. Heterogenization, however, rejects the influence of global technologies and products in favour of stressing the inherent uniqueness of localities. The former category suggests that we are becoming more alike and heading towards a uniform global culture. The latter emphasizes cultural differences and the power of the particular.

Those who see the forces of globalisation leading to the homogenisation of sport have argued that there is ample evidence to suggest that sport culture is growing more similar throughout the world. For example, the emergence of homogeneous sportscapes as manifested in standardised stadia and sports fields (Bale, 1993b) is consistent with this view.

Rowe and Lawrence (1996: 10) also suggest that cultural commentators find 'evidence' of this new phenomenon in international sports media spectacles (such as the Olympic Games and the Fédération Internationale de Football Association [FIFA] World Cup), geographically 'mobile' sports (such as basketball and golf) and US-originated advertising, promotion, marketing and 'packaging' practices (such as celebrity endorsements and the high-pressure sale of sports paraphernalia).

Yet even commentators who show some level of support for this hypothesis recognise that there are other forces at work that seem to counter the processes of homogenisation.

> Globalisation is accordingly best understood as a balance and blend between diminishing contrasts and increasing varieties, a commingling of cultures and attempts by more established groups to control and regulate access to global flows. Global sport development can be understood in the same terms; that is, in the late 20th century we are witnessing the globalisation of sports and the increasing diversification of sport cultures. (Maguire, 1999: 213)

Many sport theorists share the view of coexistent forces for homogeneity and diversification (Denham, 2004; Harvey & Houle, 1994; Melnic & Jackson, 2002; Merkel *et al.*, 1998; Washington & Karen, 2001). At an empirical level, there is also support for the thesis that local resistance ensures that there is a significant degree of difference between local sport cultures. Despite global trends to export US sports such as American football, regionally prominent sports such as Australian Rules Football and Rugby League have prevailed in Australia (Rowe *et al.*, 1994). Similarly, it has been argued that New Zealanders have negotiated the introduction of basketball on their own terms (Jackson & Andrews, 1999). In the case of the World Cup of football held in the United States in 1994, analysts concluded that while the motivations to hold the event in the United States were influenced by the desire to capitalise on forces of globalisation, the final outcome had little impact on the spread of soccer in the host country (Sugden & Tomlinson, 1996). In another context, Bernstein (2000) demonstrated through content analysis and interviews with journalists that despite powerful forces of a global media, press coverage of the 1992 Olympics in Barcelona was characterised by local or national perspectives. Nationalistic interpretations of sporting events and performances still dominate media coverage.

Organisational fragmentation

Globalisation is about increasing interconnections. These interconnections take the form of networks of interacting and interdependent actors. March and Wilkinson (2009: 461) describe them as 'complex and mutable entities that develop and evolve over time in response to environmental and organizational developments and demands'. It is challenging to articulate goals and implement successful strategies in such a complex environment. Organisational fragmentation can therefore become an issue. A prerequisite to addressing this issue is not only recognition of existing and potential networks but also a willingness and ability for these players to work together in pursuit of their common interests related to sustainable development. This outcome is most likely to occur at the level of strategic alliances and partnership.

Until recently, however, partnerships in sport tourism have been largely ineffective. For example, a study of six European states in the early 1980s identified a linkage between sport and tourism in the minds of participants, commercial providers and local authorities (Glyptis, 1991). However, despite this link, there was a lack of conscious integration by policymakers, planners and public providers at the national level. Weed and Bull (1997a) noted that by the late 1990s there were still very few joint sport tourism initiatives among the regional agencies responsible for sport (Sports Council Regional Offices) and tourism (Regional Tourist Boards) in England. Even in Australia, which is a leader in sport tourism partnerships, the primary rationale for the development of its policy on sport tourism was the lack of an identity and cohesiveness perceived in this area (Commonwealth Department of Industry, Science and Resources, 2000).

The need for partnerships and strategic alliances in tourism and in sport has been increasingly recognised over the past 20 years, especially as government resources that were traditionally directed towards these areas have been reduced (Jamal & Getz, 1994). While a broad range of models for partnership have emerged, they can generally be described as '... a voluntary pooling of resources (labour, money, information, etc.) between two or more parties to accomplish collaborative goals' (Selin & Chavez, 1995: 845). The environmental management outcomes of the Lillehammer Winter Olympic Games (1994), for example, were built upon effective partnerships and strategic alliances between central and local government, sport, tourism, environmental and community groups (Chapter 7).

Partnership is particularly important in a sport tourism context given the many stakeholders involved. In his study of the restructuring of winter resorts in the French Alps, Tuppen (2000: 337) noted that development '... results from the actions of different organisations and interest groups in both the public and private sectors, often rendering management a complex task'. In addition to the sheer number and diversity of stakeholders who may be involved, the dynamic of power shifts among these stakeholders throughout the temporal course of development further complicates these partnerships.

There are various additional constraints to sport tourism partnerships. Competition between stakeholders, bureaucratic inertia and geographic as well as organisational fragmentation are typical (Selin & Chavez, 1995). In the specific context of sport tourism, the Commonwealth Department of Industry, Science and Resources (Australia) (2000) highlighted the lack of awareness of the mutual benefits of establishing alliances and difficulties in coordinating resources and information. Bull and Weed (1999: 151) added to this list of constraints the

> reduction of funding to the national and regional tourism agencies allocated to core functions, the adoption of increasingly narrow definitions of sport, and the cutting of the only statutory link between sport and tourism agencies in the abolition of the Regional Councils for Sport and Recreation as ... policies that have limited the extent to which integration is likely to occur.

The bottom line is that successful partnerships need partners who recognise their mutual interest. Participating organisations must also be characterised by a domain focus that is goal-oriented rather than organisation-oriented. A good example of one such initiative was the development of a background paper intended to lead towards a national sports tourism strategy in Australia (Commonwealth Department of Industry, Science and Resources, 2000) and the success of the Canadian Sport Tourism Alliance initiated in 2000 (Focus point 4.2).

Focus point 4.2

Canadian Sport Tourism Alliance

Initiated in 2000, the Canadian Sport Tourism Alliance (CSTA) has grown from 18 founding members to more than 200 members, including 95 municipalities, 55 national sport organisations and various product and service suppliers to the industry. It has worked in close cooperation with the Canadian Tourism Commission to support the development of event-based sport tourism in Canada. The key to CSTA's success has been its ability to connect the various stakeholders in this realm. Sport organisations are effectively partnered with host destinations to bid on and deliver a wide range of sporting events. The CSTA bases its activities on a solid planning framework that is guided by the following:

A. Mission Statement

To increase Canadian capacity and competitiveness to attract and host sport events.

B. Objectives

To market Canada as a preferred sport tourism destination.

To facilitate networking, educational and communications opportunities.

To coordinate research, data collection, monitoring and reporting of activity within the sport tourism industry.

To build investment and involvement in the sport tourism industry from the public and private sectors.

To enhance the image and profile of the sport tourism industry.

To develop and facilitate access to national tools.

C. Action Plans

To achieve CSTA's mission and objectives, this strategy assigns responsibility for action to six committees: membership, marketing and communications, training and education, research, government relations and administration

Source: Canadian Sport Tourism Alliance website (2002) On WWW at http://www.canadiansporttourism.com/portal_e.aspx. Accessed 28 November 2010.

Conclusion

The underlying premise of this book is that the sustainability of sport tourism can be facilitated by active intervention into the processes operating in the realms of sport and tourism. Such interventions should target the event and active and nostalgic dimensions of sport tourism. Planning will help to optimise the design (or redesign) and development of sport tourism products and services and, by so doing, will impact the environment in which sport tourism functions.

Sport tourism developers need to be conscious of the challenges that they face in terms of commodification/authenticity, globalisation and fragmentation. They should, however, also be aware of the opportunities that accompany these issues. In terms of commodification and authenticity, the protection of the sport attraction should be a fundamental objective. Care must be taken to keep the spirit of sport competition and entertainment spectacle in an appropriate balance. Media representations need to be rooted in place (Chapter 6). The authenticity of the sport attraction should be retained without suppressing the dynamic evolution of a sport (Chapter 10). Relative to many other types of tourist attractions, sport has a major advantage in terms of the joys of performance and the unpredictable drama that sports embody. By maintaining the integrity of sports, spectators and active sport tourists will have access to the 'backstage' of sporting destinations.

Globalisation issues play out around the trade-off between global and local interests. In many cases, the motivation for hosting major sporting events is to establish the host city as a significant player in a global context (Case study 4.1). For this to happen, the local context of the event needs to be considered and negotiated. Active and nostalgia-based sport tourism attractions can be used to mediate global demands. Sport tourism strategies to foster a positive local identity and destination image should be driven by significant local input.

Sport tourism partnerships should be established and operationalised in a way that is mutually beneficial. One of the first steps in such an exercise is to articulate the advantages and goals of cooperative partnerships. It is particularly important for the tourism industry to demonstrate the benefits of involvement for sport groups. Sporting interests must be convinced that their cooperation will result in increased gate receipts, facility development, new participants for their sport and similar types of benefits. It is not sufficient for the tourism industry to be a silent partner, and significant beneficiary, of sport tourism. Beyond the recognition of these benefits, specific strategies need to be developed to address the constraints to alliances and partnerships that are discussed in this chapter. Unproductive competition between stakeholders is a significant barrier to development. Communication linkages that reduce fragmentation between and within stakeholder groups are one way of addressing these barriers.

Part 3

Sport Tourism Development and Space

Chapter 5

Space: Location and Travel Flows

> *Although sport tourism can boost export spending in a defined region, not all communities have an equal likelihood of successfully hosting an event, tournament, or team.*
>
> Daniels, 2007: 333

Introduction

Sport tourism development takes place within a complex milieu of spatial parameters. Different sports are reliant to differing degrees on natural and/or built resources. Some sports are rigidly anchored to specific and non-transportable natural resources. Others are relatively free of resource constraints and may be located where proximity to concentrations of population and the existence of a tourism economy offer the greatest competitive advantage (Mason & Duquette, 2008a). Distance–time–cost thresholds also shape the spatial travel patterns of sport tourists. However, sport tourism market range and travel flows can be moderated and facilitated by strategic planning actions and partnerships at a range of spatial levels. Successful strategies require that consideration be given to the relationships that exist between sport, tourism and space. This chapter discusses the locations where different forms of sport tourism take place and also the 'movement of tourists from originating markets to leisure destinations of their choice' (Mitchell & Murphy, 1991: 57). It examines sport tourism resource requirements, destination hierarchies and travel flows. The locational requirements and travel flows associated with sports that take place in central and peripheral areas are then addressed followed by consideration of spatial travel patterns associated with active sport tourism. The concept of scale, so central to geographical theory, is a recurring element of these discussions.

Sport, Tourism and Space

Space and place are concepts that are central to the geography of sport (Bale, 1989) and the geography of tourism (Lew, 2001; Pearce, 1987). Unlike recreation and free play, many sports require defined spatial delineations, such as the length of a marathon course, or the physical parameters for a football field or basketball court. The spatial boundaries that are applied to sports are written into rules and codes of regulations. These rules may be explicit in terms of player movement, as in the case of netball (where, e.g.

defenders must remain in the defensive half of the court), or implicit, where a defensive formation will be weakened or broken if a player moves out of position. 'In many cases sport involves the dominance of territory or the mastery of distance; spatial infractions are punished and spatial progress is often a major objective' (Bale, 1989: 12).

Tourism is also characterised by a spatial component. To be considered a tourist, individuals must leave and then eventually return to their home (Chapter 2). Travel is one of the necessary conditions of tourism. Various qualifiers have been placed on this dimension including a range of minimum travel distances, but the fundamental concept of travel is universal.

The spatial element of sport tourism, as is addressed in this chapter, centres on the locations and regions in which specific sports take place, travel flows associated with those sports and the ways in which these flows may be moderated and facilitated. Various questions emerge from this discussion associated with the resource base, location and management of sport attractions. For example, to what extent can sports resources be reproduced and transported? Similarly, what are the implications of changes within a sport in terms of the propensity of spectators to travel to attend a sporting event?

Spatial Analysis of Sport Tourism

The spatial analysis of sport tourism involves the study of the locations in which sports occur and the movement of tourists to these locations. Such an analysis finds its theoretical foundation in the geography of sport (Bale, 1989, 1993a; Rooney, 1988), which introduces concepts such as central place theory, distance decay and location hierarchy for consideration in the study of sport tourism. This analysis also draws on the geography of tourism, which considers the 'spatial expression of tourism as a physical activity, focusing on both tourist-generating and tourist-receiving areas as well as the links between' (Boniface & Cooper, 1994). The concept of scale, from city and state/province, to national and global scales of analysis is critical to these discussions.

The spatial elements of sport tourism also vary between sports that tend to be centrally located and those that take place in peripheral regions. Sport tourism in peripheral areas is generally based upon the presence of natural resources, which may be modified or complemented by built facilities. This distinction reflects Boniface and Cooper's (1994) tripartite classification of tourism resources as follows:

(1) User-oriented: Centrally located, intensive developments providing proximity to markets and tourism infrastructure and based upon built or artificial facilities and attractions;

(2) Intermediate: Located with a view to accessibility, based on resources that are built and/or natural; and

(3) Resource-based: Natural resources of high quality that tend to be spatially removed from centres of population and located on the basis of remote and limited resource availability.

The spatial concept of distance decay applies to both sport and tourism. For example, in the case of elite sport, a discernable pattern exists in terms of the home or away status of a sports contest, and the probability of winning. Not only is winning away less probable than at home, but 'the probability of winning forms a clear gradient according to distance from home' (Bale, 1989: 31). The further a team travels from its home venue, the less likely it is to win.

In the context of sport tourism, sports that take place in central locations are advantaged by proximity to markets. Residents of adjacent regions or from peripheral areas are less likely to travel to a sporting event or activity than those located nearby (Daniels, 2007; Pearce, 1989). The gravity model of distance decay suggests that tourist flows decrease with distance from the origin (Boniface & Cooper, 1994). In theory, therefore, the power of attraction that a sport may exert upon the travel decision process diminishes as the distance away from the site or venue increases. The distance decay function that underlies the gravity model is influenced by increasing travel costs and declining knowledge of distant locations (Mitchell & Murphy, 1991). Therefore, in the case of event sport tourism, all other things being equal, the further a team travels to compete, the less likely it is that its home-based supporters will accompany it.

In reality, a linear distance decay function is moderated by a range of factors (Miossec, 1977), such as cultural and climatic characteristics, which may act as barriers or facilitators to travel (Cooper *et al.*, 1993; Mitchell & Murphy, 1991). Travel flows may be mediated by a number of interrelated variables (Boniface & Cooper, 1994). Zonal travel patterns can be 'modified by the hierarchy of resort destinations, the spatial advantages offered by major transport routes, and locations with outstanding (unique) reputations' (Mitchell & Murphy, 1991: 63). The provision of low-cost (budget) air services is one obvious example. The distance decay function of sport tourism may also be mediated by such things as the quality of the opposition, the importance of the competition, the number of matches that will be played by a team and the travel distances between matches contested while on tour. Factors that may intervene to distort the distance decay function of the gravity model are not well understood and merit further attention.

Sport Locations, Location Hierarchies and Tourism

Modern sports exist in a continual state of change. The dynamics of change are often driven by economic processes that bear upon the structure of competitive sports (e.g. the development of new league competitions), the location of sport facilities and the rise and fall of sport attractions. Bale (1989: 77) refers to 'the growth and decline in importance of different sport locations' which parallels Butler's (1980, 2006) tourist area life cycle theory (Chapter 10). These dynamics have implications for the scale of the player and spectator catchment areas. Within the ranks of professional sports, the limitations associated with drawing players only from areas nearby the home team site are alleviated through external recruitment, player transfers and draft schemes. The spectator catchment, and the propensity for residents and non-residents in different regions to attend live sport, is a separate issue that is of particular relevance to sports marketing managers. Interests in this area may be significantly advanced in collaboration with tourism destination managers at sport locations.

Central place theory lends itself very conveniently to the study of sport and tourism (Daniels, 2007). Sports attractions exist within a hierarchical organisational structure (Table 5.1) in a fashion similar to other tourist attractions (Leiper, 1990). This hierarchy reflects the fact that some sports centres primarily draw upon a local catchment, while others

Table 5.1 Theory of sports locations

1. The main function of sports locations is to provide sports outlets for a surrounding hinterland. Sports facilities are therefore centrally located within their market areas.
2. The greater the number of sports provided, the higher the order of the sports location.
3. Low-order sports locations provide sporting facilities that are used by smaller catchment areas. The threshold population needed for the viability of a lower-order place is smaller.
4. Higher-order locations are fewer in number and are more widely spaced. They have large population thresholds.
5. A hierarchy of sports locations exists in order to make as efficient as possible the arrangement of sports opportunities for (a) consumers who wish to minimise their travel to obtain the sport they want and (b) producers of sports who must maintain a minimum threshold of customers to survive.

Source: Bale (1989)

situated higher in the sports hierarchy draw upon district, regional, national or international catchments. Bale (1989: 79) explains that sports facilities situated in central locations are located 'as close to potential users as possible in order to maximise pleasure from the sport experience and to minimise travel, and hence cost'. This characteristic has been complicated in recent years, as new factors that influence the status of sports locations have emerged. These factors include facility sharing, changing access to infrastructure and travel nodes, proximity to tourism and service developments, and associations with media markets (Stevens, 2001).

The notion that demand for sports decreases with distance from the location at which the sport is consumed applies to sport spectatorship as well as participation. Bale (1989) introduces the term 'spheres of influence', which describes the power of attraction that sports teams exert upon spectators. As noted in references to the model of distance decay, the slope and range of the spatial demand curve for sport spectatorship are elastic. It may be influenced by factors that are, to some degree, beyond the immediate control of sports managers, such as the fortunes of the team (win/loss record), circumstances of the competition, league position and weather. A distinct range of factors influences the demand curve relating to sport participation. These factors include costs of access (White & Wilson, 1999), the standard of the sport resource and the uniqueness of the sport tourism experience. Additional tourist opportunities, such as visiting friends and relatives, or achieving other desired tourist experiences at a destination may also moderate the demand curve.

The Spatial Analysis of Sport Tourism in Central Locations

In practice, 'a vast number of physical, economic and social barriers will contribute to a distortion of the central place model' (Bale, 1989: 81; see also Daniels, 2007; Mason *et al.*, 2008). For example, the catchment population required to support a professional sports franchise will vary as determined by the propensity of residents within the catchment area to support the team. Small-city teams, such as the Saskatchewan Roughriders (Canadian Football League) and Green Bay Packers (National Football League, United States), serve to illustrate that the level of support that a team receives at its stadium may bear little resemblance to the population of the host city. The Roughriders, for instance, survive because of a strong team following from across the province of Saskatchewan. This example confirms that 'human and cultural factors can upset the rationally economic world predicted by central place models' (Bale, 1989: 82). These factors help to explain the higher than expected loyalty from within and beyond the local spectator catchment that some teams are able to generate.

Inter-urban travel is an increasingly common by-product of sport. Bale (1989: 112) notes that 'in an age of relatively easy interregional and international travel, sports events are able to generate substantial recurrent gatherings of peoples ... and hence ... [they contribute] ... to the wealth and economic dominance of the big city'. Increasingly, sport events and facilities are being used as economic anchors in the entertainment districts of higher-order urban centres (Judd, 2003; Mason *et al.*, 2008). The sports location hierarchy and the spatial demand curve, both of which are subject to change over time, influence the status of a sport tourism destination. In most cases, sports teams compete at a home venue to which spectators will travel from within the host region and, possibly, further afield (Gibson, 2002; Higham & Hinch, 2000). Traditionally, competition leagues are characterised by a series of home and away games, which are attended by supporters of both teams in varying proportions. Home games tend to be dominated by hometown supporters, although sport and tourism managers may devise strategies to encourage visiting fans, casual spectators and tourists at a destination to attend a sports contest. It is also noteworthy that home team supporters are not necessarily hometown residents. As an example, since the return of Newcastle United Football Club to the English Premier Football League, an estimated 170,000 long weekend trips to Newcastle per year have been undertaken by Norwegians who support this football club (Law, 2002). Strong and enduring support for Newcastle and Liverpool football clubs in Norway arises from the initiation of regular television coverage of English football in Norway in the 1970s, when these clubs were the dominant forces of the English first division (now Premier League).

Other models do exist in the spatial organisation of sport competitions. 'An alternative form of spatial organisation is for the sport to travel to the people in order to attract sufficient business to meet its threshold population' (Bale, 1989: 85). While some sports are rigidly anchored to specific and non-transportable natural resources, others are relatively free of resource constraints and may be transported (Chapter 7). A marathon course, for example, can be relocated to take advantage of concentrations of population, distinctive urban landmarks or unique scenic settings.

The 'periodic marketing' of sports involves a tour circuit incorporating a sequence of different venues where competition occurs. These are designed to improve spectator access to sports, and are scheduled in cases such as golf (e.g. Professional Golf Association Tour) and tennis (e.g. Association of Tennis Professionals Tour) to take advantage of seasonal conditions at the destination (Chapter 9). Periodic marketing has two noteworthy implications for sport tourism. Firstly, it transforms the athlete or contestant into an elite sport tourist as the tour circuit moves from one venue, city, country or continent to the next. Secondly, it creates the opportunity for sport tourism development associated with the regularly recurring visit of the sports tour. The International Rugby Board's International Sevens circuit, most notably the annual tournament that is hosted in Hong Kong (China), has been developed and promoted as a sports festival, often in association with other urban tourist activities. Following in the same vein the Wellington (New Zealand) Sevens has been developed into a sports event that provides a festival atmosphere, a platform for the expression of contemporary culture and a prominent annually recurring sport tourist attraction.

Formula One, which currently involves 17 races in the annual Grand Prix circuit, is another example of an annual professional sport competition that has been developed on the principle of periodic marketing. So too have biennial and quadrennial sports events such as the *Federation Internationale de Football Association* football and International Cricket Council cricket world cups, International Amateur Athletics Federation world championships and the Olympic Games. However, the cities that host these events vary, as determined by a bidding process.

Sport tourism market range

The market range of a sports team varies according to a wide array of factors. These include style of play, team image, public promotion and the success of the team, which influence the status of a team as a tourist attraction (Hinch & Higham, 2001). Similar factors apply to the visiting team as well as the home team. A recent trend in North American professional sport leagues is to charge spectators a premium to watch the top-ranked visiting teams. For most sports clubs, the spectator catchment is local/regional in scale, although some successful clubs have managed to extend the range of their spectator markets, fan base and media reach.

'Hallmark teams' are those that 'regularly attract large spectator crowds (and) have now become synonymous with tourism place promotion as well as short break leisure tourism packages' (Stevens, 2001: 61). In such cases, the scale of analysis that applies to spectator flows may be international or global. Bale (1993a) notes that football clubs such as Liverpool, Arsenal and Manchester United receive high levels of media attention. This has helped to build a support base throughout England and, particularly in the case of Manchester United, all over the world. The implications for tourist market range are significant. Manchester United Premier League games played at Old Trafford regularly attract between 4000 and 6000 international tourists to the Greater Manchester area (Stevens, 2001). Similarly, 46% of all spectators that attend Baltimore Orioles (United States) baseball matches at the Camden Yards stadium are sport excursionists and sport tourists, approximately 11,000 of whom remain in Baltimore for at least one night.

The spatial travel patterns associated with a sports team may be mapped using readily available secondary data such as the places of residence of season ticket holders or fan club members. Extending the study of sport spectator travel flows to include 'casual' spectator markets requires the collection of primary data. These analyses may afford some idea of the range and specific regions from which sport tourism spectators originate. Extending market range beyond the geographical boundaries that a team actually represents may be achieved nationally or internationally through match attendance, as well as merchandise sales or supporters club memberships. The continued success of a team influences its market range, but enduring success is very rare. This factor alone cannot explain the sustained and extended fan bases that some teams enjoy. Individual star players and the aura, glamour and heritage associated with teams and the venues at which they compete contribute to the enduring allure of some sports teams. The same factors influence the propensity of visitors to engage in nostalgia sport tourism. The atmosphere of the home stadium, colour and parochialism of the home fans and public presentation of prominent team players may also bear upon the supporter catchments that are generated by sports teams. These factors apply to sports teams and professional franchises at various levels of competition and scales of analysis (Mason & Duquette, 2008b).

Sport, space and the visitor experience

The distances that sport tourists travel usually influence the sport tourist experiences that are pursued at the destination. The time–distance–cost thresholds of tourism are such that the increasing investment of discretionary time and income on travel will bear upon most aspects of the visitor experience (Chapter 8). For instance, the further sport tourists travel, the more likely it is that they will spend some time at the destination engaging in other types of tourist activities (Hinch & Walker, 2006; Nogawa *et al.*, 1996). It is also noteworthy that the area that a sports team represents may in fact require 'home' supporters to travel considerable distances to support their team. A national team performing in international competition at home may attract domestic supporters from throughout the country that it represents, who travel long distances to attend as domestic tourists. Indeed expatriates may also return to their country of origin to support or compete in sports teams. Thus, the spatial area that a sports team or club actually represents may vary considerably from the spatial extent of the team supporter and player catchments. This raises the prospect of spectators travelling as domestic or international tourists, without feeling that they are leaving 'home', or indeed feel that they are going 'home', which may have interesting implications for the visitor experience (Chapter 8).

Visitor expenditure patterns associated with the sport tourist experience are of particular interest to sport, tourism and service industries. Studies of the economic impacts of sport tourism are commonplace in North America (Schaffer & Davidson, 1985, cited by Bale 1989), particularly at the local/regional scale. Insights exist into 'both the costs and benefits to a community of attracting a professional sports outfit and the economic impact of an existing sports franchise on the city in which it is located' (Bale, 1993a: 77). The expenditures associated with the location of a sports club or franchise in an urban area may include club expenditures, or those associated with the production of the sport, and expenditures generated by local and non-local spectators. Such expenditures will vary with the size of the urban area and the definition of its geographical parameters. Bale (1993a: 81) points out, in direct reference to English football, that 'as distance from the football club increases, the positive spillover effect on retailers is likely to decline until a particular point is reached at which the club has no direct economic impact at all'. It is noteworthy that the spending patterns of different sport spectator catchments may be quite unique, with variation between local and non-local visitor expenditure patterns particularly evident (Gibson *et al.*, 2002). However, relatively little research has been committed to this aspect of sport tourism (Chapter 8).

Sport tourism and the status of sport centres

At the local scale, urban centres have been at the forefront of a new phase of entertainment consumption, which Belanger (2000) describes as the spectacularisation of space. This process is 'creating a new urban landscape filled with casinos, megaplex cinemas, themed restaurants, simulation theatres, stadia and sports complexes' (Belanger, 2000: 378). In many cases, this new urban landscape exists in nodal entertainment enclaves that may function as 'sport precincts' and 'tourist precincts' (Judd, 2003; Leiper, 1990; Mason *et al.*, 2008). 'These group-specific combinations of spatially related attractions and facilities are also called complexes' (Dietvorst, 1995: 165). The status of sports centres is enhanced when facility developments are planned in coordination with entertainment, tourism and service sector interests. Central sports locations that are situated adjacent to city service and entertainment areas have become an important aspect of the planning for sports centres.

The development of the modern stadium features prominently in advancing the status of sport centres that function as tourist destinations. The Astrodome (Houston) and Superdome (New Orleans) are examples of stadia that have been developed alongside hotel and convention centre complexes as part of urban regeneration and inner-city tourist-based development programmes (Stevens, 2001). They have also stimulated development of the service industry, including travel agents specialising in sport tourism, to accommodate the needs of tourists. These developments, in combination with ancillary tourism services such as accommodation, transport, dining and entertainment, enhance the status of sports centres. The redevelopment of Melbourne Park (see Case study 5.1 by Anne-Marie Hede and Pamm Kellett) provides a useful contemporary case in point.

Case study 5.1
Why Redevelop Melbourne Park?

Anne-Marie Hede, Victoria University, and Pamm Kellett,   .
Deakin University

Melbourne Park (incorporating Rod Laver Arena, Hisense Arena and the Melbourne Park Function Centre) is an important part of Melbourne's sporting complex – the Melbourne and Olympic Parks (MOP) Precinct. Melbourne Park is host to the Australian Open Tennis Championship (AO), which is held annually each January. Melbourne Park is nested within the MOP Precinct with AAMI Park (hosting professional football and rugby codes), Olympic Park Stadium (hosting athletics), the Westpac Centre (host to the Victorian Institute of Sport and a professional Australian Football League team) and numerous training fields for use by sporting teams and the public. The MOP Precinct is adjacent to the Melbourne Cricket Ground (an international standard event venue that also includes the National Sport Museum), and is within 1 km of the Melbourne City Centre and within 5 km of other international standard event venues such as the Melbourne Sports and Aquatic Centre and the Etihad Stadium.

Melbourne Park has proven to be an important hub in Melbourne's sport precinct – not only for the AO but also for its multi-purpose use in other events hosted in the city. The complex was crucial to Melbourne's successful hosting of the 2006 Commonwealth Games. In that instance, Hisense Arena was transformed into an international standard track cycling venue, and the offices of Tennis Australia were used for Commonwealth Games venue operations staff because of the centrality of Melbourne Park within the sport precinct. One year later, when Melbourne hosted the 2007 FINA World (Swimming) Championships, Rod Laver Arena, Melbourne Park's Centre Tennis Court, was transformed into an international standard swimming pool.

Melbourne Park became the core venue for the event, hosting both the opening and closing ceremonies.

Sports zones can give a city national and international visibility and coherence – and assist to develop new tourist and business areas for cities (Smith, 2010). Francis and Murphy (2005) suggested that Melbourne is a good example of a 'sports city'. That is, Melbourne has taken a holistic approach to the inclusion of sport facilities in its urban planning and integrated them to develop an international profile as a tourist destination. Furthermore, hosting multiple events has meant that it has developed a reputation as being a vibrant and exciting place to live, as well as a prosperous city in which to locate and do business. Melbourne's Event Strategy (which relies on its sport infrastructure) has contributed to Melbourne being ranked third in the world on the Economist Intelligence Unit's 2009 Liveability survey.

Melbourne's position as a leading destination for sports events means that it will always face the threat of competitors. Evidence suggests that Melbourne's competitors are nearby and watching Melbourne's every move. During 2008, it was revealed that Sydney, Australia, was secretly trying to secure the AO. Sydney argued strongly that Melbourne Park was outdated. A newer facility could be offered at Homebush Bay, where the 2000 Olympic Games were held. In addition, other cities through the Asia-Pacific, such as Shanghai, have also shown interested in the AO. Melbourne Park's age provides its competitors with a timely opportunity to 'muscle in' on Melbourne and lure the event to rival cities. It is, however, in the best interests of the Victorian State Government to ward off such threats. In 2009, the AO attracted more than 600,000 spectators to Melbourne Park, with one third of those attending from interstate and overseas. Furthermore, the event generated more than $160 million for the Victorian Economy. The AO has been described as one of the highlights on Melbourne's sporting calendar and, for the month of January, it is the biggest sporting event in the world.

The nearby competitors are correct in emphasising that Melbourne Park is a tired facility compared with similar facilities around the world. For 21 years, Melbourne Park has been an integral part of the cluster of sports facilities that has assisted Melbourne to position itself globally as an exciting sport and tourist destination. However, it has undergone little renovation during that time. It still has the look and feel of a facility that was built in the 1980s. Recognising the importance of Melbourne Park in both its urban and tourism development strategies, in 2010 the Victorian State Government committed $363 million to the first stage of a long-term redevelopment plan for the venue. The redevelopment is aimed at securing the AO for Melbourne until at least 2036.

Aligned with Victoria's urban planning strategy 'Melbourne 2030', Melbourne Park will be developed in association with a range of entertainment facilities. The Minister for Sport stated: 'As well as extending the life of Rod Laver Arena, Margaret Court and Hisense Arena, our $363 million investment will also help open up opportunities for other sports, such as netball and basketball, as well as concerts and other events'. The redevelopment project will transform the 21-year-old facility into a state-of-the-art sport and entertainment complex designed to not only benefit the sport of tennis but also position the MOP Precinct as a multi-sport and entertainment complex.

The Victorian Government could have sat idle and let Melbourne Park continue to mature as a sport venue and potentially head into decline. Instead, the redevelopment of Melbourne Park is designed to not only further improve the standard of the facility but also strengthen Melbourne's position as a tourist destination in an increasingly competitive marketplace. The redevelopment will better link Melbourne Park to the other sport and recreational venues in the MOP Precinct, and will also link the Precinct to the vibrant business and retail sectors in the City of Melbourne. Tourists to Melbourne, like most tourists to other metropolitan destinations, seek a mix of leisure activities. Investing in a strategy that integrates opportunities for tourists to attend events, enjoy retail experiences and visit cultural attractions, while enhancing the urban environment for its residents, makes good sense in such an intensely competitive market.

Literature cited in this case study is included in the list of references at the end of this book.

The concept of a sport centre gives rise to the concept of the sport tourism centre, sport tourism destination or sports resort. The attractiveness of sport tourism centres may draw upon the uniqueness of different sports regions that exist within a country (Rooney & Pillsbury, 1992). By definition, a sport tourism centre requires the presence of sports facilities and resources as well as tourism infrastructure and services (Standeven & De Knop, 1999). 'To the visitor the amenities appear to be related to each other; the whole is more attractive than each separate amenity' (Dietvorst, 1995: 165). Sport tourism centres have the capacity to accommodate significant inward travel flows at a destination. An established tourism economy in the form of national and/or international transport nodes, an established accommodation sector, tourist attractions to complement the sport industry and a well-developed service sector including tourism information services is critical to its functionality (Whitson, 2004).

The development and management of sport tourism centres and regions in Upper Franconia/Bavaria (Germany), requiring the existence of both sport and tourism resources, are discussed by Maier and Weber (1993). They map the regional structure of the sport tourism industry, as measured in bed night availability, and the spatial distribution of resources relating to specific sports. In a similar exercise, Pigeassou (2002) documents the sport activities, and distinct images associated with sport tourism centres and regions in France. He profiles the status of sport tourism in three regions – Brittany, Cote d'Azur and Limousin – in an analysis of printed and electronic tourism promotion materials. This study identifies the unique points of difference in a regional analysis of sport tourism, providing insights into appropriate development strategies in sport and tourism, to enhance the status of sport tourism centres in these regions.

The evolution of sport tourism in central locations

Spatial change within the sports industry continually takes place within the urban milieu (Bale, 1989). This is particularly evident in the locational dynamics of team sports in Europe and North America. Sports stadiums in Britain were originally located to take advantage of population concentrations and transport nodes. The strategy of minimum aggregate travel for sport spectators resulted in the development of sport stadia in inner-city locations. Hub and spoke public transport networks brought the majority of supporters relatively short distances by train and bus to attend sports matches at central locations. However, these locational criteria have lost much of their relevance given increasing stadium size and the demand for more parking facilities to match the growth in private car ownership. The situation of locational flux arrived relatively belatedly in British sports, although in recent times Manchester City, Liverpool and Everton football clubs have cemented the trend towards developing new stadiums, often on new sites within the same urban setting.

By contrast, the situation in North America 'has been characterised since 1950 by a state of locational flux' (Bale, 1993a: 150). Over the past 50 years, many high-profile professional football, baseball and ice hockey franchises in North America have been relocated from one city, state or country to the next. Here, a different and troubling scale of analysis applies as entire teams are relocated between cities in different states and countries. The geographic delineations of sport competition have changed dramatically through this process. The expansion of professional ice hockey franchises to the warm weather climates of California and Florida, and the relocation of teams between Canada and the United States, aptly demonstrates this point.

The heritage values associated with sports teams are invariably compromised in the process of inter-city or transnational relocation (see Chapter 6) and may, in fact, be lost to a region altogether if transferred to the new host city (Kulczycki & Hyatt, 2005). Ironically, the situation of locational flux has, in many cases, taken place in association with development of the tourism product, including tourist attractions that target the nostalgia sport tourist (Stevens, 2001). Nostalgia sport tourism has been actively developed in North America (Rooney, 1992). Sports halls of fame have often been positioned as tourist attractions, with traditional museum style presentations being succeeded by new-generation sport attractions, which feature cutting-edge interpretive techniques, designs and technologies. This has not been possible given the static location of facilities in other parts of the world. Stevens (2001: 69) notes, in reference to sport halls of fame in England, that their locations tend to be governed by non-market–related criteria, such as the location of administrative offices or the owners' desire to convert a hobby into a public display. Most are located outside the major metropolitan areas, and when compared with the geography of major league franchises, and hence major stadium developments, it is apparent that the opportunity to physically link sports stadia with visitor attractions has largely been missed.

The Spatial Analysis of Sport Tourism in Peripheral Locations

Christaller (1963/64: 95) states that tourism is 'a branch of the economy that avoids central places and the agglomerations of industry. Tourism is drawn to the periphery ... (where) one may find, easier than anywhere, the chance of recreation and sport'. Sport tourism in peripheral locations (Chapter 7) is often based on the natural resources found there. Examples of these resources include mountains, lakes and rivers that form the resource base for sports such as mountain climbing, skiing, rafting, kayaking and angling (Hudson, 1999; Orams, 1999). Sport tourism in peripheral locations is typically resource-dependent and, therefore, determined by the physical nature of the landscape rather than proximity to market areas. Sport tourism market zones, travel patterns and tourist experiences in peripheral locations stand in contrast to those associated with sports that take place in central locations. The principles governing the spatial dynamics of sport tourism in peripheral areas are proposed in Table 5.2.

Table 5.2 Spatial dynamics of sport tourism in peripheral areas

1. The main challenge of the sports areas in the periphery is to facilitate visitor access and opportunities to engage in sports in natural areas. Sports areas are located in peripheral areas where natural resources and built infrastructures rather than centrality determine site location decisions.
2. Peripheral sports areas are reliant primarily on active sport tourists as participants rather than spectators.
3. The quality of the sport environment/resource, rather than the number of sports provided, determines the order of the peripheral area within a sports location hierarchy. Quality may be determined by uniqueness, naturalness/absence of impact, remoteness and features of the natural environment.
3. Peripheral sports locations exist in clusters of critical mass, allowing the development of a high standard and range of sports facilities that enhance the standing of the destination in the sports location hierarchy.
4. Higher-order locations are clustered in peripheral areas where natural features and developed infrastructure and services facilitate sport tourism.
5. Consumers of sport tourism in peripheral areas may be motivated by the desire to (a) engage intensively in their chosen sport and/or (b) maximise the other tourism opportunities associated with the pursuit of their chosen sport.

Sports space theory applied to peripheral areas suggests that the natural resource base, rather than market access, will determine the locations where sport tourism takes place (Focus point 5.1). A ski resort, for example, is dependent on the requisite elevation, terrain and snow conditions, among other things, to allow participants to engage in their sport in favourable conditions. This is especially the case for niche sport tourism markets where specific sport motivations requiring unique natural environmental attributes often apply. As Bourdeau *et al.* (2002: 23) observe, 'the location of sites and itineraries thus depend on diverse natural conditions which do not readily lend themselves to the satisfaction of geographic (accessibility), demographic or economic needs'. The resource requirements of sports may be moderated through, for example, snowmaking technology in the case of alpine winter sports. Resources such as artificial ski slopes can be constructed at considerable expense in central locations, with immediate access provided for concentrations of population. Notwithstanding these points, the resource requirements of sport tourism in peripheral areas remain the fundamental characteristic of the locations in which they take place.

Focus point 5.1

BASE Jumping at Kjerag (Norway)

Kjerag is a Norwegian mountain (1110 m above sea level) located in Lysefjorden in south-west Norway. Lysefjord is the southernmost of Norway's great fjords. The northern face of Kjeragbolten is famous for its iconic rock (the bolt in the rock), which is wedged between two sheer rock faces that tower 984 m above the fjord. Kjerag is a popular location for various outdoor recreation activities, including hiking and climbing, which can be pursued in various mountain settings in Norway and elsewhere. However, the repute of Kjeragbolten and its iconic international profile is the pursuit of BASE jumping, which is a recreational activity that involves free jumping from a fixed platform with a parachute. BASE is an acronym that stands for buildings, antennae, spans (e.g. bridges) and earth (e.g. cliff faces). The activity may be described as skydiving without an aeroplane. It is commonly viewed by non-participants as one of the more extreme of the extreme sports, although it has also been described as a fringe activity or stunt.

The sheer rock walls of Kjerag are to BASE jumping what Hawaii (United States) is to surfing and Sipadan Island (Malaysia) to scuba diving. In these cases, unique natural resources situated in the periphery provide critical regional tourism development opportunities. The status of these tourism places is cemented by the subcultures that have become established over time and come to venerate these locations as the apex of their specific sport location hierarchies. In the case of these nature-based sports, transportability is impossible because of the unique qualities of these locations and the sport subcultures with which they have become associated. While such locations are relatively immune to the threat of replication or transportability (because of their unique natural resources), the status of sports places can be embellished through deliberate tourism development initiatives aimed at building the subcultural capital associated with iconic destinations.

Source: http://en.wikipedia.org/wiki/Kjerag. Accessed 1 October 2010.

The inescapable circumstances of sport tourism in peripheral areas provide unique challenges in terms of commercial development (Bourdeau *et al.*, 2002). Remoteness and terrain may limit access while reliance on weather conditions and climatic uncertainty may compromise the viability of sports or render them impossible (Chapters 9 and 10). The consequences include seasonal use variations, low-intensity use due to institutional factors, high mobility of visitors between sites and self-sufficiency on the part of many users in terms of service requirements (Bourdeau *et al.*, 2002).

Where favourable natural resources and market access coexist, a competitive advantage may be achieved. The development of a critical mass of sport tourism activities and facilities in peripheral areas may stimulate further investment in transportation and infrastructure, thereby improving access.

This discussion suggests that like central locations, a hierarchy of peripheral sport tourism destinations exists (Table 5.2). Higher-order destinations are generally located in peripheral areas where natural features, developed infrastructure and services are all present. Higher-order places may cement this desirable status by fostering and building unique cultures (and subcultural values) associated with specific sports. 'Depending on the resources that they offer, and their reputation and use characteristics, sites generally become established in a very clear hierarchy, in which they are identified as being of local, regional or national interest' (Bourdeau *et al.*, 2002: 24). In their study of 2000 climbing sites in France, Bourdeau *et al.* (2002) identified a hierarchy in which 85% were considered to be of local, 13% of regional and 2% of national significance. However, the existence, and the functioning of a peripheral sport tourism destination, is also determined by the level of tourism infrastructure and services. Teigland (1999: 308) states, in reference to the 1994 Lillehammer Winter Olympics, that 'the influence zone of a particular Olympic Games will vary depending on the distribution of venues in different types of satellite areas ... (and) entry and departure points to the host country or region, especially areas close to airports receiving international visitors'. These principles of sport space highlight the opportunities and potential, as well as the limitations, that apply to active and event sport tourism development in peripheral areas.

The spatial analysis of active sport tourism in peripheral areas

The discussions offered in this chapter suggest that the majority of event sport tourism takes place in central locations, while active sport tourism tends to predominate in peripheral locations. Active sport tourism has received comparatively little attention in the academic literature. One exception is an analysis of the destinations visited by active sport tourists of German, Dutch and French nationality (Table 5.3) (World Tourism Organization & International Olympic Committee, 2001). This study considers the destination preferences of 'sport-orientated' and 'less-sport-orientated' travellers, which parallels Robinson and Gammon's (2004) distinction between sport tourism and tourism sport (Chapter 3). Study findings show distinct spatial travel patterns associated with active sport tourists of different nationality and motivational profiles

Table 5.3 Top 10 destinations visited by sport-orientated and less-sport-orientated tourists: German, Dutch and French nationals (%)

Destination (top 10)	German		Dutch		French	
	Sport-orientated	Less-sports-orientated	Sport-orientated	Less-sports-orientated	Sport-orientated	Less-sports-orientated
Austria	51	3	26	34	17	
Italy	19	14	5	5	13	4
Switzerland	9		8		19	
Spain	4	32	3		33	42
France	3	5	24	21		
Czech Republic	3					
Netherlands	2	7				
Denmark	1	3				
Great Britain	1		2	1		
Poland	1					
Others	6	36	32	39	18	54

Source: World Tourism Organization and International Olympic Committee (2001) (sport-orientated and less-sport-orientated). Austria and France are the preferred destinations of Dutch nationals, just as Spain is the preferred destination of active sport tourists from France. Proximity plays an important part in destination choice (Cooper *et al.*, 1993); however, it is apparent that Austria and Switzerland are generally viewed as sport-orientated destinations, while Spain, for example, is the destination of choice for many less-sports-orientated travellers from Germany and France.

A spatial analysis of golf highlights the variations that exist in the regional supply of sport tourism products (Hudson & Hudson, 2010, Priestley, 1995). Golf sport tourism associated with championship courses takes place mainly in Britain and the United States where the Grand Slam Opens (British and United States Opens and the Professional Golf Association) are played on a rotation basis. The spatial distribution of single integrated golf resorts stands in obvious contrast. 'Numerous resorts exist in the sunniest areas of the USA (Florida, Hawaii and California), on the southeast coast of Australia (and) similar resorts have appeared in the Caribbean, South Pacific and Indian Ocean islands' (Priestley, 1995: 210). Priestley (1995) also performs an analysis of demand for golf, which identifies the United States, Japan and the United Kingdom as prominent golf travel markets. The Japanese golf market is particularly important as the demand for golf in Japan has increased beyond the capacity of domestic golf courses. These findings confirm the importance of understanding established spatial travel patterns that exist in sport tourism, as they have implications for the continuing development of sport tourism.

Conclusion

This chapter highlights the factors that determine the locations of sport sites and the spatial dimensions of sport tourism travel flows. It extends the concept of the sport centre and the hierarchy of sport locations (Bale, 1993a), within the context of sport tourism. The prominence and status of sport tourism centres are determined by the range and quality of sports experiences, in combination with levels of service development and unique sport facilities and resources. The sports event experience can be usefully considered at various spatial scales from the global to the local (Pettersson & Getz, 2009).

Sports locations may command local, regional or national travel flows that can be actively influenced by sport and tourism organisations. The location of sport tourism activities in central or peripheral areas exerts a major influence on the market range, spatial travel flows and visitor patterns. An appreciation of travel flows that exist within the spatial dimension of sport tourism is fundamental to sport tourism development.

The status of sports locations can be actively developed in an attempt to extend market range through the implementation of development strategies. The redevelopment of Melbourne Park at the costs of AU$383 million is a clear strategy to further enhance the status of Melbourne as a sports location, retain the Australian tennis grand slam, extend market range and expand visitor markets (see Case study 5.1). These goals, which are mutually beneficial, are most effectively achieved when sport and tourism management initiatives are planned and implemented in a coordinated manner (Glyptis, 1991; Weed & Bull, 1997a).

Chapter 6
Place, Sport and Culture

> *We have essentially treated sport and tourism as cultural experiences – sport as a cultural experience of physical activity; tourism as a cultural experience of place. It will come as no surprise, therefore, that the nature of sport tourism, ... is about an experience of physical activity tied to an experience of place.*
>
> Standeven and De Knop, 1999: 58

Introduction

Sport exerts a significant influence upon the meanings that people attach to space. These meanings are central to the experience of sport tourists, to the impacts felt by their hosts and to the strategies designed to shape development. The validity of these claims will be demonstrated in this chapter by considering the unique nature of sport tourism places, by examining sport and culture in relation to place identity, and by considering sport as a strategy to sell tourism places. A case study of the place attachment of rock climbers to indoor and outdoor climbing sites illustrates one way in which the meaning of sport places is changing.

Place

Place is concerned with the meaning attached to space (Tuan, 1974). Crouch (2000: 64) expands on the difference between space and place from a postmodern perspective by suggesting that

> [s]pace can be a background, a context, a 'given' objective component of leisure and tourism. In that way it is seen as a location, a National Park or a site where particular leisure/tourism happens, a distance between things. Place can be a physical image that can be rendered metaphorical as the content of brochures, 'landscape' as a foil for what people might imagine they do ... In this way it may be that place is understood to be a cultural text that people read and recognize directed by the particular intentions of a producer or promoter.

While the geometric characteristics of space can be objectively measured, place is much more subjective in nature. Individuals and groups are constantly defining and refining the meanings that they attach to spaces. As other aspects of their lives change, so do the meanings that they attach to spaces.

Place attachment is made up of two main components. The first is place dependence, which is the functional tie that individuals and collectives have to a space. Brown and Raymond (2007: 90) state that '[p]lace dependence refers to connections based specifically on activities that take place in the setting'. In the context of sport tourism, a particular location may have a combination of unique resources that facilitate certain sporting activities. An example would be the dependence of downhill skiers and snowboarders on mountainous areas that receive generous amounts of snow cover. This functional dependence typically contributes to a strong attachment to the area (see discussion on sport tourism in peripheral areas in Chapter 5). The second dimension of place attachment is place identity, which plays a role in the self-making of individuals and groups (Kerstetter & Bricker, 2009). In articulating where we are or where we play, we contribute to our understanding of who we are. Travelling for sport is therefore an important part of the way we construct our self-identity.

Tourism places

In his seminal work *Place and Placelessness*, Relph (1976) argued that the concept of sense of place was most applicable in the local environment where individuals are in a position to develop deep attachments to place. He suggested that tourists were one of the least likely groups to develop a 'sense of place' in relation to the destinations that they visit because of the superficial nature of their experience and the tendency of the tourism industry to present 'disneyfied' landscapes devoid of deeper meaning. This view of tourism contrasts markedly from the position that tourism involves a serious pursuit of meaning and authenticity (MacCannell, 1973). It also ignores the importance of the 'social world' that helps to shape visitors' bonds to a leisure-focused destination (Kyle & Chick, 2007) and Stebbins's (2007) concept of serious leisure. Cuthbertson *et al.* (1997) have argued that many types of travellers are likely to form strong attachments to the place, an example being the strong attachment that nomadic people have to the places that they travel through. Similarly, Jones and Green (2005) argue that serious leisure and travel to participate in such leisure are mutually reinforcing activities in the context of sport tourism.

Travelling for pleasure beyond the boundaries of one's life space implies that there is some experience available at the destination which cannot be found at home, and which compensates for the costs of the trip (Cohen, 1996). Standeven and De Knop (1999: 57) build on this line of argument by suggesting that the

> nature of tourism is rooted in authentic cultural experience of places away from home that have different characteristics. Those

characteristics are unique to each place, and the tourist views, feels, hears, smells, and touches them. Their differences (and their similarities) become a part of his or her conscious experience.

The destinations where authentic experience occurs become infused with meaning for those who visit them. Gu and Ryan (2008) likewise argue that tourism development can impact the locals' place identity based on their perception of distinctiveness, self-efficacy, continuity and self-esteem associated with the place. All of these dimensions can be affected by the type of tourist activity that is engaged in at that place. Such logic suggests that the concept of place is very applicable to sport tourism. From the perspective of the tourism industry, the more meaningful a destination is for visitors in a positive sense, the greater that destination's competitive advantage in the tourism marketplace (Williams *et al.*, 1992).

Sport places and tourism

The experiences of sport tourists ' – staged or real – result from tourists' interactions with place' (Standeven & De Knop, 1999: 58). There are at least four possible sources of this meaning highlighted in the literature. In the first instance, Bale (1993a) argues that there is a changing 'religious' allegiance of a substantial portion of the public. Rather than worshipping at a religion's altar, many people have substituted sport's altar. MacCannell (1973) suggests that tourist travel is analogous to a religious pilgrimage. He argues that tourists are motivated by the search for the authentic. Cohen's (1996) existential mode of tourist experience also suggests that this type of tourism represents a pilgrimage for modern humans. Like pilgrims, tourists travel from the profane (origin) to the sacred (destination) and back to the profane (origin) (Graburn, 1989). In a tourism context, individuals define the sacred and the profane in a reflexive manner. Generally, however, tourism sites act as a refuge from modernity and the sacred forms a reality separate from the ordinary lives of travellers. The search for sacred sites may reflect a response to conditions of rootlessness that are increasingly characterising the post-modern world (Higham & Hinch, 2009).

A second way that sport spaces become endowed with meaning is through the development of home-like ties to a site even though that site may be far removed from one's residence. A particular sporting venue may become home as fans or active participants develop allegiances to the site (Chapter 5). This idea of 'home' contrasts with most technical definitions of the tourist, which provide an arbitrary distance threshold that, once surpassed, define a traveller as a tourist or an excursionist. In doing so, interesting questions are raised about the meaning that these 'home' fans attach to the destination. For example, Nogawa *et al.* (1996) suggest that the distance travelled to a sport tourism destination is a significant factor in the type of behaviours demonstrated by the visitor although they did not comment on the psychological attachment of these visitors to the destination. In their study of visitors to university football games in Gainesville, FL, Gibson *et al.* (2002) did, however, find that sport tourists who identified with the 'home team' tended to participate in few non-sport tourist activities while visiting the town. Their attachment to place would seem to be a form of social bonding focused on family, friends and fandoms (Kyle & Chick, 2007). Gibson speculated that sport tourists identifying with the 'visiting team' might behave more like 'typical tourists' to a community.

A third way that sport spaces may become endowed with meaning is through aesthetics. In this case, place meaning is derived from various sporting landscape elements that contribute to the aesthetics of a sport place (Bale, 1993a). For example, football stadiums in the United Kingdom have been described as 'secular cathedrals' which are intimately tied to perceptions of place, from the perspective of both followers and non-followers of the sport (Robinson, 2010). More tangibly, the development of sports zones or quarters in a city represents a manifestation of the connection between sport and tourism. Smith (2010) suggests that such zones need to go beyond a focus on major event facilities to a concentration of other more participatory sports facilities such as halls of fame, exhibitions of sport activities and other types of active engagement.

Sporting heritage is the last element that Bale (1993a) highlights as influencing the way sport sites become endowed with meaning. The concepts of sport heritage places and sport heritage tourists fit well with the idea of nostalgia sport tourism (Fairley & Gammon, 2005; Gammon, 2002; Gammon & Ramshaw, 2007; Gibson, 1998; Redmond, 1990). Support for this view is found in the prevalence of sport museums, tours of former Olympic sites and pilgrimages to the origins of various sports such as golf at St. Andrews in Scotland.

While all of these factors infuse sport spaces with meaning to create sport tourism places, Bale (1989) notes the emergence of sportscapes as a counter-trend. In fact, these sportscapes are an embodiment of 'placelessness' as described by Relph (1976):

> In the twentieth century sportscapes rather than landscapes have tended to characterize the sports environment ... New materials had changed the shape of the stadium and the texture of the surfaces; fields became carpets and parks became concrete bowls. Most sports require artificial settings, although the degree to which the natural environment needs to change varies between sports. (Bale, 1989: 145)

Sport is relatively unique in this regard. In few other activities has there been so much pressure to make one place exactly the same as another (Bale, 1989). The rationale for this pressure is at least fourfold:

(1) an attempt to ensure spectator and participant comfort and safety;
(2) to standardise the playing fields and sites, thereby providing an 'even playing field' and, in so doing, fostering fairer competition;
(3) a reflection of technological advances that have allowed for 'improved' performance; and
(4) an outcome of mass media broadcast requirements both in terms of technological needs and in terms of market appeal.

This tension between homogenisation of sporting landscapes and the maintenance of unique natural characteristics is being played out in the growing trend towards artificial or built facilities for sports that have traditionally taken place in natural settings. Of particular interest is the nature of place attachment that activity participants develop at these contrasting sites (Case study 6.1 by Cory Kulczycki).

Case study 6.1
Place Attachment and Rock Climbing

Cory Kulczycki, University of Alberta

Rock climbing has evolved with the development of its own norms, values and meanings which distinguish it from other mountain-based sports. However, until recently, its connection to the natural environment appeared to be an enduring feature. Climbers were motivated by the remoteness of the climbing area, the physical and mental requirements of the route and the outdoor setting (Attarian, 2003).

Despite this apparent affinity with the natural environment, the attraction and use of indoor and artificial (built) climbing spaces have been growing and are increasingly where people are first introduced to the sport (Attarian, 1999). Indoor climbing walls have been built in warehouses, gymnasiums, leisure centres and numerous other urban-based facilities. Climbing walls have also been built in the outdoors as permanent or movable structures. Motivations for this proliferation of built structures include the reduction of seasonality (e.g. control weather conditions), removal of distractions such as insects, and increased accessibility (Mittelstaedt, 1997). Indoor climbing walls provide an opportunity to train, play, learn and compete within an enclosed and monitored space (Attarian, 1999). The ability to readily modify and redesign the routes on built climbing walls also provides a unique contrast to the relatively static routes of outdoor rock climbing spaces.

Place Attachment

This growth in urban-based built climbing walls raises the question of the importance of place and particularly the way that participants are connected to the places where they climb. Place attachment can be viewed as an emotional connection that a climber has towards a specific place (Hidalgo & Hernandez, 2001). It comprises place dependence and place identity. Factors related to place dependence include accessibility to the climbing area (e.g. distance from home), distance from the trailhead, length of climbing routes and style of climbing available (Kyle *et al.*, 2004b). Place identity involves the meanings and values associated with a specific place and connected to a person's self-identity (Proshansky *et al.*, 1983).

The research presented here is part of a larger study looking at how rock climbers experience the places they climb. Twenty-one interviews were conducted for this project of which the first six interviews form the basis for this case study. These interviews were analysed through inductive coding. Data analysis identified the following place themes: (1) pilgrimage to climbing meccas; (2) searching for the exotic and (3) climbing sites as social settings.

The culture of sport and the interaction of athletes, spectators and space infuse an area with meaning. Climbers often referred to certain places as meccas. For example, Participant 2 asked other climbers about rock climbing in Thailand and, '... a lot of them said you have to go to Railay Beach – you have to go to the climbing Mecca of Southeast Asia ...'.

Climbers were interested in exploring different places and attempting different routes; part of the attraction of climbing was linked to creating experiences within new places. Participant 5 described the exotic as, '... just being in that totally new environment ... I've never been in a desert environment before and it's kind of full-on, and you're just seeing this crazy red rock ... that I've never experienced before ...'.

The social aspects of climbing emerged in two distinct perspectives: positive social interaction with all climbers and a social interaction with the climbing partner(s) and the natural environment. Participant 4 explained, '... some place like Lake Louise it's very easy to get to but once you get above the trail you can't see and ... hear anybody else'. In comparing indoor and outdoor social interactions, Participant 5 stated, '... they're both fairly social... But I can choose to climb outside with just ... me and my ... climbing partner ... We purposely try to locate a crag where we know there will be minimal people. I can never do that in the indoor climbing situation'. Participant 5 went on to discuss the quality of the social interactions and found that while there were more people to talk with indoors, the amount of time spent outdoors with only his climbing partner(s) was more meaningful.

Participant 3 described her indoor gym experience, '... you go there and it's an individual thing yet it ends up being ... such a social and ... team thing all at the same time'.

Conclusion

Participants constantly evaluate the suitability of a place for their activity, that is, their place dependence, based on the characteristics of the place (Kyle *et al.*, 2004a). Study respondents evaluated their climbing place based on route types and lengths, route variety and accessibility. The indoor climbing places tended to be associated with place dependence where the key attraction was accessibility and convenience. Climbers articulated place identity with indoor facilities after a number of repeat visits resulted in the creation of social connections. At outdoor natural sites, the social element tended to focus on interactions with people the climbers knew whereas other climbers or strangers were viewed as distractions.

It is through constant interaction between people and place characteristics that individuals create, apply and begin to understand the identity of a place (Twigger-Ross & Uzzell, 1996). Through this interaction, the users of the place develop an identity linked to their meaningful places. In this study, climbers referred to certain outdoor places as meccas and the meanings were often inferred or established through the climbing culture's perceptions (e.g. magazine articles and guidebooks) of the place. Climbers who frequented indoor climbing gyms also began to identify with these spaces based on the social dimension of these facilities.

It was evident that through the social interactions and the characteristics of the place, the climbers in this study developed attachments to the place (Kyle & Chick, 2007). Climbers had favourable perceptions of their climbing partners, the broader climbing community in which they interacted and characteristics of the climbing place. For example, Participant 6 explained, 'I know one of the climbers that sort of developed this area ... and I climbed with him and his family a few times and you kind of like to be there with the people who kind of battled the bush... Like it felt like kind of a community...'. This quote highlights the elements often associated with place attachment: respect for the place, continued use and community (Low & Altman, 1992).

The climbers in this study developed place attachments to both built and natural climbing places. Differences exist in the nature of these attachments especially in terms of meanings (e.g. the mecca), accessibility and social interaction.

Literature cited in this case study is included in the list of references at the end of this book.

Culture, Place and Identity

Place is intimately tied to culture. The meanings that are attached to sport spaces are strongly influenced by the cultural context in which sport and tourism exist (Funk & Bruun, 2007). Culture relates to sport in a number of ways, but three of the most tangible associations are the following: (a) cultural programmes run in association with sport events, (b) sport as a form of popular culture and (c) subcultures in sport. Each of these cultural dimensions influences the meaning that is attached to sport spaces and, in so doing, they affect place identity and, potentially, place making for tourism.

Sport and culture

Sport and culture are often treated as separate but complementary activities. This treatment is particularly evident at major sporting events, which often have distinct cultural and sporting programmes. The opening and closing ceremonies of the Olympic Games provide a good example of the conscious juxtapositioning of sport and culture, as do the separate Olympic cultural programmes organised by host cities.

There are three types of narrative approaches associated with the opening ceremonies of major sporting events. Moragas *et al.* (1995: 105) have categorised them as history, party and show. In the first case, the ceremony is treated as a 'unique historic event taking place in that moment, although forming part of a historic chain'. The opening ceremony of the 2010 Vancouver Winter Olympics was a good example with its dramatic representation of Canadian heritage and landscape. In the second instance, the ceremony is treated as a celebration and pays particular attention to the event's cultural aspects. 'It is a peak experience; an explosion of culture, theatre and joy' (Moragas *et al.*, 1995: 107). Performing arts that are indigenous to the hosting city are often showcased. Finally, the third type of ceremony is one of entertainment. This type of ceremony downplays the 'distraction' of the cultural and ritual structures of the event and tries to provide 'an entertaining introduction to the "real" excitement: the sports competition' (Moragas *et al.*, 1995: 108). Each of these three approaches, but most particularly the first and the second, may serve the explicit positioning of culture in relation to place.

The 'fine arts' programme held in conjunction with the sporting competitions of the Olympic Games is another example of the distinct but complementary association of sport and culture. The charter of the International Olympic Committee requires that a 'fine-arts' programme be held under the auspices of the local host committee. Various approaches have been taken with this arts agenda, but it has increasingly been used as a way to promote the host city and country. For the 2000

Summer Games in Sydney, a four-year plan was developed, called the Sydney Cultural Olympiad. Its four main components were 'The Dreaming' in 1997, designed to showcase Aboriginal culture in Australia; 'A Sea Change' in 1998, which emphasised the eras of migration to Australia; 'Reaching the World' in 1999, featuring performance tours by elite Australian artists and performers; and finally, 'Harbour of Life' in 2000, an on-site Sydney exhibition of the highest quality Australian and international artists. Stevenson (1997: 236) argued that the Sydney 2000 Cultural Olympiad was principally 'concerned with constructing and promoting images and representations of Australianness that will assist the symbolic and material sale of the Games'. This view is consistent with the declaration of the Artistic Director for the Cultural Olympiad that '... the four festivals of the Cultural Olympiad ... are the greatest opportunity we have ever had to change national and international perceptions about Australia' (Voumard, 1995: 14a).

Sport as culture

Popular culture as manifested in sport is one of the main ways that humans develop personal and collective identities (L'Etang, 2006). It is through these personal and collective identities that place identity is developed. At its most basic, identity is the way we perceive ourselves, as individuals and collectives, based on prevailing social and ideological values and practices (McConnell & Edwards, 2000). It is a social phenomenon developed through social and cultural processes as found in the press, television and other dominant cultural institutions. Identity is the way in which people make sense of the self through affiliation and bonds with other people and the cultures that define these affiliations (Dauncey & Hare, 2000).

National identity is typically thought of in the way that nations differ from each other in terms of stereotypes, symbols and practices including those associated with sport (Devine & Devine, 2004; Jackson, 1994; McConnell & Edwards, 2000; Tuck, 2003) (Focus point 6.1). McGuirk and Rowe (2001: 52, 53) have captured this idea more broadly:

> Places have come to be conceptualised as constructed through a dynamic articulation of their material and representational dimensions, and place identity is understood to be mutable, contingent and fluid. Cultural stocks of knowledge about places can, however, constitute a prevailing, often stubbornly persistent balance of forces that name, interpret and project place meanings. A place in this sense is a 'text', the meaning of which is continually being made, reproduced and re-made.

Focus point 6.1

Sport Tourism in Mongolia: The Ulaanbaatar Naadam

The Eriwyn Gurvan Naadam, or the Naadam in its short form, translates to the Festival of the Three Manly Sports although females now participate freely. It is the biggest festival of the year for Mongolians, with the largest gathering occurring in the capital of Ulaanbaatar from 11 to 13 July each year. It is estimated that about 50,000 people attend this gathering including an increasing number of international visitors. The festival begins with a colourful opening ceremony followed by two days of horse racing, archery and wrestling competitions followed by a day of socialising and feasts. Each of these sports is deeply rooted in Mongolian heritage and, as such, offers locals the opportunity to celebrate their identity and visitors a unique opportunity to share in a genuine celebration of cultural heritage. The horse-racing event is linked to traditional rituals related to the consecration of mares which were traditionally left to run free on the steppes for the summer. Such ceremonies were followed by the racing of the stallions with the focus on the horses rather than the riders. Traditionally, the winning stallion was consecrated to the gods and allowed to run free. The archery competition had its roots in both war and hunting. In the past, archers competed in pairs, with princes alongside of herders. Finally, Mongolian wrestling is a combination of music, ritual and dance along with the physical competition of the match itself. The wrestlers personify the strength, skill and courage of the 'ideal man'. Victorious wrestlers shared their victory with the spirits of nature and with the spectators by offering cheese to the mountains, sky and the crowd. While the rich heritage that underlies each of these events is difficult for an uninitiated guest to fully understand in a short visit, the cultural relevance of the festival is clear, and the festival is appreciated as a rare opportunity to be exposed to the 'backstage' of this destination. For a brief few days, visitors are allowed unique access into place-based identity in Mongolia.

Source: O'Gorman and Thompson (2007)

Place identity is influenced by many cultural attributes, but sport certainly appears to be one of the most dominant. Nauright (1996: 69) suggests that not only is sport a factor in the process of constructing place identity but that it

> is one of the most significant shapers of collective or group identity in the contemporary world. In many cases, sporting events and people's reaction to them are the clearest public manifestations of culture and collective identities in a given society.

It is not just high-profile sporting competitions that influence and reflect place identity. Sports and leisure pursuits that occur on a daily basis in local communities are also important (Harahousou, 1999; Nauright, 1997b). Typically, insights into cross-cultural differences related to sport are gained incidentally as a by-product of travelling to another culture as a sport participant or spectator, or by being exposed to cultural differences through the media. Increasingly, however, sport is consciously being used as a lens to develop an understanding of cultural differences as exemplified through sport-based study abroad trips by US universities (Fairley & Tyler, 2009).

Place identity through sport is constructed in at least four ways that have particular relevance to tourism. These include the following: (1) the association of particular sports to specific regions, (2) the unifying forces of competitive hierarchies found within sport, (3) identification with sporting success, and (4) the personification of place through sporting heroes and heroines.

Specific sports are commonly associated with particular nations. This connection may be based on various factors, but one of the most powerful is the role that a given sport has played in a nation's heritage. An example of this type of association is that of rugby union in New Zealand. Fougere (1989) has suggested that rugby

> served from the end of last century [1900] as a mirror to New Zealand society. It symbolized a pattern of social relationships that, in New Zealand eyes, made New Zealand both distinctive and admirable. As such it provided an important basis for the construction of a sense of national unity and individual identity.

The competitive hierarchy that exists in many sports is also an important factor in the promotion of place identity (McGuirk & Rowe, 2001). The principle reflected in the Bedouin saying 'I against my brother, I and my brother against my cousin, I and my brother and my cousin against the world' reflects the aggregation of territorial interest that occurs within a competitive hierarchy (Fougere, 1989: 116). Place identity is fostered through a growing territory as successively higher levels of the competitive hierarchy are reached. In this process, many of the real differences and disparities that are found within these places are overshadowed or subsumed.

The relative success of a region in terms of its sport performance also influences the connection between sport and place identity. In addition to being in the 'news' more frequently, places with teams that consistently win major championships tend to be characterised as winners in their own right. Such success can provide a sense of common identity even when there may be numerous other social and economic divisions that exist within the region (Bale, 1989, 1993a; McGuirk & Rowe, 2001). One has only to look at the national celebrations associated with World Cup Football to see evidence of this dynamic (Dauncey & Hare, 2000).

Finally, sport heroes and heroines can have a strong impact on the way that we identify with place (Dauncey & Hare, 2000; Nauright, 1996). Recent international examples include Yao Ming from China and Ronaldinho from Brazil. Yao Ming is the 2.29-m (7 ft 6 in) National Basketball League superstar playing for the Houston Rockets and idolised in his home country of China. Brazilian football superstar Ronaldinho is noted for his penalty kick and ball-control prowess. Ronaldinho has spent the majority of his peak playing years playing professional football in Europe for Italian Serie A club AC Milan while still being revered in Brazil partly for his contribution to their national team. Both players have acted as unofficial ambassadors for their home countries where their compatriots have taken great pride in their international success.

Sport subcultures

Sport subcultures represent a third cultural dimension of sport that contributes to place identity in a tourism context. These subcultures are generally characterised by commitment to a particular sport, distinguishing symbols or cultural capital, and various career stages in terms of subculture membership. The use of the term 'subculture' in this instance is meant to be inclusive of lifestyle and neo-tribe concepts of sporting cultures that are distinguishable from dominant cultures (Wheaton, 2007). They are of interest because they are characterised by unique relationships to place including place identity.

For example, the subculture of windsurfing has been described as a culture of 'conspicuous commitment' (Wheaton, 2000). This commitment is expressed in a number of ways, but it is essentially reflected in the prowess, dedication and skill that members demonstrate in relation to their sport. Identifiable communities form around sports such as windsurfing, and these communities tend to share characteristics that go beyond the sporting activity itself. Green and Chalip (1998: 280) describe women's football as a sport subculture that '... gives participants much more than the opportunity to play together. It is a statement about who they are and the conventions by which they refuse to be constrained'. More generally, the adoption of subculture identity through sports is seen as a way of asserting cultural identity and a sense of community in a society fragmented by divisions of class, race and gender (Beezer & Hebdige, 1992). In many cases, such as surfing (Law, 2001) and snowboarding (Heino, 2000), and adventure sports in general (Breivik, 2010), sport subcultures represent a form of 'counterculture' in that members deliberately distance themselves from the mainstream norms and practices of society.

Style incorporates the symbolic representations of subculture. This form of cultural capital is found in the dress, hair and speech styles of surfers (Law, 2001), snowboarders (Heino, 2000), climbers (Donnelly & Young, 1988) and many other sport subculture groups. For the 'hard-core' members, these subculture symbols permeate all aspects of their life:

> Participation in this (subculture) lifestyle is displayed in a range of symbols such as clothes, speech, car, and associated leisure activities; however, for the dedicated, often-obsessive participant, windsurfing participation is a whole way of life in which windsurfers seek hedonism, freedom and self-expression. For 'core' members …, windsurfing dictates their leisure time, their work time, their choice of career, and where they live. (Wheaton, 2000: 256)

Membership status within these subcultures is characterised by career stages that are based on the demonstration of commitment and prowess. These stages include (a) presocialisation or information gathering about the subculture, (b) recruitment and selection by the subculture, (c) socialisation in the subculture and (d) acceptance or ostracism from the subculture (Donnelly & Young, 1988). As a result, there are various levels of membership in these subcultures, ranging from 'outsiders' gathering information so that they can obtain membership through to the hard-core members who have achieved widespread acceptance. Membership and cultural identity within the group are, however, dynamic.

In the context of the mode of leisure experience framework (Williams *et al.*, 1992), sport subcultures tend to be more focused on activity and companionship than on place. Green and Chalip (1998: 275) arrived at this conclusion in their study of women football players participating in a tournament in Florida. They suggested that these particular sport tourists ' … seek opportunities to share and affirm their identities as football players. It is the occasion to celebrate a subculture shared with others from distant places, *rather than the site itself*, that attracts them'. In this case, the host destination provided a social space for female football players to celebrate their subculture. Participants were able to distance themselves from their regular lives, they enjoyed a sense of camaraderie with their teammates and other members of the subculture and they were given the opportunity to parade their subculture identities. The destination was described as facilitating the primary purpose of the visit to the tournament site.

At another level, sport subcultures are intimately connected and dependent on specific places for their sport. This is true of climbers, surfers, wind surfers, snowboarders and many other 'extreme' sport subcultures that are currently enjoying popularity. Traditionally, these groups tend to be very dependent on natural resources found in the periphery (Chapter 5). Their strong subculture commitment provides them with the motivations to overcome the constraint of distance. More recently, however, urban landscapes have become popular with these groups (Breivik, 2010; Wheaton, 2007). In either setting there appears to be an attempt to become 'one with the environment'.

Often, the spaces used by these subculture groups are contested. For instance, skiers did not welcome snowboarders when the sport was initially introduced to the slopes of the major ski resorts (Heino, 2000; Hudson, 1999). Because of financial necessity, effective management and on-site modifications, snowboarders and skiers increasingly share these slopes in harmony. Nevertheless, while the space associated with these sports is increasingly shared, subculture place identity may be quite distinct.

Subculture groups also recognise special places through access to 'insider information' (Donnelly & Young, 1988). As members of sub-culture groups progress through their subculture careers, they become privy to information about 'special' sites in the context of their group. The very act of travelling to selected destinations may garner social capital for an individual within their subcultural group (Shipway & Jones, 2007). Experience at these sites may be closely tied to a member's status within his or her subculture. Place can become one with the activity. Hard-core subculture members will tend to live near to where they can be active in their sport and will use their vacation time to travel to destinations that are 'sacred' to their sport.

Marketing Place Through Sport

The tourism industry is in the business of selling places, and this is done through the process of marketing. Place marketers construct new images of the place to replace either vague or negative images previously held by residents, investors and visitors (Page & Hall, 2003). In doing so, they are actively trying to influence place identity. Carter *et al.* (2007) suggest that place identity can be imposed by globalising forces of development such as tourism. They raise questions about the ethics of such manipulation, and their work advocates that the promotion of place identity should be consistent with the sense of place prevalent in the community.

The logic that underlies place marketing is twofold. Firstly, it is based on an understanding of the way that place consumers, such as sport tourists, make decisions about the destinations that they visit. Baloglu and McCleary (1999: 870) summarise this view stating that destination

> image is mainly caused or formed by two major forces: stimulus factors and personal factors. The former are those that stem from the external stimulus and physical object as well as previous experience.

Personal factors, on the other hand, are the characteristics (social and psychological) of the perceiver.

In place marketing, personal factors can be addressed through target marketing while the stimulus factors can be modified through product development and promotion. The belief that destination image or place identity can be consciously manipulated is a fundamental assumption of place marketing (Gallarza *et al.*, 2002).

In the case of consumer tribes such as sport subcultures, the image/ experience is the product. For example, revered status within the surfing community of selected destinations makes them relatively easy sales in this market segment (Moutinho *et al.*, 2007). The second line of logic that explains increased attention to place marketing is that destinations are facing increasing competition from other places (Hall, 1998). In fact, Kotler *et al.* (1993: 346) argue that we are living in a time of 'place wars':

> The globalization of the world's economy and the accelerating pace of technological change are two forces that require all places to learn to compete. Places must learn to think more like businesses, developing products, markets, and customers.

Page and Hall (2003: 309) highlight the need to commodify particular aspects of place in the process of place marketing.

> In the case of urban [or regional] re-imaging, marketing practices, such as branding, rely upon the commodification of particular aspects of place, exploiting, reinventing or creating place images in order to sell the place as a destination product for tourists or investment.

Sport is one of the most powerful ways of establishing place identity as culture is one of the key factors in distinguishing places. By harnessing the cultural dimensions of sport, place marketers are able to commodify 'the ways of living' in a place. In a sport context, this can be done by developing (1) major facilities, (2) hallmark events, (3) focused tourism marketing strategies and policies and (4) broad-based leisure and cultural opportunities within a destination (Hall, 1998) (Focus point 6.2).

Focus point 6.2

Infrastructure Plans for the FIFA World Cups in 2018 and 2022

The winning bids by Russia and Qatar to host the FIFA World Cups in 2018 and 2022 'reflect a new world order as ambitious developing countries level the playing field with cash strapped Western nations' (Grant, 2010: A12). Along with the 2008 Olympics in China, the 2010 World Cup in South Africa, the 2014 World Cup scheduled for Brazil, the success of the Russian and Qatari World Cup bids establishes a clear break from the traditional practice of circulating the major sport events between Europe and North America. In hosting these events, a strong message is being sent about the emerging importance of these countries in the global world order. Part of the rationale for Russia and Qatar committing to the huge investment of hosting these events is the anticipated impact that the events will have in terms of place making statements. In order to help ensure this result, a major portion of the investments for the FIFA World Cups in Russia and Qatar is going to build and upgrade sport facilities and transportation networks. Qatar plans to build nine new stadiums and renovate three more. Each one will be fitted with state-of-the-art, zero-emission solar-powered cooling systems, and at least one stadium has been designed to include a membrane on its outer walls that will serve as a massive projection screen. In Russia, a commitment has been made to a $4 billion construction program to build 13 new stadiums and upgrade three more. Both countries are investing many more billions of dollars on transportation upgrades.

Sources: Attfield (2010) and Grant (2010)

Establishing a critical mass of visitor attractions and facilities has proven to be one of the most popular strategies for re-imaging a city. An obvious benefactor of this trend has been the real estate sector, but the sport and tourism sectors have also been active promoters of this strategy.

Another high-profile strategy for re-imaging places is the hosting of hallmark events (Getz, 1997; Hall, 1992a). Sporting events are particularly attractive given the media attention that they tend to attract. The Australian Tourist Commission actively tried to capitalise on the opportunity to re-image Australia in connection with the Sydney 2000 Olympic Games (Morse, 2001). It did this by developing a detailed strategy that included joint promotions with Olympic sponsors, a visiting media programme prior to, during and after the Games, the provision of logistical support for television broadcasters, the provision of press facilities for non-accredited media as well as accredited media, business development support, specially targeted promotions at high-yield markets and an assortment of other activities including a detailed post-games strategy. At a broader level, Australia made a conscious attempt to reposition its overall brand. In fact, the International Olympic Committee's Director of Marketing stated that

> Australia is the first Olympic host nation to take full advantage of the Games to vigorously pursue tourism for the benefit of the whole

country. It's something we've never seen take place to this level before, and it's a model that we would like to see carried forward to future Olympic Games in Athens and beyond. (Payne as cited in Brown *et al.*, 2002: 175)

Birmingham, Manchester and Sheffield are three UK cities that have consciously used sport to re-image themselves. Birmingham attempted to re-position itself as an international city through the construction of the National Indoor Arena, a bid to hold the 1992 Olympic Games and the hosting of Davis Cup tennis and international athletics. Manchester also bid on the Olympics, hosted the 2002 Commonwealth Games and built a new 45,000-seat stadium. Sheffield staged the 1991 World Student Games and developed many new facilities including major swimming and arena complexes. In his assessment of these re-imaging initiatives, Smith (2005) noted that the sporting reputations of these cities were strengthened. However, he also noted limitations to this re-imaging including the lack of control that the cities had over the message that was expressed by sport media and the lack of impact on image by the facility investments.

A third popular approach to re-imaging places for tourism is non-event-related tourism marketing that attempts to capitalise on a positive association between sport and place. A 1998 New Zealand promotional strategy linked rugby to place. In announcing the campaign, the Minister of Tourism stated that 'the upcoming promotion will leverage off the popularity of the All Blacks in rugby-mad South Africa to create an awareness of New Zealand and all its attractions' (New Zealand Tourism Board, 1998: 2). Sport-related marketing slogans, such as Edmonton's (Canada) 'City of Champions', also reflects this type of place marketing strategy.

Finally, the widespread development of sport-related leisure and cultural services is a fourth type of approach used to sell places based on sport. This approach goes beyond the support of high-profile professional sports to the development of a sporting ethic within the place through such things as park land and shorefront development that encourages active sporting pursuits such as jogging, cycling and sailing. Glasgow has used this approach to re-position itself as an active healthy community both in terms of self-identity and in terms of destination image (Hooper, 1998; Porteous, 2000).

Conclusion

This chapter highlights the importance of place in the context of sport tourism. Place was defined as space which has been infused with meaning, and it should be clear now that tourism spaces are increasingly infused with meaning through sport. Sporting culture is particularly important in terms of three variations: sport and culture, sport as culture and sporting subcultures. Each can have major impacts on the way that sport tourists see and experience a destination. Given sport's powerful influence on the way place identity is understood, it is not surprising that it is manipulated to market tourism places. Place marketers attempt to use sport events, activities and nostalgic attractions to create desirable place images.

A number of issues need to be considered in association with the numerous opportunities to market 'place' through sport. Bale's (1989) spectre of the trend towards homogenous sportscapes poses a threat to the critical elements of uniqueness, which, in turn, is a threat to the sustainability of sport tourism development. Taken to its extreme, in a homogeneous sportscape, the need or desire to travel to different areas for sport is greatly reduced.

The integrity of the sports being commodified for sport tourism must be protected. Place marketers should avoid the temptation to sensationalise or spectacularise featured sports in a way that erodes the essence of the sport competition. While place marketers are in the business of commodifying both place and sport, if the meanings associated with sport are compromised or destroyed in this process then the sports resource, and the attractiveness of sport as a tourist attraction, will also be compromised.

Finally, it must be recognised that there are multiple views on place in tourism spaces (Schollmann *et al.*, 2001; Sherlock, 2001). Place marketers who use sport as a marketing tool need to appreciate the contrasting perspectives of place held by different groups within the community. Distinct place meanings are not just associated with hosts and guests but with the complex array of subgroups that exist therein (e.g. in the case of alpine resorts: long-term, short-term residents, second-home owners, skiers, snowboarders, climbers and numerous others). The failure of place marketers to account for these differences may result in conflicting views on place, which are non-optimal at the very least, and may in fact be non-sustainable in the long run.

Chapter 7

Environment: Landscape, Resources and Impacts

Sport tourism's link to the environment is both as victim and as aggressor.
Standeven and De Knop, 1999: 236

Introduction

Sport-related tourism development is tied more closely than many other forms of tourism to the geographical resource base at a destination. The extent to which tourists find a destination to be attractive is strongly influenced by the physical environment, including landscapes and climate (Boniface & Cooper, 1994; Burton, 1995; Krippendorf, 1986). Many sports are closely tied to the physical geography of a destination. For instance, Priestley (1995: 210) observes that single integrated golf resorts '... have mushroomed in the hotter climates where traditional sun, sand and sea tourism could or does exist'. In sports such as surfing, hang-gliding, and scuba diving, there tends to be a hierarchy of destinations based on the experiential value of the physical environment. Destinations may be managed and promoted to develop new or exploit existing links to specific sports. For example, the development of integrated golf resorts in Spain capitalises on increasing levels of visitor demand for this sport (Priestley, 1995), in conjunction with the hypermobility of European nationals, particularly with the growth in demand for low-cost air travel as an increasingly instituted social practice (Randles & Mander, 2009).

The sport tourism development potential of a destination is also determined by cultural influences on the landscape. Event sport tourism development at a destination requires, in most cases, constructed resources, including sport facilities and tourism infrastructure. Sports in central locations often use facilities that are purpose-built, such as stadia, marinas, sports arenas and gymnasiums. Alternatively, sports may temporarily make use of buildings or infrastructures that are developed primarily for purposes other than sport. Examples include roads, central parks and urban tourism icons (e.g. New York's Central Park and the Sydney Opera House) which may figure prominently as locations or backdrops to sporting scenes. An understanding of the spatial elements of sport tourism development is therefore incomplete without some consideration of the physical environment. This is an important starting point to understanding the resource requirements and impacts of sport tourism development. Natural and built resources for sport tourism, and impacts associated with each, are considered separately in this chapter.

Sport Tourism Landscapes, Environments and Resources

'Landscape' is a term that is commonly associated with attractive scenery. Natural landscapes (and seascapes) are central to the pursuit of many sports. However, sports are not natural forms of movement and, therefore, 'the landscape upon which such body culture takes place is part of the cultural landscape' (Bale, 1994: 9). Even sports that rely on natural elements take place in environments that are subject to varying degrees of anthropogenic change. For instance, ski slopes are subject to change through the grooming of ski trails, the construction of facilities such as ski jumps and slalom courses, snowboard half pipes and ramps, snow making, and the development of visitor services (Hudson, 1999). Golf courses, which are very 'green' in appearance, represent highly modified natural areas and are characterised by significant ecological impacts (Priestley, 1995).

While the popular use of the term landscape often implies naturalness, the landscapes of sport are, to varying degrees, cultural landscapes. The term 'sportscape' is used in the geography of sport to describe the highly modified (e.g. modern stadium or arena) and technologised (e.g. corporate suites, closed circuit television) sports environment (Bale, 1994). Relph (1985: 23) notes that landscapes can 'take on the very character of human existence. They can be full of life, deathly dull, exhilarating, sad, joyful or pleasant'. This observation certainly applies to the landscapes of sport. The manner in which the landscapes of sport are developed, and the impacts arising from the use of those landscapes, are important to the sustainable development of sport and tourism.

The landscapes of sport

The values and interpretations associated with the landscape are highly subjective (Tuan, 1974). Sportscapes are no exception. Bale (1994) applies Meinig's (1979) 'ten versions of the same scene' to the landscape of sport in an exercise that is relevant to the study of sport tourism (Table 7.1). These 'versions' are important in understanding the resources and impacts of sport tourism. The development of resources and infrastructures for sport tourism should take place with consideration given to the values and interpretations of landscapes noted in Table 7.1.

Table 7.1 Interpretations of sport landscapes

Interpretations of sports landscapes	Description
1. Sport, landscape and natural habitat	It is possible for sport participants to encounter and utilise the natural landscape for certain sports events and, when the event is over, never return to it. They remain landscapes and never become sportscapes. Landscapes therefore may be used for sports but never 'sportised' in any permanent sense. Impressions of nature and environment are important elements of the athlete's experience.
2. Sport, landscape and human habitat	The sport landscape may also be regarded as part of the human habitat. Conscious decisions can be made for slopes, soils, elevations, sites and routes, channels or relief features to be used as homes for sport. Humans rearrange nature into sport-related forms; an adjustment rather than a conquest of nature.
3. Sport landscapes as artefacts	Many sport landscapes disregard the natural or semi-natural landscape upon which they are found. This view sees humankind as the conqueror of nature, with concrete, plastic and glass, totally flat synthetic surfaces and indoor arenas in which nature has been neutralised.
4. Sport landscapes as systems	Sports landscapes can also be viewed as part of intricate economic or physical systems. A sports stadium, for example, does not exist in isolation; it generates flows of people and spatial interactions over an area much greater than that of the stadium itself. For example, the Tour de France is part of an extensive economic system that affects the places through which it passes. Sports events are also part of physical systems. Snow conditions influence performance in ski races and rain may deter attendance at sports events.
5. The sport landscape as problem	The excessive dominance of sport over nature may be seen to lead to social or environmental pollution, erosion and visual blight. Problem landscapes occur in various sports in quite different ways. Traffic congestion and crowding can result from hosting a sports event in an inner-city stadium. Erosion of soil and damage to plant cover on ski pistes in alpine regions are also examples. Impacts also differ in terms of their permanence. When the sports landscape is perceived as a problem, it can lead to political activism and the rejection of sporting events that might have induced landscape change.

Table 7.1 (*Continued*)

Interpretations of sports landscapes	Description
6. Sport landscape as wealth	The sports landscape may also reflect the view that land is a raw material. The long-term returns of lands given over to sport are important. So, too, are the significant economic benefits that one-off events generate in local areas. Sport may be a form of place-boosting for purposes of attracting investment, and may influence rental profits. The sports landscape is littered with advertising hoardings and other evidence of sponsorship.
7. Sport landscape as ideology	The sports landscape may be viewed as a reflection of various ideologies. Sports landscapes may be explicit responses to nationalism. New national sports may be invented to distance countries from more dominant neighbours. The stadium may be an expression of modern technocentric ideology.
8. Sport landscape as history	The present-day landscape of sport is a result of the cumulative processes of historical evolution. Sports landscapes are often accumulations. Size, shape, materials, decorations and other manifestations tell us something about the way people have experienced sport over time.
9. Sport landscape as place	This view sees landscape as a locality possessing particular nuances and unique flavours possessing a sense of place. For the sports participant – athlete or spectator – the experience of place, therefore, could be argued to contribute to the overall sporting experience.
10. Sport landscape as aesthetic	Landscapes can possess aesthetic qualities predisposing the observer towards one and against another. Aesthetics are related to the artistic quality of the sports landscape. The aesthetics of the sport landscape are also portrayed in paint, film, photograph and print. Such portrayals may be accurate representations of what exists in the physical landscape. It is also possible that landscape icons may become mythical landscapes (e.g. the landscapes of English cricket and American baseball).

Source: Adapted from Bale (1994)

The resource base for sport tourism

The potential for sport tourism development at a destination is determined by the existence of requisite sport and tourism resources and infrastructures. A sport tourism resource analysis may include natural environments, constructed sports facilities, tourism transport and infrastructure and information services. These need to be provided in the required balance and combination, or developed in a planned and coordinated way as determined by the development goals of the destination. The importance of coordinated planning and development arises from the considerable overlap that exists between the resource requirements for sport and those for tourism (Standeven & De Knop, 1999). Domestic and international airline services are used by travelling sports teams and leisure travellers for the same purpose, whereas both use stadia, albeit for different reasons (competition and spectatorship, respectively). The existence or systematic development of sport and tourism infrastructures is required for any location to function as a sport tourism destination (Table 7.2).

Considerable opportunity exists, therefore, for sport and tourism resources to be developed in a synergistic fashion that maximises the mutual benefits of the stakeholders. Event sport tourism, for example, offers the potential for the inner-city resource base for sport, recreation, entertainment, retail and service to be transformed in a planned and coordinated manner. This course of strategic development may generate the advantages of enhanced profile and destination image vis-à-vis sport tourism, thereby improving the standing of the destination in the hierarchy of sport tourism locations (Chapter 5). The status of a ski destination, for example, is a function of high-quality ski resources (e.g. terrain, elevation, snow conditions, weather), in combination with the required tourism services and infrastructure.

The reproducibility of sports

The tourism resource base may be classified in various ways. One approach draws on the distinction between those that can be reproduced, or transported, and those that are non-reproducible (Boniface & Cooper, 1994). Resorts, theme parks and stadium experiences are readily reproduced and can be developed in, or transmitted to, various locations (Weed, 2010). In contrast, natural landscapes and cultural heritage are generally non-reproducible (despite efforts, generally of limited success, to the contrary). Sports resources may also vary on the basis of their transportability. Nature-based sports such as downhill skiing and rock climbing tend to be dependent on certain types of landscapes or specific landscape features. Attempts to create artificial ski slopes in central

Table 7.2 Resource-base for sport tourism development

Tourism industry resource requirements	Sport sector resource requirements
Natural features National parks, scenery, lakes, mountains, rivers, coastlines.	**Natural features** National parks, open amenity spaces, wilderness areas, geographical features (mountains, rocks, spas, coastlines, marine environments).
Facilities and infrastructure Transport services, places of accommodation, dinning and entertainment.	**Facilities and infrastructure** Stadia, arenas, sports halls, transport infrastructure, dining and entertainment.
Built amenities Public toilets, parking facilities, signposts, shelters.	**Built amenities** Public toilets, parking facilities, signposts, shelters.
Tourist information services Visitor information services, internet-based information services, booking and ticketing services, travel agents.	**Sport services** Coaching and leadership, equipment/clothing hire and/or purchase, storage and management, supervision and safety, hiring, operations, training facilities, injury prevention and medical facilities, science and research facilities.
Tourism organisations Planning and development, strategic planning, destination image, tourism marketing, place promotion, visiting media programmes, tourism research, industry coordination and liaison.	**Sport organisations** Sports clubs, volunteer groups, and community groups. Administration, facility development, funding, sponsorship, information services, marketing, merchandising.
Transport services Road, rail, air, sea, domestic and international; plus scenic journeys, gondolas, tourist routes, rides, heritage rail tourism, historic routes, tour coaches, hot air balloons.	**Transport services** Road, rail, air, sea, domestic and international.
Entertainment and activities Attractions, casinos, cinemas, zoos, shopping, nightlife, nightclubs.	**Entertainment and activities** Sports halls and venues (ice rinks, leisure centres, gymnasiums, swimming pools, climbing walls), golf courses, marinas, sports museums, halls of fame, shopping, nightlife.

Source: Adapted from Standeven and De Knop (1999)

locations have met with moderate commercial success (see Chapter 10). The reason for this is that the experiential value of the mountain environment, which forms an important part of the participant experience for many sport tourists, is not transportable (although spectators may dramatically experience alpine skiing through film media, such as the Banff Film Festival).

The same is true of indoor climbing walls. While they present an exciting new variation of rock climbing, they cannot duplicate the unique challenge of outdoor climbing sites (see Case Study 6.1). Green sports are those that are dependent on the integration of a physical activity with specific environmental attributes (Bale, 1989). Sports such as surfing, cross-country skiing, windsurfing, sailing, mountain climbing, and orienteering are examples of green sports, as they are built around specific features of the natural environment as sources of pleasure, challenge, competition or mastery. A case in point is the way that hang-gliding, parapenting and windsurfing harness the natural forces of air and sea. As a result, participants enjoy a heightened sense of environmental awareness because of the role that it plays in their performance. The experiential value of these sports is largely dependent upon the mood of the landscapes where they are performed. These landscapes are inherently non transportable.

In contrast, other sports are more readily transported. For example, ice skating has been successfully transported from the high to mid- and equatorial latitudes with the development of improved ice-making technology and expanding markets. Indeed, indoor arenas have transformed sports such as ice hockey from outdoor to indoor activities, impacting their spatial and temporal distribution (Higham & Hinch, 2002; Case study 6.1). Spatially, these sports have spread from high to low latitudes and temporally from winter sports to year-round activities. Outdoor winter sports such as ski jumping may also be transported from peripheral to central locations in the high latitudes to capture the advantage of proximity to markets. The Holmenkollen (Oslo, Norway) and Calgary 1988 Olympic (Canada) ski jumps are examples of constructed ski jump facilities that have been developed adjacent to central locations.

Many sports, such as competitive swimming, diving, squash and racquetball, are performed in indoor sports centres and have become very transportable. These sports are also characterised by highly prescribed spatial rules and standards. Other sports that are traditionally played in outdoor settings can also be transported and performed in indoor sports centres and arenas. Examples include tennis, netball, athletics and even equestrian activities. These sports demonstrate what Bale (1989: 171) refers to as the 'industrialisation of the sport environment', which relates closely to the concept of transportability. Indoor cricket, for example, is a sport that takes place in air-conditioned centres that are typically housed in unused industrial buildings and warehouses located in industrial landscapes (Bale, 1989).

The application of technology to the modern stadium demonstrates the height of sport transportability. The reproducibility of the sportscape facilitates the transportation of sports and the sport experience. For instance, in 2002 the Australian Rugby Union (ARU) considered hosting the 2002 Mandela Trophy test match between the Wallabies (Australia) and the Springboks (South Africa) in Hong Kong (China) rather than one of the Australian state capitals. Rugby is an example of a transportable sport, which offers opportunities for generating new markets and revenue. Viewed another way, sports facilities may be built, permanently or temporarily, at locations designed to maximize market access. Such developments offer the potential to enhance the status of sports, such as snowboarding and beach volleyball, through increased public awareness and spectatorship (Focus point 7.1). However, the transportability of sports also presents the threat of the displacement of a sporting activity from its original location. The importance of retaining and enhancing the idiosyncrasies and elements of uniqueness associated with a tourism site is an important strategy to mitigate this threat (Bale, 1989: 171).

Focus point 7.1
Wanaka Snowfest: Bringing Extreme Sports into the Urban Environment

The town of Wanaka, New Zealand, hosts an annual winter sports festival which includes a series of events such as the World Heli Challenge and the Wanaka Snowfest. The World Heli Challenge, which has been at the cutting edge of modern winter sports competition since its inception in 1995, involves 70 skiers and boarders who are transported by helicopter to remote alpine regions to contest extreme, free-ride and downhill competitions. The Snowfest features Masters ski races at ski fields in the Wanaka region. These events take place in the surrounding alpine environments. Other events such as snowboarding, ski jumping and acrobatic competitions have proved to be relatively transportable sports. The culmination of the two-week World Heli Challenge and the Wanaka Snowfest is the 'Pulsate Wanaka Big Air'. This event 'brings the snow to the town, with over 8,000 spectators, international headline bands and a host of the world's premiere new school aerialists'. These sports are contested in the main street of Wanaka. This requires the development of a temporary extreme ski facility, featuring snow-making equipment. Streetlights provide floodlighting, and the shops and sidewalks become galleries for spectators. For the duration of the festival, the streetscape of downtown Wanaka becomes a snowscape for extreme sport. This innovation has brought significant benefits to sports such as acrobatic snowboarding due to enhanced spectator access. The status of Wanaka as a tourist destination has also been enhanced by the success of the annual Wanaka Big Air event.

Source: http://www.lakewanaka.co.nz/new-zealand/Annual-Events/

Environmental Impacts of Sport Tourism

From a geographical perspective, 'the environment is the totality of tourism activity, incorporating natural elements and society's modification of the landscape and resources' (Mitchell & Murphy, 1991: 59). An understanding of the impacts of sport tourism, and management techniques appropriate to those impacts, is central to the sustainable development of sport and tourism. 'Inevitably, the growth and continuing locational adjustments made by modern sports have created significant changes in the landscape' (Bale, 1989: 142). Many such impacts are fleeting, or temporary. Triathlons, marathons, cycle races, car rallies and festival or exhibition sports are often conducted on circuits, courses or courts that may be constructed temporarily in urban areas. The impacts of these sports, which may include a sizeable body of spectators, are rapidly dispersed at the conclusion of the contest. The immediate negative consequences of stadium-based sports may include traffic congestion and crowding, and undesirable impacts such as vandalism, antisocial behaviour, littering and noise. These impacts are generally short term, but they can cause disruption to a great number of community residents (Bale, 1994). They may also result in aversion effects upon visitor flows into or within a destination as non-sport tourists choose to visit other destinations or cancel their intended visit (Faulkner *et al.*, 1998).

Other sports may have a longer term, or indelible, impact in cases where naturalness forms an important, perhaps central, element of the sport tourist experience. While environmental impacts in natural areas may be 'permanent but, paradoxically annoying to few' (Bale, 1994: 11), one significant consequence may be a compromise on the quality of the sport tourist experience (see Case study 7.1 by Ghazali Musa). This is illustrated by the stagnation of ski markets in Europe and North America as a demand-led response to the unsustainable management of environmentally sensitive alpine environments (Flagestad & Hope, 2001).

Case study 7.1

Sipadan: A jewel in the Scuba Diving Crown

Ghazali Musa, University of Malaya

Sipadan is a tiny Malaysian island (16.4 hectares) in the north-east of Borneo. Geologically, it was formed by a volcanic thrust which surfaces 600 m from the floor of the Celebes Sea. Its unique underwater scenery displays glorious landscapes of walls adorned with hundreds of species of soft and hard corals. Located at the heart of the Indo-Pacific basin, the island's waters have more than 3000 fish species, a diversity which is similar to Australia's Great Barrier Reef (Jackson, 1997). Sipadan has more marine life than any other spot on this planet (Sipadan, 2010). It is also perhaps the only location where sharks and turtles are seen regularly (Wood, 1981). Another unique feature of Sipadan is the 'Turtle Tomb', an underwater limestone cave with tunnels and chambers, some of which contain many skeletal remains of turtles. Sipadan consistently appears in lists of the world's top 10 dive sites in scuba magazines.

The island was 'discovered' by Ron Holland, one of the founders of Borneo Divers in 1983. Sipadan was brought to international attention following a documentary with worldwide circulation produced by Jacques Yves Cousteau in 1988: 'Ghost of Sea Turtles' and he described the island as an untouched piece of art. Musa (2002) criticised this, arguing that the event was the beginning of what might have led to the island's over-exploitation in the decade of the 1990s. Responding to the unceasing demand to experience Sipadan, extensive development was carried out on the island and threatened its delicate resources. Many had commented that Sipadan was simply being loved to death (e.g. Musa, 2002; Wood *et al.*, 1995) and became a victim of the 'tragedy of the commons'.

Despite concerns about the impacts of over-development on the island (Mortimer, 1991; Universiti Kebangsaan Malaysia [UKM], 1990; Wood, 1981; Wood *et al.*, 1993, 1995), by the end of the 1990s there were six resorts perched on the northern rim of the island. These were Borneo Divers (1988), Pulau Sipadan Resort (1991), Abdillah Sipadan Resort (1991), Sipadan Dive Centre (1992), Borneo Sea Adventure (1995) and Pulau Bajau (1997). Musa (2002) estimated that all these resorts would have accommodated a total of 360 divers. Adding divers from elsewhere (nearby islands and the mainland), Sipadan could have hosted up to 500 divers a day during the peak season. Intensive land development on the island expanded alarmingly throughout the 1990s and the 2000s: 8% (UKM, 1990), 13.5% (Wood *et al.*, 1993), 33.4% (Wood, *et al.*, 1995) and 50% (Musa, 2002) of the land area of the island. The physical, environmental and social impacts of tourism development on the island were considerable.

The clearing of vegetation and undergrowth had increased evapotranspiration and destabilization of sediments. This led to erosion. Beachfront vegetation clearance, excessive lighting, and noise had reduced the frequency of turtle nesting by 31.7% from 1992 (1470 turtles) to 1997 (1001 turtles) (Musa, 2002). Mortimer (1991) commented that the practice of relocating turtle nests from their natural site to the sun-exposed beach area could affect the gender balance of turtles. The underground water had been utilized faster than rain replenishment, causing the encroachment of salt water inland and the destruction of up to 20% of Sipadan's original vegetation (UKM, 1990).

The septic tank used was ineffective, and the flushing of toilets with seawater reduced the biodegradability of the sewage. Partially treated sewage leaked to the sea, causing neutrophication, which resulted in plankton blooms with subsequent reduction of the underwater visibility (something that divers particularly value). The previous 40–60 m underwater visibility recorded by Cousteau in 1988 had now decreased to 20–30 m. Wood *et al.* (1995) commented that even though coral damage was still minimal, the reefs were not exactly pristine. Boats anchored around the island had also resulted in oil spillages, posing a threat to the marine environment. Wood *et al.* (1995) was critically concerned at how the island's development had been dictated by political and economic precedence. In a study of scuba divers' satisfaction, Musa (2002) noted that divers were gravely concerned about over-development, crowding (on the island and underwater), litter and noise, as there was nowhere on the island that the noise of resort generators could not be heard.

All the resorts formed Resorts Consortium in 1998 to centralize scuba diving operations in Sipadan. The effort was self-imposed and self-regulated. Collectively, they bought turtle nests from traditional turtle egg collectors and transferred them to a hatchery. The newborns were released to the sea. The Consortium also pooled resort services which pollute, overlap and are costly if handled separately. The best example of this was the centralization of transportation. However, efforts to centralize other important elements such as water, waste, compressors and power generators did not materialize.

Both Wood (1981) and Musa (2002) proposed that the island should be left alone without any serious human interference. Musa (2002) suggested that all resorts on the island should be relocated to nearby islands or the mainland. Efforts then should urgently be carried out to determine the island's carrying capacity or limit of acceptable change together with the necessary rehabilitation in order to re-establish its ecological balance. He added that because of the island's small size, zoning for recreational users may not be practical. The sole recreational activity permitted should be scuba diving and only experienced divers should dive in Sipadan. Musa (2002) also proposed that the island should be designated as a World Heritage Site because of its unique geological features and marine life.

Musa (2002) commented that the irresponsible development on the island in the 1990s could be attributed to uncertain governance due to the disputed status of the island, which was claimed by both Malaysia and Indonesia. The area was attractive to both countries due to the multi-million-dollar scuba diving tourism industry and the possible lucrative deep oil reserve. While the dispute was referred to the International Court of Justice, the governments may have been reluctant to take action by way of control which might be construed as pre-empting the court's decision. However, in 2002, the Court declared that Sipadan belonged to Malaysia, based on effective occupation and the absence of other superior title.

With growing international criticism, the central government of Malaysia firmly ordered all six resorts on the island to be closed and moved to nearby islands or the mainland by 31st of December 2004. The majority relocated to Mabul Island. The decision was regarded as a victory and culminating success for conservation. Only day trips were allowed to Sipadan, and the daily carrying capacity was set at 80 divers. After decades of over-exploitation, Sipadan was declared a Protected Marine Park Reserve on 1st January 2005, under the management of Sabah Park. With pressure from dive resorts on the island of Mabul, the Resorts and National Security committees subsequently increased the Sipadan quota to 120 divers a day.

Not everyone agreed that the presence of operators on the island had contributed to the damage of the island's ecosystem. Alin *et al.* (2006) for example argued that the presence of the operators on the island not only had deterred illegal and destructive fish bombing but also slowed down the extinction process of endangered turtle species. The increased naval presence in the area as a direct result of a dispute with Indonesia resulted in higher levels of security on the island and protection of its marine life.

Even though Sipadan is yet to be designated as a World Heritage Site, the island can no longer be regarded as belonging to Malaysia alone. Sipadan is overseen by a vigilant international diving community. Evidence of this arose on 15 May 2006 when a barge carrying thousands of tonnes of building material beached on the island, destroying a significant portion of reef (372 m^2). Within hours there was a global outcry from the diving community demanding an explanation and criticizing the Malaysian government for mishandling their precious island.

In terms of management, the Marine Research Foundation works together with Sabah Parks, which have a mandate from the Sabah State Government to develop management plans for the island under International Union for Conservation of Natural Resources (IUCN) Category IV Protected Area Status. The organisation provides technical expertise to restore the damage of the reef ecosystem. The immediate target is get the island designated as a World Heritage Site under the Convention Concerning the Protection of the World Cultural and Natural Heritage. This would ensure that the island's management would be monitored in the international interest by the IUCN under UNESCO's World Heritage Trust.

Education is being targeted at divers, dive operators, and residents of Sipadan's nearby islands and the mainland. These stakeholders need to be acknowledged for behaviour that impacts the marine environment. In Mabul – the main island of the relocated resorts and new resort developments catering to divers to Sipadan – operators regularly hold marine educational workshops and programmes as well as beach clean-ups. Since the island of Mabul is also inhabited by thousands of local people, the majority of whom rely on traditional fishing for their livelihoods, other than establishing, carrying capacity, monitoring and enforcement, a sustainable management model should consider greater community involvement (extending to compensation schemes if necessary). Anecdotal evidence suggests that turtle nesting is currently increasing and Sipadan vegetation is recovering. Marine life appears to be resilient, and the island appears to be returning to its former glory.

Further reading

Alin, J.M., Primus, D.D. & Razli, I.A. (2006). The roles of eco-entrepreneurs in conserving common pool resources: Wildlife and natural areas in Sipadan Island. Paper presented at Survival of the Commons: Mounting Challenges and New Realities, the Eleventh Conference of the International Association for the Study of Common Property Location, Bali, Indonesia, 19–23 June. On WWW at http://hdl.handle.net/10535/627. Accessed 2.7.2010.

Mortimer, A.J. (1991). *Recommendations for the Management of the Marine Turtle Population and Pulau Sipadan*. Kuala Lumpur, Malaysia: Worldwide Fund for Nature. Musa, G. (2002). Sipadan – A SCUBA-diving paradise: An analysis of tourism impact, diver satisfaction and tourism management. *Tourism Geographies*, 4 (2), 195–209.

Sport Tourism in the Built Environment

Much of the existing literature on the environmental impacts of sport tourism has focused on natural areas (Standeven & De Knop, 1999). However, sport tourism development in urban areas presents unique environment, resource and impact issues, which require informed consideration. Sport tourism in the urban context may include the following:

(1) Active sport and physical exercise in the built sports landscape (leisure centres, hotel gymnasiums, squash, badminton and tennis courts, swimming pools), recreational running along urban parks and developed littoral zones;
(2) Recreational or club sport in dedicated sports fields or improvised settings (e.g. skateboarding and street basketball);
(3) Recreational or competitive sports that take place in largely unmodified (e.g. kayaking, surfing) or reproduced nature (e.g. orienteering in an urban conservation reserve); and
(4) Event sport tourism.

Active, recreational and competitive sports in the urban context generate relatively benign impacts although they may require management of social impacts or recreational conflict between participants. Sport tourism events that take place in central locations, in the form of elite or non-elite sports that require dedicated or temporary facilities, offer considerable potential for impact, both positive and negative. The impacts of event sport tourism in the built environment are a function of the scale of the event and the infrastructure capacities of the destination.

Issues of scale in event sport tourism

Scale, be it global, regional or local, is critical to the study of sport tourism in central locations. 'The idea of scale, or geographical magnitude, keeps in focus the area being dealt with, and can be likened to increasing or decreasing the magnification on a microscope or the scale of a map' (Boniface & Cooper, 1994: 3). The capacity for locations to accommodate flows of tourists is determined in large part by the scale of the destination, and its capacity to absorb tourists. The tourist function index, for example, employs the number of tourist beds, and the total resident population of a destination as indices of tourist capacity. The concept of tourism carrying capacity considers the maximum level of tourist activity that can be sustained without adversely impacting the physical environment, or the quality of the visitor experience with consideration given to the views of the host community (Archer & Cooper, 1994; Mathieson & Wall, 1987).

'[M]ega-events are short-term events with long-term consequences for the cities that stage them' (Roche, 1994: 1). Unfortunately, interests in the impacts of event sport tourism are often restricted to economic development (Burgan & Mules, 1992), positive image and identity, inward investment and tourism promotion (Getz, 1991; Hall, 1992a). This focus ignores the potential for sporting events to create negative impacts, which tend to increase with the scale of the event (Olds, 1998; Shapcott, 1998). Where the scale of a sports event is too great for the social and infrastructure capacities of the host city, significant potential for negative impacts arise (Hiller, 1998). Host community displacements and evictions (Olds, 1998), increases in rates and rents (Hodges & Hall, 1996), the disruption of daily routines due to crowding and congestion (Bale, 1994), security issues (Higham, 1999) and the exaggerated behaviour of 'sports junkies' (Faulkner *et al.*, 1998) may be associated with large-scale sporting events. Shapcott (1998: 196), for example, reports that

> 720,000 room-renters (were) forcibly removed in advance of the 1988 Olympics in Seoul, thousands of low income tenants and small businesses forced out of Barcelona before the 1992 Games (and) more than 9000 homeless people (many of them African-American) arrested in the lead-up to the 1996 Olympics in Atlanta.

Sporting events and competitions of more modest scale include regular season domestic sport competitions, national/regional championships and non-elite sports events. At these more modest scales, the potential for serious negative impact is reduced (Higham, 1999). Crowding and infrastructure congestion are less likely to occur and are more rapidly dispersed. Nonetheless, the positive impacts of sports events of more modest scale are, within the geographical parameters of the destination, very similar to those of mega events (Hall, 1993), although easily oversold (Whitson, 2004). The issue of scale in event sport tourism is important. It mirrors the 'alternative tourism/mass tourism' debate (Krippendorf, 1995; Wheeller, 1991). Although the economic imperative that 'bigger is better' remains prevalent (Weed, 2009a), the achievement of a match between the capacity constraints of host cities or regions and the scale of the sports events that they seek to host represents an important element in achieving sustained success in event sport tourism.

Managing the compatibility of sports in the built environment

Consideration of the compatibility of multiple sport demands is an important sport tourism issue in the built environment. Different sports may be viewed as

(1) Compatible: Sports that can use the same area of land or water at the same time.
(2) Partially compatible: Sports that can use the same area of land or water but not at the same time.
(3) Incompatible: Sports that cannot use the same area of land or water and need to be zoned into exclusive spaces.

The extent to which different sports demonstrate compatibility with other landscape users varies considerably. For example, motor sports and sports involving dangerous equipment (e.g. field archery) are essentially incompatible with other sports. The incompatibility of sports generally increases at higher levels of competition. Competitive or elite levels of sport require specialised and sometimes exclusive use of facilities. The sports manager, then, must be mindful of the required balance between specialisation and multiple use in the design of sports facilities. The Montreal stadium developed for the 1976 Olympic Games is an example of a specialised facility which has proved inappropriate for subsequent use due to its sheer size (Olympic Co-ordination Authority [OCA], 1997).

The development of multiple-use facilities, particularly those that cater to sports at various levels of competition (ranging from local/ recreational to international/ championship), may diversify and expand the user and spectator market catchments for a facility. Consideration should be given to both the spatial (e.g. dimensions of the playing surface, parking and spectator capacities) and the temporal (e.g. daily/ week use patterns, sport seasonality) compatibility of sports that may derive mutual benefit from the use of a single multiple-use facility. In some cases, however, the development of generalised or multiple-use facilities can cause unacceptable compromises to the sport experiences of both participants and spectators. Stadia with running tracks, for example, typically are characterised by non-optimal viewing for a high proportion of spectators (Bale, 1989).

The issue of compatibility in the built landscape extends to reconciliation of sport/non-use interests, particularly at sites that are designed primarily for purposes other than sport. For example, the marathon and distance running boom, with race fields exceeding 20,000 participants in some cases, has '... put pressure on municipal authorities to control and redirect traffic on race days' (Bale, 1989: 163). Streetcar rallies, cycle races, and a host of festival sports may also cause disruption to normal use of the urban landscape. Such impacts, however, tend to be short term and rapidly dispersed. They do, however, require that sport managers and event organisers consider security, safety and liability issues relating to their sport.

Landscape to sportscape: The impacts of sport facility development and design

It has been noted that 'the search for regional diversity in the landscape has remained an important motive for travellers, despite the standardisation and homogenisation of the tourism industry' (Mitchell & Murphy, 1991: 61). There exists an evolutionary tendency to confine and homogenise the sporting environment. A transition from landscape to sportscape represents one aspect of standardisation and homogenisation in sport tourism which may seriously threaten the uniqueness of specific places. The modern stadium has an ancient history, and has evolved through phases that have been influenced by the formalisation of sports rules, and the imposition of spatial limits in sport, which allowed the development of facilities for spectators to observe games at close proximity (Bale, 1989).

More recently technological developments, such as video screens, virtual advertising, floodlighting and retractable enclosures, have been imposed on the modern stadium (Bale, 1989). This course of development has given rise to an increasing sameness of stadium design in many parts of the world (Higham & Hinch, 2009), which may significantly alter the overall sporting experience from the viewpoint of both competitors and spectators. One implication may be erosion of 'the cultural mosaic that encourages tourism' (Williams & Shaw, 1988: 7). The potential contribution to sport tourism development of unique stadium design, contiguous markers, distinctive elements of the destination and the natural elements that differentiate destinations must be carefully considered in relation to the design and development of sports resources.

Sport Tourism in the Natural Landscape

Natural features are central to sport tourism experiences in peripheral areas. They also present a distinct range of management issues.

> Sports like hang-gliding create pressure on rural hill and scarp country, surfing on beach areas, skiing has placed pressure on mountain regions and water sports compete with one another for precious room on the limited amount of suitable inland water space. (Bale, 1989: 163)

These landscapes can be quite fragile and sensitive to disturbance (Hall & Page, 1999). Sport activities on these landscapes, therefore, need to be managed in order to mitigate negative impacts (Weed & Bull, 2003). Equally, it may be that extreme nature-based sports may foster feelings of connectedness with nature that give rise to strong desires to care for nature, and be environmentally sustainable in practice (Bryner *et al.*, 2009).

The challenge of sustainable sport tourism development in natural areas arises for various reasons. One reason is the dynamic nature of sport as reflected by the speed with which new sports are developed and diffused. The transition from an emerging sport pursued by relatively few to a mass participation phenomenon may take place in a short space of time (Standeven & De Knop, 1999). Recreational running, which emerged and developed in popularity in the 1970s, is a case in point. So, too, is the rapid expansion in participation in golf (Hudson & Hudson, 2010). Other sports that have demonstrated a rapid rise in popularity include mountain biking, snowboarding, scuba diving, windsurfing, triathlon, jet skiing and kite surfing. This dynamic presents fascinating development opportunities at tourist resorts and destinations, but it also requires proactive action to establish and implement appropriate policies and management strategies to protect the natural landscapes (Focus point 7.2). In some cases, the development of participation sports has taken place in the absence of a relevant legislation framework, management structure or administrative authority. Sports such as BASE jumping and bungee jumping demonstrate the challenge that management agencies may encounter with the development of new sports innovations. Extreme sports such as these often defy a single management authority (Mykletun & Vedø, 2002).

Focus point 7.2
Cavo Sidero and Golf Developments

The sport of golf has moved far from its ancient beginnings in Scottish sand dunes, when it was played in an unaltered landscape by shepherd-boys and kings and did nobody any harm. It was transformed by Americans who industrialized it, bulldozed it and watered it into unsuitable parts of the world. Modern golf in the wrong places can do immense environmental and social damage. Golf-courses now try to keep green all through the year, even the rainless summers of the Mediterranean, and use immense quantities of water and polluting chemicals. (Care2, 2010)

This viewpoint, expressed in emotive terms by an online environmental agency, is representative of the groundswell of concern associated with the unsustainable development of golf courses and resorts in unique local ecologies. These views are reflected in the contentious case of Cavo Sidero (Crete).

In 2007, a development proposal by Minoan Group and its subsidiary Loyalward sought to create five integrated golf resorts at

Cavo Sidero. The proposal included five resort villages, a harbour development and three golf courses, causing a vociferous debate that revolved around sustainability and the destruction of the ecology as well as the archaeological value of Cavo Sidero.

The Cavo Sidero controversy is built upon concern for large-scale environmental destruction associated with resort and golf course development. The island of Crete, and particularly the eastern region of Crete, has high ecological value given its predominance of drought- or salt-adapted vegetation which includes some of the world's rarest plants. Cavo Sidero, on Crete's north-eastern peninsula below Cape Sideros, is also an area of archaeological importance dating to Greek and Roman times prior to the decline of the Byzantine empire. Neo-lithic and Minoan farms, terraces and associated archaeological sites remain largely unmodified from classical times. Widespread concerns and legal objections remain unresolved in what has become an entrenched and costly case.

Source: Care2 (2010) Save the Cretan landscape: Stop golf development on Cavo Sidero. On WWW at http://www.thepetitionsite.com/1/ Save-the-Cretan-landscape/. Accessed 22.11.2010.

The management of the impacts of sport tourism in natural areas is a complex task. Indeed, simply measuring the impacts of tourism is fraught with difficulty. Rarely do baselines exist from which to assess change, and the impacts of tourism can seldom be disaggregated from the direct or indirect impacts of other human activities (Mathieson & Wall, 1987). The impacts of littoral sport tourism on marine flora and fauna, for example, are difficult to distinguish from those of fishing, aquaculture or the inappropriate dumping of waste materials from towns, industries, agriculture and forestry (Bellan & Bellan-Santini, 2001). The impacts of sport tourism in fragile alpine ecologies may, due to extremes of altitude and climate, require extended recovery and regeneration timeframes (Flagestad & Hope, 2001). Although the visual impacts of development may be immediately apparent, more subtle changes on fragile alpine flora, growth and regeneration rates, water regulation (May, 1995) and the breeding success of rare alpine bird species (Holden, 2000) require intervention programmes and long-term monitoring.

While it is sometimes possible to identify positive and negative impacts within the social, cultural, economic and environmental contexts of the destination, these impacts are connected in a complex web of relationships. The acceptability of different impacts in combination is also viewed subjectively by different stakeholder groups, and different individuals within stakeholder groups (Hunter, 1995; Mathieson & Wall, 1987; McKercher, 1993). The extensive literature on sustainable tourism development and impact management is of high relevance to sport and tourism managers, who should be cognizant of the environmental impacts of sport tourism (Cantelon & Letters, 2000; Hunter, 1995).

The compatibility of sport tourism in the natural landscape

Hunter (1995) observes that sustainable tourism development requires reconciliation of human needs, as well as environmental limitations. Human needs, and the benefits and costs of tourism, accrue to two main groups: the hosts and the guests (Archer & Cooper, 1994). The excessive or inappropriate promotion of sport development interests over the stewardship of natural areas may give rise to congestion and crowding, social and environmental impacts, or modification of the landscape in ways that are unacceptable to the host community. The sustained quality of the visitor experience must also enter into considerations of the appropriate direction and level of sport tourism development.

Sports that are pursued in the natural landscape may also demonstrate varying degrees of compatibility with other sports. Incompatible motivations and goals of participation in sport may give rise to symmetric or asymmetric conflict between participants in *different* sports (Graefe *et al.*, 1984). Symmetric conflict describes a situation in which participants in two sports feel the existence of social conflict arising from the presence of the other. Jet skiers, surfers and swimmers may experience symmetric conflict, giving rise, in some cases, to situations of physical danger. Asymmetric conflict arises when participants in one sport are adversely impacted by the presence of those engaging in a second sport, while participants in the latter may be oblivious to or even welcome the presence of those engaged in the former. The intrusion of technologies such as global positioning systems and cellular telephones in nature-based sports is an increasingly common cause of social impact and conflict between sports participants (Ewert & Shultis, 1999). Sports such as orienteering and downhill skiing may be compatible with other sports, if segregated in space and/or time through appropriate management techniques. Sports that take place in coastal environments offer varying degrees of compatibility. Examples include diving, surf skiing, swimming, jet skiing, windsurfing, kayaking and recreational fishing. Consumptive (e.g. hunting) and mechanised sports (e.g. jet boat racing) are fundamentally incompatible with other uses, as they may either irrevocably compromise alternative sporting pursuits and/or present physical danger to participants in other sports. This issue dictates that sports that take place in the sport tourism periphery must be carefully managed to reduce conflict.

The psychographic profile of the sport participant (Chapter 3) also determines the compatibility of different sports, and different participants in the same sport. Conflicts may arise between participants *within* a sport if the motivations of participants are incompatible. Wilderness cross-country skiing and surfing are sports that take place in environments that can be contested by numerous participants when conditions are favourable. Access to waves is managed within the surfing community by an unwritten surfing etiquette (Wheaton, 2000, 2004). The reconciliation of conflicts between incompatible sports may require careful management intervention. Once again, the compatibility of sports in the natural landscape tends to decrease with the seriousness of the participant or the competitor. Yachting and canoeing are compatible at the recreational level, but not at the higher levels of competition (Bale, 1989). Similarly, recreational skiing cannot take place simultaneously on the same runs as competitive forms of skiing take place.

The Impacts of Event Sport Tourism: A Paradigmatic Shift

Events hosted in central and peripheral locations offer similar opportunities to foster environmental interests, as well as implement negative-impact mitigation techniques. The legacy of the 1992 Albertville (France) Winter Olympic Games is one of considerable and irreversible disfigurement of the natural environment due to intense and poorly planned development (May, 1995). By contrast, the 1994 Lillehammer Winter Olympic Games have been coined the 'Green-White Games' because new approaches to environmental management were pioneered in the planning of that event (Kaspar, 1998). In all aspects of capacity and scale, Lillehammer, a town of only 24,000 residents, would generally be considered ill-equipped to host a large-scale event such as the Winter Olympic Games. Obvious challenges included traffic congestion, crowding, waste management and irreversible environmental impacts. Commitment to an environmental plan was articulated in a joint statement issued by the Chief Environmental Officers of Lillehammer and Oppland County. It stated in reference to Project Environmental Friendly Olympics (PEFO) that any

> ... development must conform to the natural and cultural landscape and other regional features. In the long run this will be crucial in preserving and enhancing qualities that are already assets to tourism. For local people it will be most important to construct the arenas and other buildings needed for the event in an environmentally friendly way. (Chernushenko, 1996: 66)

Event planning and innovation in the design and development of sports facilities and tourist infrastructure were central to this success, despite the existence of conflicts and comprises in the planning of the event (Lesjø, 2000). The Olympic Environmental Charter, as ratified in

1996, now requires that Olympic organising committees articulate and implement an environmental protection policy. This Charter was used for the first time in the planning of the 1998 Winter Olympics in Nagano (Japan). Cantelon and Letters (2000: 294) argue that 'it was the widespread environmental damage at the 1992 Albertville and the Savoie Region Games, and the subsequent Green Games of Lillehammer, Norway (1994), that were the historical benchmarks for the development of this policy'.

The Sydney 2000 Olympic Games represents not only an entrenchment but also a significant advancement of the environmental achievements of Lillehammer 1994. Conservation, ecological restoration and the remediation of industrial sites formed an integral part of the Sydney Olympic Games development programme (OCA, 1997). These sport events provide evidence of new perspectives on the sport tourism – environment nexus. The environmental legacies of the 1994 Winter (Lillehammer, Norway) and 2000 Summer (Sydney, Australia) Olympic Games represent a paradigmatic shift from impact mitigation to proactive environmental stewardship and habitat creation associated with event sport tourism (Chernushenko, 1996; Cowell, 1997). Environmental planning for the London 2012 Olympics includes targets such as 90% of materials used in construction will be recycled, 20% of Olympic site energy requirements will be renewable and 50 miles of walking and cycle ways around the Olympic Park will assist in achieving the goal of a 'car-free' event. While quantifying the environmental impacts of events (at all spatial scales) will inevitably become more important, the complexities of sports event impacts, which vary in terms of spatial scale and time, demand careful consideration of both assessment methods and organisational actions (Collins *et al.*, 2009).

Conclusion

Sport tourism environments and resources form an important part of the foundation upon which sport tourism development occurs. Landscape and climate are key determinants of the attractiveness of tourist destinations. They also bear considerable influence over the sport and recreational activities that tourists associate with a destination, thereby influencing destination image. The relationship between sport and the environment is a dynamic one (Standeven & DeKnop, 1999). By understanding this relationship, sport tourism managers achieve a competitive advantage in harnessing trends that offer opportunities and, equally, by recognising those that may pose a threat to sport tourism development. Reproducible or transportable sports offer a valuable example in this respect (Bale, 1994; Weed, 2010). The development of sport technologies, which may challenge established views of the reproducibility of sports, should be a concern of sport tourism managers. Transportability, while representing the threat of relocation from a sport's place of origin, may also provide an opportunity to develop new or existing sports resources at specific tourism places.

This chapter also considers the sharp distinction that lies between sport tourism development in the built (central) and natural (peripheral) environments. The importance of this distinction lies in the contrasting sport tourism impacts and management issues that apply to sport tourism in differing contexts, and at various scales of analysis from the local (e.g. see Pillay & Bass, 2008) to the global (e.g. see Otto & Heath, 2009). How these impacts are perceived at the local level will have a considerable bearing upon the future of sport-related tourism development (Hritz & Ross, 2010; Schulenkorf, 2009; Smith, 2009).

Part 4

Sport Tourism Development and Time

Chapter 8
Sport and the Tourist Experience

The (sport tourism) experience is created by the interaction between the activities and the places provided by the destination and the internal motivations and meanings brought by the visitors.
Morgan, 2007: 363

Introduction

This chapter considers sport tourism themes in the short term and, in doing so, focuses on the tourist experience. The tourist experience represents the sum of several distinct processes that unfold in five phases: anticipation, travel, visitor experiences at the destination, travel back and recollection (Clawson & Knetsch, 1966; Manfredo & Driver, 1983). The anticipation phase of the tourist experience requires an understanding of information search, decision making, planning and the formulation of expectations, each of which is affected by travel motivations. Travel to the destination forms an important part of the tourist experience as it influences the length of stay, and the infra-structure and service needs of the tourist. The activities, feelings and behaviours of sport tourists are key dimensions of their visitor experience. These may vary significantly with, for example, the relative priority placed on the pursuit of sport and other tourist activities at a destination, as well as the interplay of sport and tourism in terms of activity, people and place (Higham & Hinch, 2009; Morgan, 2007; Weed, 2006). The experience concludes with processes of evaluation and recollection. Visitor experiences at the actual destination, therefore, form only one part of the subject of this chapter, given that they are set within the wider context of people's lives prior to and following the tourist experience (Morgan, 2007).

The Anticipation Phase

Information search, decision making, planning and the formulation of expectations are important aspects of the visitor experience in the anticipation phase. The typology of sport tourists presented in Table 8.1 serves as a starting point from which to consider the pre-trip phase of the sport tourist experience. Different sport tourist types are likely to vary considerably in terms of information search, decision-making and planning. Anticipation of spectator events, for example, may be situated

Table 8.1 Sport tourist typologies

Sport tourist typology (Glyptis, 1982)	Parallels with subsequent typologies
General holidays with sport content	Incidental (Jackson & Reeves, 1997) Incidental (Reeves, 2000)
Specialist or general sport holidays	Sport activity holidays (Standeven & De Knop, 1999) Independent sport holidays (Standeven & De Knop, 1999) Sporadic (Reeves, 2000) Occasional/regular (Jackson & Reeves, 1997) Occasional sports (wo)men (Maier & Weber, 1993) Mass sports (Maier & Weber, 1993)
Upmarket sport holidays	Organised holiday sports (Standeven & De Knop, 1999) Occasional/regular (Jackson & Reeves, 1997)
Elite training	Top-performance athletes (Maier & Weber, 1993) Dedicated/driven (Jackson & Reeves, 1997)
Spectator events	Passive sports on holiday (Standeven & De Knop, 1999), including casual and connoisseur observers Passive sports tourists (Maier & Weber, 1993)

within wider team fandoms and the search for collective experiences in association with team support and identity building (Jones, 2000).

Information sources and decision-making

Use of a diverse range of information sources is typical of the way most tourists plan for their trips, but different types of tourists use different search strategies (Page *et al.*, 2001). Information may be obtained through word-of-mouth, advertisements and promotions, professional outlets such as travel agencies and information centres, internet searches and many other sources. The information requirements of different sport tourist types, and, therefore, avenues of information search in the pre-trip phase, stand in significant contrast. Differences in information search also differentiates first-time and repeat visitors (Taks *et al.*, 2009).

Elite athletes tend to focus on the availability of competition and suitable high-quality training facilities, while destination choice may be determined by acclimatisation or altitude training requirements (Maier & Weber, 1993). In this context, destination requirements are focused around preparation for and achievement of sport performance. Requisite information is likely to be sourced from specialised packages that are developed by sports managers and disseminated through targeted niche marketing. The travel information needs of elite athletes include competition schedules and training itineraries, which are usually developed by national sports bodies through initiatives such as reciprocal international training programmes. Relatively little autonomy in destination choice exists within this market segment (Reeves, 2000), although differing philosophies towards training may be associated with alternative training venues and destinations. The search for settings that reflect team culture (Morgan, 2007) and leisure and tourism environments that facilitate the desired 'tour balance' (Hodge *et al.*, 2009) may also influence the decision making of elite athletes and professional sports organisations (Higham & Hinch, 2009).

The processes of decision making for specialist or general sport holidays offer several notable contrasts. Access to sports training facilities of high standard, diversity or uniqueness may be an important consideration in the planning processes relating to this market (Maier & Weber, 1993). However, access to holiday regions, tourist attractions and activities may also feature prominently in the decision-making process. This is a consequence of the high autonomy in destination choice enjoyed by this market segment (Reeves, 2000). Those who pursue specialist or general sport holidays demonstrate a greater propensity to use standard tourism information services, such as travel agents and destination brochures, in the decision-making and travel planning processes. They are also more likely to respond to attraction markers, both contiguous and detached (Chapter 2), to establish or raise awareness of a destination. For tourists within these market segments, sport may be one of various activities pursued while on holiday (Getz & Cheyne, 1997). Differences between sport and tourist interests in the planning phase are important points of distinction.

Sport tourism and visitor expectations

Visitor expectations may vary significantly among participants within a given sport (Chapter 3). Expectations and desired experiences are a function of the lifestyles, attitudes and personalities of individual sport tourists and are likely to vary considerably with demographic profile, travel career stage, sport and personal experience, or involvement in a sport or sports team (Pearce, 1988; Schreyer *et al.*, 1984; Watson & Roggenbuck, 1991). The study of tourist expectations relating to sport is in its infancy, although notable contributions have emerged in relation to a small number of activities such as golf, skiing and scuba diving (Hudson, 1999; Priestley, 1995; Tabata, 1992). Little or no attention has, as yet, been paid to the visitor expectations of event or nostalgia sport tourists (Gibson, 1998; Gammon, 2002), although Morgan's (2007) work provides intriguing insights into the centrality of personal and subjective sports histories to the performance of sport-related tourist experiences of activities, people and place. This, he argues, gives emphasis to the importance of allowing visitors to 'co-create' their experiences, rather than to manage and impose event experiences. There is little doubt that national and/or regional tourism organisations, as well as sports organizations and event managers, need to better understand the expectations and desired experiences as having 'emotional, symbolic and transformation significance for the individual involved' (Morgan, 2007: 362). These will clearly vary between discrete sport markets (see Case study 8.1).

Case study 8.1
The British and Irish Lions Experience

Mike Morgan, Bournemouth University

In 2009, an estimated 40,000 people (del Carme, 2009) from England, Wales, Ireland and Scotland travelled in support of the British and Irish Lions rugby union team tour which culminated in a three match Test series against reigning world champions South Africa. The four countries constituting the British Isles normally compete as separate international rugby teams, but the tradition of Lions tours with a combined elite squad to the major rugby-playing countries of the southern hemisphere dates back to 1888, and, since rugby union became a professional sport in 1995, has survived to become a major sports tourism brand (Lions Rugby, 2005). The numbers travelling to follow these fixtures has increased significantly as long-haul tourism has become affordable to a larger proportion of the population. The 2001 Lions tour of Australia, for example, brought an estimated 10,000 fans to the country (Mintel, 2004), whereas in 2005, an estimated 20,400 travelling supporters followed the Lions squad to New Zealand (Vuletich, 2005).

The Lions tours take place every four years, giving them a rarity and significance above the regular cycle of international matches. The distances involved, the demand for tickets, hotel beds and flights all make the tours a premium product (average price £5000 for a three-week package). The tickets are made available by the host national Rugby Union governing body to a small number of approved operators, who compete not on price but on added features such as the best seats, free Lions jackets, bags and other merchandise, the services of expert representatives and star speakers, and the option of tailor-made itineraries. The market has so far been dominated by independent sports specialists such as Gulliver's Travels and Titan Tours, but major multinationals such as Thomas Cook have recently begun to enter the sports tour market.

Because of the high prices and the upscale profile of rugby generally (Mintel, 2004), the Lions supporters tend to come from affluent segments such as empty nesters, retired couples or young professionals. Interviews suggest that motivation to do a Lions tour is an expression not only of a long involvement with the history and traditions of the sport but also of a complex sense of rewarding oneself, marking a life stage or commemorating departed friends and relatives (Morgan, 2007). Such sports tourism experiences can be best understood in terms of how they fit into the visitor's perceived identity and the long-term narrative they tell themselves about their lives. Satisfaction is therefore derived from a holistic impression rather than an evaluation of discrete attributes of the tour programme.

The premium pricing of match tickets, while accepted by the UK tourists as part of the package, can become unaffordable to local supporters, and this, in turn, can adversely affect the visitor experience if matches are held in half-empty stadiums dominated by the visiting supporters, as happened with the warm-up games between the 2009 Lions and South African provincial teams.

Despite the dominance of the official tour operators, there are signs of a demand for independent travel, in keeping with overall trends in tourism, particularly in these affluent experienced segments. In New Zealand in 2005, many supporters attempted to undercut the official packages, choosing indirect cheaper flights, hiring camper vans or staying in backpacker hostels, encouraged by the itineraries and booking systems available on the Tourism New Zealand website. From the way people talked about it, this was not just a solution to the accommodation problem, it was part of the fun and a way of optimising the experience (Morgan & Wright, 2008). Even with the constraints of the greater distances and higher perceived risks of independent travel in South Africa, examples were found of individuals claiming to have saved money through organising their trips directly with hotels and picking up tickets on the match day. Two men from Swansea proclaimed their independence by wearing T-shirts with a slogan 'Gullible Travel: no t-shirt, no bag', parodying the 'uniform' of the tour operator's clients with their branded jackets and caps.

While the rugby games were the main attraction, Lions tourists were also keen to sample the sights, activities and experiences offered by the host country as part of a 'trip of a lifetime' – for example whale-watching or glacier-walking in New Zealand and safaris in

South Africa. This is in contrast to the more single-minded behaviour of sports excursionists when travelling in their own country or within Europe. To pay for these peak experiences, however, they may seek to economise by shopping around (online) for cheaper travel and accommodation options (Morgan & Wright, 2008).

In the traditions of rugby union, socialising with local supporters, in their own clubs and bars or at South Africa's traditional pre-match braais (barbecues), is also an important part of the experience. Fans proved less likely to remain in specially provided fan villages and hospitality areas than supporters of other sports such as cricket or football. For example, attempts by the 'Barmy Army' cricket supporters club in New Zealand in 2005 to provide organised entertainment for the rugby followers provoked some resentment and the tented villages which local businesses were encouraged to set up were underused (Morgan, 2007).

Unique or infrequent elite spectator sporting events such as the Lions tours, World Cups or Olympic Games present the sports and travel organisers with many logistical problems (Morgan & Wright, 2008) and the tendency is to limit the supply of tickets and other resources to a small number of approved operators and agents. However, this can have the effect of restricting the benefits of sports tourism to the economy from spreading to other geographical areas and to smaller tourism businesses. It can also lead to the tourists having what they perceive to be a less authentic experience of the country and its sporting culture. The movement away from package tours makes visitor flows and demand for specific accommodation, entertainment and facilities harder to predict, but it also creates opportunities for a wider range of tourism businesses to benefit from the event, including non-sports-based attractions and locations away from the sports tour fixtures (Morgan & Wright 2008).

Literature cited in this case study is included in the list of references at the end of this book.

Sport and the Study of Tourist Motivations

Research into tourist motivations is concerned with why people travel, the benefits that they seek and the experiences that they pursue to satisfy their needs and desires (Cooper *et al.*, 1993). Tourist motivation is a function of self-perceived needs of the traveller, which drive the decision-making process, and the purchase of tourism products (Collier, 1999). The motivational profile of the traveller is a combination of intrinsic and extrinsic factors. These factors have been described in terms of push (psychological) and pull (cultural) factors (Dann, 1981). The former are intrinsic and unique to each tourist as they are determined by the personality and attitude of the individual. In the context of sport specifically, push factors may extend to the desire to achieve sport career or serious leisure objectives that cannot be achieved at home.

Pull factors include price, destination image and marketing and promotion. Destination image, which is a function of physical and abstract attributes (Echtner & Ritchie, 1993), plays an important part in the formulation of expectations. Physical attributes include attractions, activities, sporting facilities and physical landscapes. Abstract attributes are less readily measured, and include atmosphere, crowding, safety and ambience. Again, specifically in terms of sport experiences, pull factors may relate to the search for desired competition or the achievement of sporting experiences that are unique to particular places. Unique experiences are usually bound in both space and time. These pull factors may also influence the perceived needs of tourists in the anticipation phase of the travel experience.

Sport tourism, like other forms of travel, entails a set of motivations that are established in anticipation of the fulfilment of desired needs. Stewart (2001) identifies a range of factors that motivate fans to travel to support their teams and these fall within the gambit of push and pull factors. Push factors include release from everyday life, the search for camaraderie, to develop friendships and a sense of belonging, and the opportunity to do things that cannot be done at home (e.g. to enhance one's standing within a sport subculture). In contrast, pull factors that may motivate event sport tourism include the unique interplay of a significant sports activity, people and place that distinctive tourism destinations offer. Pull factors may extend to the significance of a spatially and temporally bound context and the state of flow that may be associated with uncertainty of outcome and post-competition revelry and celebration (see Focus point 8.1). Tourist motivations are critical to understanding why people do or do not travel, their choice of destination and other aspects of tourist behaviour.

Focus point 8.1
Sport Experiences that are Bound in Space and Time

Canada's victory over the United States in the Vancouver 2010 Winter Olympics men's ice hockey final triggered scenes of jubilation among Canadians in Vancouver (and elsewhere around the world). The spontaneous celebrations that occurred in Vancouver were spatially and temporally bounded – it was *the place to be* at that moment in time. Similarly, the 1998 FIFA World Cup was hosted, and the final won in front of the home crowd, by France. The path that the French team negotiated to the final was a tenuous one. Their quarter-final against Paraguay was won in extra time by a 'golden goal'. In the semi-final, France was victorious over Italy, a two-time champion, in a game that was level after full time and extra-time, and decided in a nail-biting penalty shootout. In the final, on 12 July 1998, the French team administered the *coup de grace*, in a complete performance 'defeating the ultimate adversary, the football nation of legend, Brazil' (Dauncey & Hare, 2000: 344) by the convincing margin of 4-1.

> On the night of 12 July ... there was an outpouring of joy and sentiment that was unprecedented since the Liberation of 1944 ... Huge numbers of people poured onto the streets in spontaneous and good-humoured celebration. In Paris, hundreds of thousands gathered again on the Champs Elysées the next day to see the Cup paraded in an open-topped bus. For all, the victory was an unforgettable experience. (Dauncey & Hare, 2000: 331)

> A global television audience, at the time the largest television audience for a single sport, watched these events unfold. Based on the knife edge quarter- and semi-final victories of the French team, it is clear that the width of a crossbar can bear heavily on the emotions, experiences and behaviours that occur spontaneously in response to the performances and outcomes of football championships (Dauncey & Hare, 2000). There can be little doubt about the emotion associated with defining sporting moments that are experienced only at a given place in a given moment of time. Laidlaw (2010), in reference to sport and identity, describes some sports as a 'barometer of feelgood', noting that 'nobody who was around when ... South Africa won the (rugby) World Cup in 1995 would be under any illusion as to the collective high that those moments brought to a whole nation' (Laidlaw, 2010: 51).

The sport of golf demonstrates the diverse range of tourist motivations held by sport participants (Hudson & Hudson, 2010). Approximately 150 million people travelled internationally to golf destinations in 1999 (Bartoluci & Čavlek, 2000). The motivations underpinning this travel and, as a consequence, the sport tourism experiences of golfers differ between distinct sport tourist types (Table 8.2). These cannot be generalised directly to other sports because of the unique rules, competition structures and elements of play that characterise each sport (Chapter 2). However, an understanding of the motivations that sport tourists hold towards their chosen sports is critical to fostering desired visitor experiences. Similar studies that examine the tourist motivations associated with other sports are certainly justified.

Table 8.2 Sport motivation profiles of sport tourists who play golf

Sport tourist types (Glyptis, 1982)	Primary motivations	Destination attributes	Secondary activities
General holidays with sports content	Various business or leisure travel motivations	Vary with primary motivations (existence of a golf course is incidental)	Playing golf, among other things
Specialist sport holidays	Pilgrimage to the heartland of golf. Emulating icon players	Grandslam and other championship courses	Nostalgia sport tourism
General sport holidays	Golf as one part of a suite of visitor activities	Single integrated resorts	Family-based activities
Upmarket sport holidays	Golf as a specialised visitor activity	High degree of luxury. Second home developments adjacent to golf courses	Domestic and social activities
Elite training	Seek competition and be challenged by a range of golf courses	Networks of golf courses forming golf regions	Coaching clinics, professional advice, purchase of equipment

Source: Adapted from Glyptis (1982) and Priestley (1995)

It is useful to consider the relative importance of sport and tourism motivations held by sport tourists (Robinson & Gammon, 2004). Those motivated by elite training are less likely to concern themselves with tourist activities available at a destination. The focus of elite athletes is on preparation and performance. They may be oblivious to the experiential opportunities arising from being a tourist, at least in advance of and during the period of competition. In some cases, however, 'the touristic element may act to reinforce the overall experience' (Gammon & Robinson, 1997: 8) even when there is an intense focus on competition. Hodge's *et al.* (2009) concept of 'tour balance' describes the need for elite athletes to escape occasionally from the pressures of preparation for, and anticipation of, competition. On the other hand, those who pursue general holidays with a sport content hold quite a distinct motivational profile, such that sport tourist activities may be incidental or secondary to other tourist experiences, which form the primary travel motivation.

   Sports fans also vary in the extent to which they are motivated to travel in support of a sports team. For some fans, involvement in the sport itself is the dominant travel motivation. Social identity can be constructed and reinforced through fandom membership in which 'sport becomes a pivotal means of signifying loyalty and commitment, producing enduring leisure behaviour' (Jones, 2000). Stewart (2001) has developed a typology of Australian team sport watchers which demonstrates the diversity that exists within this travel market. The motivations held by each of these fan categories influences visitor experiences at the host destination.

(1) *Passionate partisans:* Hardcore supporters who attend games reg-ularly, regardless of inconveniences; their moods and identities are closely linked to the successes and failures of their team.
(2) *Champion followers:* Less fanatical, and change their allegiance or their allegiance remains held in abeyance until their team starts winning some games.
(3) *Reclusive partisan:* Interest in the game, and commitment to the team is strong, but they attend games infrequently. Interested in the team, more so than the game.
(4) *Theatregoer:* Primarily seek entertainment through sport but are not necessarily attached to a particular team.
(5) *Aficionado:* Attracted to exciting games, and also to games that involve star players. Interested in the demonstration of skill, tactical complexity and aesthetic pleasure, which take priority over the outcome of the game.

   Sport tourists who attend other types of sports events may demon-strate quite different motivations and preferences (Pyo *et al.*, 1988). Delpy Neirotti *et al.* (2001) examined the motivations of event sport tourists attending the 1996 Atlanta Olympic Games. They distinguished factors that motivated the decision to attend from motivations that evolved after the decision to attend had been reached. The former centred on the event offering a once-in-a-lifetime opportunity. Respondents reported that having arrived at the decision to attend, experiencing firsthand the excellence of athletic competition, international party atmosphere, cultural experience and historical significance became important moti-vations. The potential to combine sports travel with other leisure activities at the destination is evident in this case. In contrast, spending time with family may be an important travel motivation for those who participate in small-scale sport events (Carmichael & Murphy, 1996). This motivation is particularly applicable to female participation in sport, which is more likely to take place with other family members (Thompson, 1985).
   In many sports, consumer identification with a sport subculture may be an important travel motivation (Chapter 6). Green (2001: 5) notes that

'interactions with others are at the core of the socialisation process and provide avenues through which values and beliefs come to be shared and expressed'. Sport tourism may, therefore, be motivated by a celebration of subculture through participation, or, equally, through non-sport activities at the destination (Green & Chalip, 1998). This discussion confirms the importance of understanding the motivations that exist within sport tourism market segments, and the tourist experiences that they mediate.

Sport Tourism Visitor Experiences

The visitor experience can be described and studied in various ways. At one level, it is important to understand the tourist experience in terms of length of stay, the activities pursued and general tourist behaviour. It is also important to note that the visitor experience is a combination of tangible (physical attributes) and intangible (emotions and feelings) elements (Weed, 2008a). The experiential approach to studying the visitor experience involves understanding the emotions and feelings that comprise the visitor experience. These emotions may include joy, relief, exhaustion, euphoria and dejection, which arise from victory, defeat, camaraderie, sense of history or simply through participation in physical activities. Visitor experiences are a function of the motivations and desired experiences of the tourist. Walker *et al.* (2010), for example, use 'activity mode' and 'task orientation' to explore the experiences of active sport participants competing at the World Masters Games, highlighting similarities and differences in visitor experiences among discrete groups of competitors. Visitor experiences are also influenced by the sport and tourism systems at a destination. The three sections that follow examine the elements of the sport tourism visitor experience illustrated in Figure 8.1.

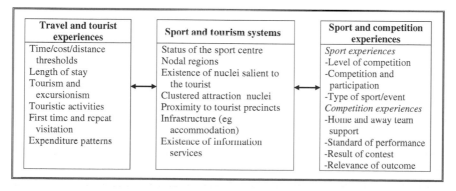

Figure 8.1 Factors influencing the sport tourism visitor experience

Travel and Tourist Experiences

Time/cost/distance travel thresholds and length of stay

The investment of time, money and energy in accessing a destination will generally influence length of stay and, as a consequence, most aspects of the visitor experiences (Collier, 1999). For example, the distance decay function associated with different modes of transportation influences levels of accessibility, and the use of tourism infrastructure. Similarly, the standard and capacity of transport infrastructure, including the perceived security and efficiency of transit and arrival procedures, influence the travel phase of the tourist experience and visitor satisfaction. Moreover, the travel time/cost/distance function of tourism may be modified by the development of transport nodes, infrastructure and services. The rapid rise of budget airline services, and the development of a new generation of rail services, has greatly influenced time/cost/distance travel thresholds in Europe (Page *et al.*, 2001). Proximity to transport nodes and services may reduce time/cost/distance constraints, resulting in altered spatial travel patterns and desired visitor experiences.

Tourism and excursionism

Length of stay at a destination relates closely to visitor engagement in tourist activities at a destination. The status of the sport tourist as a tourist or an excursionist influences the visitor experience. Nogawa *et al.* (1996) define sport excursionists as day-trippers who do not stay overnight at a destination. Their study identified statistically significant differences between sport tourists and sport excursionists in terms of engagement in non-sport activities while on their trip. The former were more likely to undertake tourist activities such as sightseeing, even in cases where the length of stay at the destination was a single night. Participation by sport tourists in tourist activities at a destination may be fostered, then, where extended length of stay can be encouraged, and where appropriate planning facilitates participation in such activities.

Tourist activities and visitor expenditures

Sport events offer significant potential to generate tourist activity at a destination. Stevens (2001) identifies that on baseball game days at Oriole Park (Baltimore, USA), double- and triple-digit percentage increases in trade are experienced by tourism businesses in the city. Spectatorship at professional baseball games in Baltimore was found to generate a 20% increase in hotel occupancy rates in the vicinity of the stadium. This sport was also found to generate significant increases in business for various attractions and activities including the Babe Ruth Museum, Balls

Sports Bar, the Baja Beach Club, National Aquarium and Maryland Science Centre (Stevens, 2001). Engagement in tourist activities and patterns of expenditure differ between local fans, event sport tourists and event sport excursionists (Bale, 1993a). A study of the expenditure patterns of spectators at Atlanta Falcons American Football games revealed that the costs of purchasing tickets represented 77% of the total expenditures of local spectators, as opposed to 41% of the expenditures of non-local spectators (Schaffer & Davidson, 1985). The majority of expenditures engaged by non-local spectators were directed towards food and entertainment, accommodation, transport and parking, concessions and shopping. Law (2002) notes that the greatest contribution of the stadium to tourism will be felt in cases where stadia are developed in close proximity to attractions, tourism services and infrastructure. It is not surprising, therefore, that there is a trend to integrate contemporary stadia developments with malls, plazas, hotels and other sport and entertainment facilities, such as theme parks, halls of fame and cinemas (Judd, 2003; Mason *et al.* 2008; Stevens, 2001).

First-time and repeat visitation

Visitor experiences and expenditures differ between first-time versus repeat visitors (Taks *et al.*, 2009). While sports may offer great variety, uncertainty of outcome and authenticity in the tourist experience (Chapter 2), Godbey and Graefe (1991) observe that in the case of college football, the spectator experience for repeat visitors may take on a predictable routine:

> The drive to the college community in question, choice of lodging and dining, the institution of 'tailgating' (eating, drinking and socialising in parking lots or other areas close to the stadium before or after the game), the choice of travel companions, even the people sitting in adjoining seats may not change radically from game to game. (Godbey & Graefe, 1991: 219)

This situation may influence spending patterns in two ways. On the one hand, the likelihood of repeat visitation may be eroded because of lack of novelty in the visitor experience. Alternatively, the sport tourist may combine the sport experience with new activities or events at the destination to achieve the level of novelty and stimulation required to warrant repeat travel. Godbey and Graefe's (1991) study of non-local season ticket holders visiting the Pennsylvania State University to experience college football identified a strong negative correlation between repeated attendance at football games and levels of visitor expenditure (Table 8.3). It seems evident, therefore, that sports producers and tourism managers need to innovate and perhaps collaborate to offer

Table 8.3 Average visitor expenditures ($US) at state college football games

Expense category	Number of games attended						
	1	*2*	*3*	*4*	*5*	*6*	*7*
Restaurants	20.78	13.92	11.14	10.83	8.79	6.61	6.44
Retail food and beverages	2.94	4.34	1.59	1.76	1.90	1.77	1.50
Admission fees	0.45	0.36	0.41	0.35	0.30	0.26	0.25
Night clubs/bars	6.15	4.30	3.34	2.59	2.94	1.90	1.79
Game clothing and equipment	6.67	3.24	2.19	2.07	2.57	2.18	2.24
Other retail shopping	19.60	10.44	7.20	5.23	6.23	4.45	4.77
Lodging	12.85	12.82	12.14	11.63	6.50	5.07	4.18
Personal health expenditures	0.11	0.03	0.11	0.06	0.26	0.15	0.09
Private auto expenses	6.00	6.83	4.17	3.67	3.02	3.59	2.52
Commercial transportation	3.52	7.42	5.29	0.95	0.91	0.34	0.08
Babysitter fees	0.21	0.82	0.00	0.15	0.03	0.10	0.05
Equipment rentals	0.00	0.00	0.00	0.17	0.06	0.03	0.02
Charitable donations	0.41	0.30	0.43	0.35	0.32	0.27	0.22
Total per game expenses	**79.69**	**64.82**	**48.01**	**39.81**	**33.83**	**26.72**	**24.15**

Note: n = 1600, surveyed over a one-year period
Source: Godbey and Graefe (1991: 221)

novel experiences for repeat visitors. The development of sport and tourism systems over time may facilitate this search for novelty in repeat experiences, although it must be balanced carefully against elements of heritage and nostalgia, which may be critical to the repeat visitor experience.

Sport and Competition Experiences

The sport experience

The defining qualities of different sports mediate the sport tourist experience in various ways. This experience also varies with levels of competition and types of involvement in sport (Chapter 2) (Figure 8.1). Tourist experiences and expenditures vary between levels of competition, particularly between amateur and professional sports (Reeves, 2000). Professional sports attract a wider catchment of sports fans and, potentially, the interest of other businesses and sponsors. As may be expected, 'travellers who go to a youth sports championship ... tend to spend less than those who are attending a major event such as a Super Bowl' (Loverseed, 2001: 35). In general, expenditure patterns associated with event sport tourism are similar to other forms of leisure-based travel. However, the magnitude of the expenditure is likely to vary between competitive and non-competitive events.

The competitiveness of the active sport tourist influences the tourist experience (Walker *et al.*, 2010). Competitive sports are often pursued with a single-minded focus. However, this generalisation does vary between sports and competitors. Walker *et al.* (2010) use 'mode of experience' (Williams, 1988) and 'achievement orientation' (Ames, 1984; Dweck, 1986; Nicholls, 1989) to obtain detailed empirical insights into the profile of competitive athletes attending the World Masters Games specifically as it relates to trip characteristics in a sport tourism context. They found considerable variation in the extent to which different athletes seek to experience the places that they visit primarily for competition. In the past, recreational participation in sports has been viewed as being relatively free of rigid time constraints, and therefore high in opportunity to engage in a wide variety of tourist activities through the duration of the visit. In fact Walker *et al.* (2010: 302) contributes to 'identifying and describing discrete groups of tourists who are otherwise treated less critically as an homogeneous and undifferentiated group within the unitary term "active sport tourists"'. In doing so, they highlight that active sport tourists may be no less inclined to experience the place of competition, either before, during or sometime following the conclusion of competition.

Opportunities for event and active sport tourists to engage in tourist activities at a destination also differ between sports. Sports that take place in natural areas offer quite different leisure and tourist opportunities compared with those that are contested in urban tourism destinations. The timing, pacing and duration of an event or sport contest may also facilitate or inhibit engagement in other tourist activities at a destination. The visitor experience and economic impacts of the 1999 Rugby World Cup (Wales), for instance, were inhibited by the spatial and temporal planning of the event. Jones (2001: 247) notes that 'the low gate receipts and visitor expenditure in general, were due in no small part to the fact that only eight of the 41 games were held in the Principality (of Wales)'. This effectively compromised the efforts of marketing and tourism agencies to portray the event as 'Welsh'. It also resulted in 'fixture gaps' (periods of up to 12 days between games scheduled in any host city), which contributed to a lack of atmosphere at the host destinations (Jones, 2001).

Gratton *et al.* (2000) present an economic impact study of six sports events hosted in British cities and towns in 1997 which provides valuable insights into the varied visitor experiences and tourism impacts associated with different sports. Their study included the World Badminton Championship (Glasgow), European Junior Boxing Championship (Birmingham), England versus Australia Ashes cricket test (Edgbaston), International Amateur Athletics Federation (IAAF) Grand Prix (Sheffield), European Junior Swimming Championship (Glasgow) and the Women's British Open Golf Championship (Sunningdale). These sports events were placed on a continuum to illustrate the extent to which each was competitor and/or spectator driven. Cricket and golf were identified as being spectator-driven, while badminton and swimming were competitor driven. Swimming, badminton and boxing attracted various competitors, officials and representatives from governing bodies. The extent to which these different types of sport tourists are able to leave their sports event and take free time to experience the destinations that they visit stand in significant contrast.

The duration of sports events also influences the visitors' experience and the economic impacts of the event (Gratton *et al.*, 2000). The boxing and swimming championships lasted nine and four days, respectively, while the IAAF Grand Prix was completed in less than five hours. Different sports, contested at different levels, offer different degrees of opportunity to engage in tourist activities at a destination. International test match cricket is a sport that includes long days of play and practice sessions on days of non-play. The duration of an amateur boxing contest stands in marked contrast to Test match cricket. The opportunities for competitors in these sports to engage in leisure activities at a destination differ accordingly. However, the relative degrees of constraint that these sports impose upon their participants do not necessarily apply to spectators.

The profile of sport tourists also varies significantly between sports. Popular organised sports such as soccer and baseball are dominated by spectator markets made up of young males. These markets are generally characterised by low disposable incomes when contrasted with the more mature spectator markets associated with sports such as golf and test cricket (Loverseed, 2001). Gratton *et al.* (2000) report that international cricket generated the greatest economic impact of the six study events, due to high spectator appeal, the relatively long duration of the contest (five days) and the high spending profile of attendees.

The competition experience

The status of a competition, stage of the season and outcome of a contest may also influence the visitor experience (Figure 8.1). Sports that are contested within a league (or within divisions of teams) provide at different stages of the competition season varied opportunities to foster and encourage leisure and tourist activities at a destination. 'Big time North American college football each fall provides the impetus for lots of tourism and considerable monetary spending' (Godbey & Graefe, 1991: 219). This potential varies from week to week with the circumstances of different games. While event sport tourists generally travel to support a team that is playing away from home, it is also the case that sport tourists may travel considerable distances to support their team at home. Gibson *et al.* (2002) demonstrate that sports tourists may perceive themselves as 'host resident' or 'visitor', based on the team that they support, with implications for the visitor experience. The standard of a team or individual performance, which may be worthy of celebration or condemnation, and the competitive outcome of a contest may also influence the overall visitor experience, especially at higher levels of competition. A famous victory may be followed by days of street celebration, whereas an ignominious loss may send fans hurrying for the first train home.

Sport and Tourism Systems

The visitor experience of sport tourists is influenced by the sport and tourism systems at a destination. The spatial distribution and accessibility of sports facilities and venues in central and satellite areas influence the sport experience for both hosts and guests. Bale (1982) makes reference to 'sports nodes' that are functionally delineated areas where the sport experience takes place. These nodal areas can be managed to minimise negative impacts such as congestion, noise and unruly behaviour. Equally, as Smith (2010) notes, 'sport city' zones may be developed to enhance the sport and tourist experience. Similarly, 'Fan Fest zones' (Smith, 2010), which were a feature of the 2006 FIFA World Cup in Germany, and 'experiential hot spots' (Pettersson & Getz, 2009), which may be micro-locations within the local event setting, are defined in space and time.

The 'tourism system' that serves sports nodes is equally important. Tourists often embark on a trip with one attraction or one particular experience in mind (Leiper, 1990). In sport tourism, as in any other form of tourism, tourists typically engage in combinations of attraction nuclei that are salient to the desired experiences of the tourist. The importance of the tourism system in fostering the visitor experience is emphasised by Leiper's (1990) concept of 'clustered nuclei'. Clusters of symbiotic attraction nuclei are a significant element of the contemporary tourism system. Leiper (1990: 375) explains that 'tourists' precinct seems a useful expression for describing a small zone within a town or city where tourists are prone to gather because of clustered nuclei with some unifying theme'.

The development of stadia within tourist precincts illustrates the potential for tourist experiences to be fostered in association with event sport tourism (Judd, 2003; Mason *et al.,* 2008, Stevens & Wootton, 1997). A unifying force exists where sports facilities are developed in association with sports bars, museums, halls of fame and other forms of entertainment. The development of complementary activities (e.g. non-sport entertainment) and tourist services (e.g. transport nodes, accommodation, banking and information services) enhances the status of the tourist precinct. These developments may or may not be permanent. The temporary creation of tourist precincts is a strategy that attempts to leverage sports events to encourage a wider experience of the destination. Nash and Johnstone (1998), for instance, describe the development of exhibitions, promotions and community events in the cities of Liverpool and Leeds, which hosted the 1996 European Football Championship.

The visitor experience is also influenced by external tourism systems. Main entry points to a destination region may act as major points of concentration for tourists. This was the case during the 1994 Lillehammer Winter Olympics, which generated economic benefits for the gateway city of Oslo, more so than it did for the host town of Lillehammer (Teigland, 1999). Where event sport tourism takes place in a major urban tourism destination, such as the Sydney Olympic Games (2000), the reverse may occur. Nearby secondary sport tourism centres can leverage the event in their own tourism development interests (Chalip, 2004). It is apparent, then, that 'intervening attractions along major travel corridors, and competing tourist destinations' may influence the visitor experiences (Teigland, 1999: 308).

Sport Tourism and Visitor Behaviour

An understanding of the visitor experience is incomplete without consideration of the manifestations of sport tourist behaviour. The theory of planned behaviour states that tourist behaviour can be predicted employing attitudes and subjective norms (Ajzen & Driver, 1992). Tourist behaviours are evaluated based on instrumental costs and benefits, as well as the positive or negative feelings that the behaviour may bring about. Studies that investigate the motivational characteristics of sport tourism niche markets may be extended to the tourist behaviours that are associated with sport tourism in its various forms. Tourist behaviour is a critical element for sustainable sport tourism development. Individual sports are characterised by sport tourist behaviour profiles that may or may not benefit the tourist destination. Active sport tourism is generally constructive in the immediate outcomes of participation, including exertion, fitness, camaraderie, social contact and subcultural identity.

The behaviours associated with sport team fans and spectators are highly varied and in many cases unpredictable (Getz & Cheyne, 1997; Giulianotti, 1995, 1996; Weed, 2002) (Focus point 8.2). Bale (1989) describes team-based contests, such as soccer and ice hockey, as ritualised conflict. Team sports foster the emotional involvement of spectators, bringing rival fans together into an intense setting (the stadium or arena) that can give rise to confrontation and antagonism. The manifestations of such behaviour may be displayed by players (e.g. ice hockey and baseball), coaches (e.g. basketball and American football) and/or spectators (e.g. soccer and cricket).

Team sports may be associated with tourist behaviours that vary in the extreme. The behaviours of spectators at the International Rugby Board Hong Kong Sevens contribute to a carnival atmosphere, whereas the passionate support of football clubs may produce behaviours that are confrontational and violent. Manifestations of sport tourist behaviour influence visitor experiences, expenditures and social impacts at a destination. The management and regulatory responses to these behaviours include restrictions on movement (segregation), alcohol bans and heavy police presence. Individual sports, such as tennis, golf and surfing, offer the contrasts of entertainment and demonstrations of individual skill. Appreciation of individual performance is commonly associated with these sports, which may still be the subject of collective behaviour, but are less likely to be associated with antagonistic behaviour on the part of participants or spectators.

Focus point 8.2
Team Sports and Visitor Behaviour

The behaviours associated with team sports vary considerably between sports, and between regions and countries. Cricket in Australia and New Zealand has at times been associated with instances of unruly crowd behaviour, as have Test matches between India and Pakistan. By contrast, in England cricket is a sedate and traditional affair, while in the West Indies cricket is a sport of carnival and celebration. Rugby spectatorship in England is closely tied to social class and is generally a refined and serious spectator experience. Rugby and Rugby League in the South Pacific, Australia and New Zealand have occasionally been associated with political demonstrations, unruly crowd behaviour and rioting, although these generally pale alongside the more serious occurrences of football hooliganism. Professional soccer has, since 1908, been associated with acts of football hooliganism in more than 30 countries in Europe, Asia, Africa and South America (Dunning,

1999). Yet Giulianotti's (1996) ethnographic study of Ireland's football fans at the 1994 World Cup finals in the United States was notable for the absence of football hooliganism and, instead, 'carnival fandom' and the promotion of a fresh sense of Irish identity beyond nation-state boundaries.

Disorderly sport spectator behaviours may have negative effects on host communities, and raise the potential for host/guest conflict (Weed, 2002). Jones (2000) applies the concept of serious leisure to football fandom in an attempt to explain the behaviours of football fans as part of the social identity process. The characteristics of serious leisure in this context include longevity in the support of a chosen team, strong identification with the chosen leisure activity, investment of significant personal effort and the existence, in some cases, of a career path involving stages of achievement and recognition. Modelling is an important aspect of this form of social identity construction, whereby 'the neophyte member begins to deliberately adopt mannerisms, attitudes, and styles of dress, speech and behaviour that he or she perceives to be characteristic of the established members of the subculture' (Donnelly & Young, 1988: 223). Two important behavioural consequences of serious leisure identification include 'in-group favouritism' and 'out-group derogation'. The preferential and derogatory attitudes of each are based on group membership, rather than the individual characteristics of members of the group. 'Hostility towards out-groups may be demonstrated if the goals of the two groups are seen to be mutually exclusive' (Jones, 2000: 291).

It is apparent that spectators at sports events can either foster or counter tourism development interests through individual and collective behaviours. Event sport tourists can create a carnival atmosphere and bring colour, excitement and atmosphere to a destination that is attractive to tourists, or generate noise and security risks and create offence that may be repulsive to tourism (Higham, 1999; Weed, 2002). 'Sports junkies' are tourists whose behaviours are indicative of a strong commitment to their sport, or support for their team. The behaviour of these sport tourists may create aversion effects (Faulkner *et al.*, 1998), while contributing to accommodation shortages that displace other forms of tourism, such as corporate, business and conference travel. These varied and contrasting manifestations of tourist behaviour demonstrate the importance of considering all aspects of the sport tourist experience along with the economic impacts of different forms of sport tourism at a destination (Higham, 1999).

Recollection and Visitor Satisfaction

Travel home and recollection form an important part of the visitor experience (Clawson & Knetsch, 1966). Visitor satisfaction influences whether the experience will predispose a visitor to return to the destination or explore new places (Ryan, 1995). Multiple criteria are assessed in the recollection process, and the weighting of criteria vary between different forms of sport tourism. Satisfaction with spectator events may be based on an assessment of its drama, standards of performance and the behaviour of other fans (Bale, 1989). Tourist experiences, such as crowding and congestion, standards of service and uniqueness of the destination, may also feature prominently in the recollection phase.

Event sport tourism experiences, if satisfactory, may promote and generate tourist activity beyond the timeframe of the initial event. 'People who attend the event may return for a vacation, or those who watch the event on television may decide to visit the destination later' (Gibson, 1998: 60). One of the most comprehensive research studies addressing this aspect of the sport tourist experience was conducted by Webb and Magnussen (2002) following the 1999 Rugby World Cup (RWC) hosted by Wales. Their initial research phase estimated that the short-term impact of the RWC was £82.3 million. A follow-up survey of non-Welsh respondents conducted in 2002 indicated that 44% of the sample had subsequently returned to Wales, and 77% had recommended Wales as a place to visit. Over one third (36%) of recommendations had resulted in visits to the destination (Webb & Magnussen, 2002). More recently, Taks *et al.* (2009) have performed a detailed analysis of the means by which medium-sized one-off sports events can be developed to create 'flow on' tourism, repeat visitation and positive word-of-mouth. Their empirical study demonstrates that visits to iconic tourism attractions (e.g. sightseeing attractions) '... were motivated by a desire to learn about the destination, and encouraged future visitation and likelihood of recommendation'. On the basis of these findings, the authors call for effective collaboration between sport event organisers and destination marketing management agencies in order to better integrate event and destination experiences. Integrating sports event planning with experience of the destination is clearly critical to 'flow on' tourism objectives.

Carmichael and Murphy (1996) provide one of the few empirical studies into behavioural intentions towards a destination following small-scale sports events. They provide insights into the various forms that repeat travel to a destination may take, including investment, the development of business interests and retirement, as well as leisure travel. Furthermore, they raise important questions regarding the role of small-scale sports events in tourism. These include the following:

(1) significance of the event itself, as against other factors that may influence future travel to the destination;
(2) relative significance of sport and tourist elements of the event experience that influence future travel intentions; and
(3) translation of travel intentions into future travel actions, and the decay of travel intentions generated by sports in the weeks and months following an event.

The factors that feature in the recall phase of the sport tourism visitor experience remain poorly understood. These factors are certain to differ between sport tourist types. High-performance athletes are likely to be influenced by the standard of training facilities, personal performance and the outcome of the sport contest (Maier & Weber, 1993). The experiences of event spectators may be judged by casual spectators based upon the uniqueness of the sport experience while more serious sports fans will judge it by the opportunities that it provides to enhance social identity and self-concept (Gibson, 1998). By contrast, those pursuing general holidays with some incidental sport content may assess the uniqueness of the tourist experience of the destination in the recollection phase (Glyptis, 1982). In each instance, perceptions of the destination, and the propensity for repeat travel, are influenced by different factors.

Conclusion

This chapter considered the short-term temporal dimension of sport tourism development. It addressed how sport may influence the frequency, timing and duration of sport tourism experiences, and how different aspects of sport and tourism mediate visitor experience at a destination. One of the pressing challenges in the academic study of sport tourism is to develop insights into the relationship between sport tourist motivations/expectations and tourist experiences/behaviours at the destination. The fact that sport tourism experiences and, as a consequence, patterns of visitor expenditure can be influenced by planning and management strategies is an important point that emerges from this discussion. Scheduling and programming of sports events and competitions have direct implications for the tourist experience. The creation of tourist precincts, permanent or temporary, through the provision of ancillary entertainment, and complementary attractions and services is another important management strategy that may contribute towards this end. Success or failure of sport tourism development initiatives will be determined to a large degree by the effectiveness of these strategies to enhance sport tourist experiences at a destination.

Chapter 9

Seasonality, Sport and Tourism

It is not known with any certainty whether tourists travel in peak season because they want to, because they have to, or because they have been conditioned to.
Butler, 2001: 19

Introduction

Seasonality is the mid-point on the sport tourism development temporal framework (Chapter 1). In the context of this chapter, seasonality is defined as 'a temporal imbalance in the phenomenon of tourism, which may be expressed in terms of dimensions of such elements as numbers of visitors, expenditure of visitors, traffic on highways and other forms of transportation, employment and admissions to attractions' (Butler, 2001: 5; see also Koenig-Lewis & Bischoff, 2005). It is one of the most common characteristics of tourism, yet probably one of the least understood. More often than not, it is viewed as a problem that needs to be fixed.

Seasonality is not generally seen as a major issue in sport (Higham & Hinch, 2002). It is dynamic though, with sport seasons changing and, in most cases, expanding dramatically over the last 30 years. The purpose of this chapter is to examine the way sport influences tourism seasonality, with an emphasis on how sport can be used to alter tourism seasons in targeted destinations. This is done by examining seasonal patterns and issues in a tourism context and then in a sporting context. Consideration is given to the factors that influence these patterns followed by a review of sport-based strategies that have been used in an attempt to alter tourism seasonality. Case study 9.1, by Debbie Hopkins, considers narratives of climatic change in the Scottish ski industry, with consideration given to seasonality.

Seasonal Patterns and Issues in Tourism

BarOn's (1975) pioneering study of tourism seasonality consisted of an analysis of tourism data from 16 prominent tourism destination countries, covering a period of 17 years. His work confirmed 'most statistical series of arrivals and departures of tourists, bed nights in accommodation, employment in hotels and other branches of the tourist industry show considerable fluctuations from month to month due to seasonality and other predictable factors, which can be measured' (BarOn, 1975: 2). More recently Lopez Bonilla *et al.* (2006) distinguished a number of different seasonal tourism patterns found across the most popular regions of Spain. 'The Andalusia and the Valencian Community display single-peak seasonality; the Balearics and Catalonia have a multiple-peak pattern; and the Canary Islands and the Community of Madrid display non-peak seasonality' (p. 255). Such analysis demonstrates a significant breadth of patterns and the fact that they can differ dramatically by region even when they are in relatively close proximity to each other.

In Canada, Stanley and Moore (1997) confirm that a peak travel season exists in July and August, with a decline in the fall, followed by slight upswings in December and February. They also found distinct seasonal patterns associated with tourists travelling for pleasure, visiting friends and relatives, travelling for business, and attending conventions. In contrast to those travelling for leisure purposes, convention and business tourists demonstrated a propensity to travel in the spring and distributed their trips relatively evenly during the rest of the year, but for a marked decline in July (the high point in the leisure travel season). Similar seasonal travel patterns throughout Canada have been confirmed, with slight variations on the basis of trip purpose (business or leisure), location (urban or rural, province/region) and market segment (families, group tours, meetings/conventions) (Canadian Tourism Commission and Coopers and Lybrand, 1996; Murray, 1996). Weighill (2002) found that event sport travellers in Canada were more likely to travel from January to March while active sport travellers were busiest during the July to September period.

Tourism seasonality tends to be more exaggerated in peripheral areas than urban areas (Jeffrey & Barden, 2001). One of the reasons for this is that the central place characteristics of urban areas mean that there is a greater concentration of year-round attractions in cities than in peripheral areas (Daniels, 2007). These attractions include museums, art galleries, historic buildings, shopping and entertainment venues, many of which are indoor facilities that offer protection from the natural elements. Sporting events, facilities and programmes represent a significant part of this suite of attractions (Chapter 5). In contrast, peripheral areas are characterised by a much narrower range of attractions (Butler & Mao, 1996) that are more sensitive to weather and climatic conditions. They are also remote by definition, which may present various access problems at certain times of the year (Baum & Hagen, 1999).

Seasonality as a problem

The prevailing view of tourism seasonality is that it is a problem that should be resolved by destination managers. Advocates of this position point out that tourism seasonality has many negative effects on the destination (Allcock, 1989; Gomez Martin, 2005; Koenig-Lewis & Bischoff,

2005; Laws, 1991; Lockwood & Guerrier, 1990; Lopez Bonilla *et al.*, 2006; Poon, 1993; Roselló Nadel *et al.*, 2004). McEnnif (1992: 68) captures the essence of the view that seasonality is a problem by highlighting

> underutilisation of capacity at one end of the scale and congestion, environmental damage, saturation of transport infrastructure, increased risk of road accidents, higher prices and a negative impact on the quality of the tourism product at the other. Although some countries suffer from traffic congestion and damage to ... tourism products through overutilisation, most are chiefly concerned with off-peak underutilisation of capacity.

Different regions of the world report many of the same problems associated with seasonality, despite experiencing quite different patterns of seasonal variation. For example, Great Britain's high season occurs in the summer months of July and August, with a marked decline in tourism during the winter months. Jamaica, in contrast, has a busy winter season but a slow spring season (Robinson, 1979). Seasonality tends to be more of an issue for destinations that depend upon specific climatic conditions as attractions (e.g. winter sports, summer sports and certain adventure sports) than destinations where climatic conditions provide an environmental context rather than the central attraction (e.g. ethnic tourism).

With a few notable exceptions (e.g. Ball, 1988, 1989; Butler, 1994; Mourdoukoutas, 1988), little attention has been paid to the possible benefits that may be attributed to seasonality. Hartmann (1986: 31–32), however, argues that tourist low seasons offer 'the only chance for a social and ecological environment to recover fully. A dormant period for the host environment is simply a necessity in order to preserve its identity'. Similarly, Butler (1994: 335) suggests that '... while areas may experience very heavy use during peak seasons, in the long run they may well be better off than having that use spread more evenly throughout the year'. In fact, the off season has been described as having a 'fallow effect' in that it offers the destination a period of recuperation (Baum & Hagen, 1999; see also Koenig-Lewis & Bischoff, 2005).

The dynamic nature of tourism seasonality

Although tourism seasonality implies that the variations in tourism activity over the course of a year are relatively predictable, they are also dynamic in the longer term (Kennedy & Deegan, 2001). Two significant factors that may influence long-term patterns of tourism seasonality are globalisation and climatic change (Case study 9.1). In the first instance, the 'relative level of affluence of residents of industrialized countries, coupled with legislated free time and ease of transportation has meant that many tourists can overcome real seasonal (climatic) problems and pursue the sun or snow at whatever time of the year they prefer, often creating inverse seasonal peaking in destinations with different climates to that of their home region' (Butler, 2001: 14). However, rather than balancing out seasonal patterns in their home regions, these tourists often exacerbate seasonal peaking in the destination areas. An example is downhill ski enthusiasts from Northern Hemisphere countries who follow the ski season to the Southern Hemisphere in June, July and August.

Climatic change may have the effect that as some areas of the world become warmer, their summer seasons will be extended and winter seasons shortened (Harrison *et al.*, 1999). Climate 'is the prevailing condition of the atmosphere deduced from periods of observation', while weather is 'the state of the atmosphere in a given place at a given time' (Gomez Martin, 2005). Climate is experienced by tourists as weather. Both of these phenomena are changing. Climatic change trends suggest that the locations of climatically ideal tourism conditions will shift pole ward (Amelung *et al.*, 2007; Harrison *et al.*, 1999). In Europe, this will mean that ideal summer climatic conditions will shift north but that the spring and fall conditions will expand in the Mediterranean region. Specific tourism activities will be impacted differently. For example, even a slight warming trend may have quite dramatic effects on the viability of ski resorts (Tuppen, 2000). A study of the potential impacts of climatic change on winter recreation in Ontario, Canada, highlighted the vulnerability of four major activities (Scott *et al.*, 2002). Even relatively small increases in temperature were shown to result in major decreases in Nordic skiing, snowmobiling, ice fishing and downhill skiing activities. The least affected of these activities was downhill skiing because of the availability of snow-making equipment that increases the range of temperatures for which snow cover can be guaranteed. Notwithstanding this technology, a relatively small increase in temperature was shown to reduce the average ski season by between 21% and 34%. Given the dispersed nature of the other activities, the current snow-making technology is not seen as a feasible way to mitigate the potentially drastic impacts of global warming in this area. Climatic change has impacted seasonality in the ski industry and will continue to do so in the future (Case study 9.1 by Debbie Hopkins).

Case study 9.1
Climatic Change Narratives in the Scottish Ski Industry
Debbie Hopkins, University of Otago

Few tourism activities are more dependent on specific climatic conditions than snow sports. Sufficient snow depth in a mountainous region is 'conditio sine qua non' for the development of winter sports tourism (Gössling & Hall, 2006: 1). Alas, climate models have forecast dire scenarios for resorts around the world. This has motivated various research centred in North America (Dawson & Scott, 2007), Canada (Scott *et al.*, 2007), Europe (Elsasser & Burki, 2002) and Australia (Bicknell & McManus, 2006). Organisational adaptive strategies have been conceptualised, with Scott (2006) distinguishing between 'hard' technical strategies and 'soft' business choices, yet literature discussing social adaptation and the perceptions of resort decision-makers is still underdeveloped. Furthermore, it could be assumed that given the intrinsic relationship between snow sports and stable weather patterns, resorts would perceive the risk and be highly motivated to adapt. However, research has shown that there is a narrative of optimism promoted by ski industry management (Burki, 2000; Wolfsegger *et al.*, 2008). The reasons for this and the implications it may have on adaptation to climatic changes are worthy of close academic attention.

Scotland is often overlooked as a ski destination, yet it is of great national economic importance, with the Scottish Office estimating that a 'good season' can generate over £20 million of tourist expenditure for the local economies, thereby preventing out-migration and boosting rural employment. However, tourist behaviour has become increasingly opportunistic; this has been attributed to the increased availability of low-cost foreign skiing holidays, unreliable snowfall (in comparison to overseas competitors) and relative size of resorts (Harrison *et al.*, 2001).

It has been proposed that perceptions of climatic change will predict adaptive behaviour (Bicknell & McManus, 2006; O'Connor *et al.*, 1999; Wolfsegger *et al.*, 2008); however, this has been critiqued as overly individualistic and rational (Lorenzoni *et al.*, 2007). The complexity of climatic change and environmental risk perceptions makes it a challenging field of study, especially within an organisation that relies on a stable climate. Furthermore, organisations are not objective entities; they are intertwined with irrational stakeholders who are bound by their own subjective realities which are created by beliefs, attitudes and judgements along with social and cultural norms (Bickerstaff, 2004; Lorenzoni *et al.*, 2007). In addition, informal networks and 'communities of practice' will create frameworks for perceiving the environment (Wenger, 1999, cited in Pelling *et al.*, 2008). For the purpose of this study, O'Connor *et al.*'s (1999: 462) conceptualisation of risk perception is adopted as 'the perceived likelihood of negative consequences to oneself and society from one specific environmental phenomenon: Global Warming'.

Climatic change vulnerability and adaptive capacity are particular to individual geographical locations (Wilbanks, 2003); therefore, working on a micro-scale is beneficial for risk perception and adaptation research. In Scotland, this is demonstrated by site-specific daily weather disparities and timing of annual snowfall. For this reason, qualitative research was conducted at one site in the Scottish Highlands. Twenty-six semi-structured interviews were undertaken with resort decision-makers and 'informal communities of social interaction' (Nonaka, 1994: 17), thus following Collins and Evans' (2002: 237) advice to move 'beyond the core'.

Midwinter thaw and fluctuating seasons were identified by inter-viewees as presenting the greatest threat to the resort's winter season operations. They posited that shifts in snowfall patterns often resulted in insufficient snow prior to the Christmas holiday period. However, this was not echoed by the resort's decision-makers, who felt that it was the demand-side perceptions and demands which had altered, in line with the operating seasons of European and American resorts. Decision-makers stressed that the season often ends because of insufficient visitor numbers rather than snow. The media and experts were blamed for 'scaremongering' without understanding the specific microclimate, which was seen to have a direct influence on ticket sales, 'if the media says climate change is happening, people won't ski in Scotland because they think there's no snow' (Interviewee O). Decision-makers argued that the global (Northern Hemisphere) norms of skiing during the Christmas period were attributing to an inaccurate appearance of climatic change. This maintains an optimistic stance with the risk perceived to be the relatively targetable and manageable demand-side behaviour (compared to anthropogenic climatic change).

Because of the reliance on specific and stable climatic conditions, one would be forgiven for thinking that ski resort operators would be engaging with the climate change dialogue. However, this research found a consensus amongst employees attributing the perceived climatic changes (such as increased extreme events) to natural climate cycles, unconnected to human actions. This denial of the anthropo-genic climate change discourse could be explained by the scale and scope of the problem, where lay people (including decision-makers) are unable to envision their role in mitigative or adaptive efforts.

'How much power or control do I have over it (reducing green-house or carbon emissions) anyway?' (Interviewee B).

These findings concur with those of Sjoberg (2000), who identified that whilst lay people are unable to engage with the issue, or perceive a level of control, they may deny the risk. The detachment with the climate change discourse is further perpetuated by the relationship between lay people and experts which seems to be entrenched in mistrust, with interviewees questioning the subjectivity of expert interpretations of data.

The resort actively participated in adaptation through 'soft' strategies including diversification into year-round operation, attributed to business sense, and also through 'hard' adaptation. Despite the Managing Director asserting that 'I'm convinced it's snowing as much as it used to, if not more', resort decision-makers frequently made reference to the future possibility of artificial snow production in order to ensure operationality before the Christmas period, thus contradicting their argument that snowfall had not reduced and relying on hard adaptation to reduce vulnerability.

'We struggle to make snow [pause] we've tried [pause] and may do again eventually in the future, it depends on the technology ...' (Managing Director).

Bleda and Shackley (2008) assert that organisations will only take adaptive action when the perceived risk of climatic change is attributed to human behaviour. Yet in this example, it appears that the resort decision-makers reject anthropogenic climatic change whilst also adapting, which contradicts both the interviewee's stated perceptions and Bleda and Shackley's (2008) findings.

This research identifies a need for further investigation into the social processes influencing climatic change adaptation including identification of vulnerability. The lay public's rejection of the anthropogenic narrative transcends into organisational structures and thus affects decision-making on this scale. Furthermore, the acute risks forecast for the ski industry could explain a formal narrative of optimism in order to reflect a 'business as usual' outlook. This research supports Bicknell and McManus's (2006) conclusion that for some organisations the rhetoric of climatic change could be more damaging than the physical consequences. Furthermore, climatic changes will not affect all countries or organisations in the same way, thus creating 'winners' and 'losers' on various scales (international, national, regional and local). This will be in terms of both the physical effects of changes to the climate and also the adaptive capacity of the individual organisation or system which will have implications for vulnerability assessments. The social and behavioural responses to climatic change by individuals and organisations require further investigation and should work alongside technical responses to provide a holistic outlook for the ski tourism industry in these uncertain times. This should include understandings of demand-side adaptation, in terms of perceptions and behavioural adaptations, which will impact upon the supply-side industry.

Seasonal Patterns, Trends and Issues in Sport

A significant part of the dynamic evolution of sport over the last 30 years has been the expansion of traditional sporting seasons. While the reasons for this development include an assortment of technological innovations, changing social conditions and general forces of globalisation, one of the most significant factors has been the professionalisation of many sports at the elite level of competition. In conjunction with this trend, partnerships with broadcast media have generated pressures to increase the length of the competitive season as a business strategy (McPherson *et al.*, 1989). In many cases

> the restrictions of functioning within a traditional sports season have ... been cast aside. The professional development of numerous sports, where teams compete virtually year round, has, in those cases, largely eliminated the notion of sport seasonality. (Higham & Hinch, 2002: 183)

European football is one of the many examples that illustrate this trend. The professional football season in Europe has been transformed through the development of international league competitions, from a domestic winter sport, to an international club sport that takes place across most of the calendar year. Other examples exist where sport seasons have been altered to revolve around the summer rather than winter months. The Norwegian Football League, which takes place in summer to exploit favourable playing and spectator conditions, is one example. Similarly, the development of the Super League realigned Rugby League from a winter to a summer sport in the United Kingdom and France as part of a strategy to develop a global competition season involving teams based in the Northern and Southern hemispheres.

Figure 9.1 illustrates the expansion of rugby union competition season in New Zealand from 1975 to 2002, 2010. Using data drawn from New Zealand Rugby Union statistics published on a season-by-season basis in the New Zealand Rugby Almanac, the dramatic expansion of the rugby season is evident. This expansion of the sport season was advanced by the introduction of the National Provincial Championship in 1976 and the transition to professionalisation of rugby union in the Southern Hemisphere in 1996 (Higham & Hinch, 2002). Continued league expansion and adjustment to accommodate broadcast interests continue to extend and shift seasonal patterns (Higham, 2005a). Features of the 2010 New Zealand rugby calendar (see also Figure 9.1) include the expansion of the early season Super 12 competition in 2009 (now Super 14). It also included a further expanded international rugby calendar, specifically the expansion of the TriNations competition (from four to six games per team), which now extends through August, and the establishment in

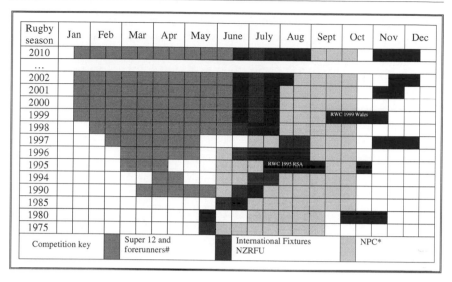

Figure 9.1 Expansion of the New Zealand representative rugby season (1975–2002, 2010)
Source: New Zealand Rugby Almanac 1975–2002, 2010 as cited in Higham and Hinch (2002a)
Notes: # Rugby Super 12 (1996–), Super 10/CANZ (1990–1995). Includes preseason warm-up games. *NPC: National Provincial Championship. RWC: Rugby World Cup. Years prior to 1994 and from 2002 are not continuous

recent years of the 'Autumn tests' played in Europe (November/ December), with a feature test match played in an Asian capital city en route to Europe in early November each year. Such has been the continuing expansion of the international programme in June to August that it now overlaps with an expanded national championship competition in August, which precludes the involvement of national representatives in that competition (because of their higher international rugby commitments at that time of year). The Super 14 competition is set to become the Super 15 in 2014.

The development of all-season sport facilities represents another change that has facilitated the extension of sport seasons. Examples include summer skiing facilities in Scandinavia, the all-season Millennium Stadium in Cardiff (Wales) and the proliferation of smaller-scale leisure sport facilities that effectively provide climatically controlled environments or ones dominated by new technologies (Bale, 1989; Focus point 9.1). For sports that are conducted in the outdoors, an assortment of equipment and clothing innovations have expanded the range of climatic conditions in which they may be comfortably pursued.

Notwithstanding these changes, it is evident that seasonal patterns still exist in sport. This is most obvious in the case of winter sports such as those that require snow or summer sports such as sailing and scuba diving, which are much more attractive to participants in warm-water conditions. The reality of these sport seasons has a direct impact on the seasonality of sport tourism.

Focus point 9.1

Bring on Winter

While the majority of tourists tend to seek warm climates for their vacations, winter sport enthusiasts will traverse the globe in search of the right conditions to partake in their sport. This pursuit of optimal conditions means that winter sport destinations such as alpine areas are characterised by challenging seasonal variations in visitors. Such destinations work hard to attract spring, summer and fall visitors. Technology is beginning to play a role in these strategies. For example, the Vuokatti Ski Tunnel is an indoor cross-country ski track, located 600 km north of Helsinki, in Vuokatti, Finland. The ski tunnel, which is 1212 m in length and features significant changes in elevation, was developed in close association with the tourist infrastructure of Vuokatti. Its starting point is the Vuokatti Sports Hotel and Sot-kamo-Vuokatti tourist information area. The Sports Hotel provides the service centre for skiers, reception and information services, refreshments, ski waxing and sport shops. For reasons of landscape management, the ski tunnel is partly subterranean and covered with a protective and concealing layer so that from the exterior, the ski tunnel has the appearance of a ridge that is typical of the surrounding landscape. The air and snow temperature inside the ski tunnel, as well as the air conditioning, are monitored and controlled by computer. The inside air is normally maintained between -5 and $-9°C$, but can be dropped to $-18°C$ as needed. The tunnel's snow-making system consists of high-pressure cannons which replenish the trail surface at night when required. The ski trails are groomed mechanically. This facility has positioned Vuokatti as the world's leading training centre for Nordic ski disciplines and an all-season ski destination.

Destinations in higher latitudes no longer hold a monopoly on sports that require snow or ice. Refrigeration units have been used in ice hockey arenas for decades and have enabled the expansion of the sport to southern North America and Europe. More recently, large indoor downhill skiing and snowboarding facilities have been developed near major urban centres and destinations. Ski Dubai is a classic example – a downhill ski resort in the desert. It features five runs of varying difficulty including what is purportedly the world's first indoor expert ski run. Indoor air temperatures are kept at a comfortable -1 to $-2°C$, with appropriate clothing and equipment supplied. The ski slope attraction is further supported by a St. Moritz Café themed restaurant and associated winter activities. All in all, a great break from the heat.

More recently, the fast growing sport of indoor climbing has featured a fascinating twist on its version of climate control. CityRock Climbing Center in Colorado Springs, Colorado, held an indoor ice climbing competition in 2010, called the Pro Indoor Ice Brawl. Climbers raced to the top using a combination of ice axe techniques and adapted climbing holds. While the technology for these indoor ice-climbing walls is still at an early stage of development, it is not difficult to imagine that ice climbing may be the next-big-thing in the indoor rock climbing world.

Sources: http://www.vuokatti.fi/eindex.html. Accessed 17 April 2011. http://www.skidxb.com/home/about-ski-dubai/factsheet.aspx. Accessed 17 April 2011. http://rockandice.com/news/1241-indoor-ice-comps-next-big-thing. Accessed 17 April 2011.

Sport as a factor of tourism seasonality

At a general level, tourism seasonality has been attributed to 'natural' and 'institutional' factors (BarOn, 1975; Frechtling, 1996; Hartmann, 1986; Koenig-Lewis & Bischoff, 2005). Natural seasonality refers to regular temporal variations in natural phenomena, particularly those associated with cyclical climatic changes throughout the year (Allcock, 1989; Butler, 1994; Gomez Martin, 2005). These variations impact demand as well as supply. For example, climate is of fundamental importance to sport tourism in higher-latitude destinations, although it is often considered as a nuisance factor or constraint to tourist development. Kreutzwiser (1989: 29–30) contends that

> [c]limate and weather conditions... influence how satisfying particular recreational outings will be. Air temperature, humidity, precipitation, cloudiness, amount of daylight, visibility, wind, water temperature, and snow and ice cover are among the parameters deemed to be important. ... In summer, air temperature and humidity can combine to create uncomfortable conditions for vigorous activities, while wind and temperature in winter can create a wind chill hazardous to outdoor recreationists.

These climatic variations are closely correlated with other cyclical events in the natural realm, such as plant growth and animal migration, the latter of which has a direct bearing on sport hunting.

By contrast, institutional factors reflect the social norms and practices of society (Hinch & Hickey, 1996; Koenig-Lewis & Bischoff, 2005). These include religious, cultural, ethnic, social and economic practices as epitomised by religious, school and industrial holidays. Two of the most prevalent institutional constraints on the scheduling of sport travel are school and work commitments (Butler, 1994; McEnif, 1992). Tradition also plays a large part in the scheduling of these vacations. Changing religious views, social norms, transportation options and technological advances may moderate these forces.

Butler (1994, 2001) has identified three additional causes of seasonality. The first of these is social pressure or fashion, which is usually set by celebrities and other privileged classes within society. A sport example of this factor would be media attention given to celebrities at yachting regattas and horse racing meets. Inertia or tradition is a second seasonality factor. People tend to be creatures of habit and if they have traditionally taken their holiday during a given time of the year, they will likely continue to do so. For example, even upon retirement, many individuals will take an 'annual vacation' during the same period that they were previously constrained to because of their jobs. Finally, the scheduling of sporting seasons is a factor in its own right. Butler (2001) makes the case that sport seasons have a direct impact on tourism seasons. Winter sports such as skiing, snowboarding and snowmobiling are perhaps the most obvious examples, but summer-based activities such as surfing and golf also influence travel patterns as tourists search for the best seasonal conditions for the pursuit of their sporting passions. Climatic conditions appear to be influential in all of these examples, yet even sports that are played within climatically controlled settings, such as competitive basketball, normally have distinct seasons. If an inclusive definition of the 'institutional' category of determinants were adopted, then sporting season would seem to be closely associated with this category. Indeed, sport sociologists have long argued that sport is a social institution (McPherson *et al.*, 1989).

Butler (2001: 8) has suggested that it

> is the interaction between the forces determining the natural and institutionalized elements of the seasonality of tourism in both the generating and receiving areas as modified by actions of the public and private sector which creates the pattern of seasonality in tourism that occurs at a specific destination.

Natural and institutional factors are active in both the receiving and the generating areas of tourism. They can be thought of as pull and push factors which interact with each other (Butler & Mayo, 1996; Koenig-Lewis & Bischoff, 2005; Lundtorp *et al.*, 1999). While the interactions

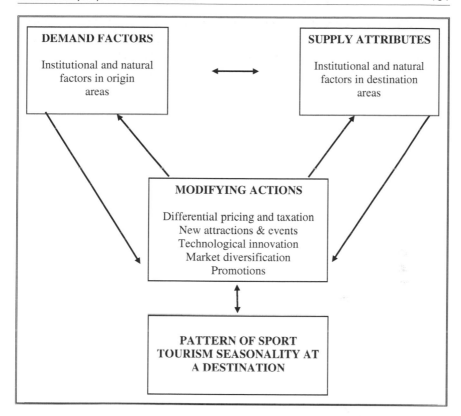

Figure 9.2 Sport influences on patterns of tourist seasonality
Source: Based on Butler (2001)

between the factors that influence seasonal patterns of sport tourism visitation are complex, their basic relationship is relatively straightforward (Figure 9.2). Institutional and natural factors influence tourism demand as well as tourism supply. Policy-makers, planners and managers may intervene in this process by modifying supply attributes through strategies such as the development of climatically controlled sport facilities. They may also modify institutional and natural factors on the demand side through such strategies as promotional information that dispels misconceptions that potential tourists might have about sport participation during the off season. Amelung *et al.* (2007) point out that seasonality will be impacted by climatic change and associated movement in terms of natural factors. The big question that they raise is whether institutional factors can be manipulated or whether they will prove to be intransient. If the latter response is the case, a strategic approach to the manipulation of these factors will be challenging.

Differential influence across the hierarchy of sport attractions

The degree to which a sporting activity influences tourism seasonality is in part determined by the placement of that sport within the traveller's hierarchy of attractions (Chapter 2). Trip behaviour varies on the basis of the centrality of sport as the tourist attraction or how prominently the sport features as a travel motivation. Where sport is the principal focus of the trip (i.e. the primary attraction), travellers demonstrate a greater propensity to travel in the tourism 'off season' (World Tourism Organization and International Olympic Committee, 2001). More casual sport tourists (i.e. those who see sport as a secondary or tertiary attraction) show higher levels of seasonal variation in their travels. Where sport is the primary motivation, sport tourists are willing to negotiate through institutional and natural constraints that might otherwise be insurmountable for more casual sport tourists (Hinch *et al.*, 2001). For example, outbound tourists from Germany, the Netherlands and France who have a strong sport focus are more likely to travel from January to April than are outbound tourists with a more casual approach to sport. The latter group is much more likely to travel from May to August (Table 9.1).

In the case of casual sport tourists (Table 9.1), a single peaked pattern of seasonality emerges that reinforces typical summer peaks for general tourism visitation to destination countries. A similar pattern was found for sport tourists in Canada (Weighill, 2002).

The degree to which a sporting activity is dependent on natural resources is also an important factor in terms of seasonal patterns of

Table 9.1 Seasonal travel patterns of outbound sport tourists from Germany, the Netherlands and France with both strong and casual sport focus (1999)

	Jan–April	*May–Aug*	*Sept–Dec*	*Total%*	*Trips (1000s)*
Strong sport focus					
Germany	44	32	24	100	11,000
The Netherlands	39	46	15	100	7,000
France	40	51	9	100	500
Casual sport focus					
Germany	11	57	32	100	21,000
The Netherlands	10	70	20	100	3,000
France	20	57	23	100	3,000

Source: Abstracted from World Tourism Organization and International Olympic Committee (2001)

activity. Sports such as skiing and sailing are directly tied to specific natural attributes such as snow and wind conditions, respectively. Other sports, even though they occur outdoors, may be enhanced by natural attributes, but these attributes are not necessarily central to the experience. In the latter case, natural factors such as weather may serve as the general context rather than having a direct bearing on the essence of the sporting performance. In cases such as mountain biking and beach volleyball, natural conditions which deviate from what is perceived as the ideal may be a significant deterrent to sport tourism at certain times of the year. Alternatively, advantageous or extreme weather conditions (e.g. unseasonably warm temperatures leading to snow melt and high river flow volume) may be promoted as a positive characteristic for many types of extreme sports (e.g. white water rafting and kayaking).

Strategic Responses

Tourism managers, planners and policy-makers have addressed seasonality issues in numerous ways. Responses have included attempts to lengthen the main season and/or establish additional seasons by diversifying markets, using different pricing and tax incentives throughout the year, encouraging staggered school holidays, encouraging distinct domestic and international seasons, introducing differential pricing at different times of the year, adjusting supply inventories, and introducing new festivals and conferences during periods that traditionally experience low visitation (Baum & Hagen, 1999; Butler, 2001; Capo Parrilla *et al.*, 2007; Koeing-Lewis & Bischoff, 2005; Lee *et al.*, 2008). More generally, Weaver and Oppermann (2000) categorised these approaches into six basic strategic responses: increase, reduce or redistribute demand and increase, reduce and redistribute supply. Strategies that have the most relevance in a sport tourism context include changes to the sport product mix, market diversification and the adoption of a leisure constraints framework to target unique seasonal barriers.

Changes to the sport product mix

Individual sports are characterised by their own patterns of seasonality. By capitalising on these unique characteristics, it is possible to manipulate seasonal patterns of tourism visitation in a destination. Two subtypes of sport-based product mix strategies are particularly prominent. The first is the introduction of sporting events during the off-peak tourism periods and the second is the introduction of new or improved sport facilities and programmes.

The introduction of new events and festivals is one of the most common strategies for altering seasonal tourist visitation (Hinch & Jackson, 2000). Many special events do not require large capital expenditures, are relatively transportable and can be targeted to specific or combinations of distinct market segments. Sporting events may offer the additional advantage of utilising existing facilities and infrastructure at off-peak times in the destination. A good example of product diversification through the introduction of sporting events is provided by the Isle of Man (Baum & Hagen, 1999). The Isle of Man has traditionally been a popular summer tourist destination in the United Kingdom, but a sharp decline in the 'sun seeker' markets in the early 1980s prompted the development of a product diversification strategy designed to increase sport tourism in the shoulder seasons. Two new sporting events were introduced. The first was the development of the Manx TT road race scheduled during the shoulder tourism period of late May and early June. Recent event evaluations show that it attracts approximately 37,000 visitors who spend in excess of £15 million at the destination. This major event is supported by a series of other motor sport events throughout the year that each attracts between 3000 and 6000 visitors.

The second type of sporting event that was introduced on the Isle of Man to increase visitation during the tourism low season was the Student Festival of Sport (Isle of Man Sports Challenge, 2010). This festival was

> started in 1985 as part of the Isle of Man's 'Year of Sport'. In its inaugural year, a total of 1000 participants were welcomed; by 1997, this number had increased to 2700, taking part in a wide range of sporting activities (archery, badminton, basketball, cricket, cycling, fencing, field hockey, netball, rugby, soccer, shooting, ten pin bowling, triathlon, swimming and water polo). (Baum & Hagen, 1999: 306)

The Student Festival of Sport was reported to have cost the local government £29,100 to run in 1997 with a return of 7884 bed nights and £500,000 in direct visitor spending. A distinguishing feature of both of these sport events was the close collaboration of the sport and tourism sectors. For example, a budget priced inclusive package for sea travel to the island and one week's accommodation proved to be very successful for the Student Festival of Sport.

Product diversification designed to modify seasonal visitation can also take the form of physical development. In a sport context, a classic example of this type of strategy is the development of all weather resorts, such as Centerparcs in Europe, which provide year-round sport-based facilities for family groups. Golf developments have also been used effectively to modify seasonal visitation. For example, Baum and Hagen (1999: 309) report that the

> development of Prince Edward Island, Canada, as a recognized golf resort with in excess of a six month season (compared with the

traditional two to three month beach season), is the result of a planned strategy, public and private sector investment and a focus on quality outcomes in all aspects of the development cycle.

This development was accompanied by targeted promotions to senior and retired markets interested and able to visit during the shoulder seasons.

Perhaps the best example of this type of strategy can be found at ski resorts (Tuppen, 2000). In the face of falling visitation in the 1980s, ski resorts in North America and Europe made a concerted effort to improve and diversify their product. One of the key improvements was a major expansion in snow-making equipment which allowed heavily used runs between the upper slopes and the base of the resort to open sooner and close later in the year, thereby facilitating an extended season. Just as importantly, it built consumer confidence within active sport tourism markets that there would be snow at the resorts during what had previously been considered a very marginal period. Many resorts also expanded the range of winter-based activities that visitors can partake in through the provision of indoor sports and fitness centres, as well as facilities for other types of winter sports such as snowboarding, cross-country skiing and snowshoeing. Some, such as the resort of Whistler, British Columbia, Canada, developed summer attractions such as golf courses to provide all-season attractions.

Notwithstanding these successes, Baum and Hagen (1999) advise caution in the use of product diversification through facility development as a strategy for addressing seasonality. Careful financial analysis is required, especially in the case of peripheral destinations, to verify that an adequate return on investment will be achieved. The lower costs of product diversification through a new events strategy explain the popularity of this approach over more expensive facility redevelopment strategies.

Market diversification

There needs to be a corresponding demand in the marketplace for product diversification strategies to work. It is, therefore, necessary to verify market needs prior to investing in product development. In a tourist seasonality context, there are a number of market segments that are traditionally recognised as having fewer constraints relating to the timing of travel. These groups include senior citizens, conference delegates, incentive travellers, empty nesters, affinity groups and special interest tourists (Baum & Hagen, 1999). The success of Prince Edward Island's product expansion into golf was largely due to their parallel strategy of marketing to seniors and empty nesters who have greater flexibility to travel outside of the peak summer months. While there are many market segments that have relevance in terms of sport tourism seasonality, one of the most promising is the special interest segment (Hall & Weiler, 1992). Individuals that are passionate about a given sport, including members of sporting subcultures (Chapter 6), will be much more motivated to overcome constraints to travel during the off season than general tourists. They represent niche markets (Chapter 3) that can be targeted during the off season and who are willing to travel long distances to pursue their sporting passions. The development of the Internet as an information source for tourism and sport enables communication with what is potentially a widely dispersed market.

Another form of market diversification addresses the institutional constraints that sport markets face at different times of the year. A good example of this type of approach to the resolution of a seasonal visitation problem is illustrated by the use of geographic market segmentation by Eurocamp (Klemm & Rawel, 2001). This company specialises in self-drive holidays in Europe that feature active sporting amenities at the campgrounds on route. Initially, the company targeted British families, but because of the institutional constraint of school holidays, bookings were concentrated in August. A conscious strategy to promote their product to other European countries that had different school holiday periods was successfully pursued over a 15-year period. The outcome of the market diversification strategy was a consistently high level of bookings from May to September rather than the single month of August.

Jang (2004) presented a variation of this type of strategy through the application of financial portfolio theory. He argued that marketers should select a mix of tourism segments that fall along a Seasonal Demand Efficient Frontier, given a demand-risk target. At the very least, destination marketers should know the priority segments in the mix and should consciously consider sport tourism markets as part of this mix.

Leisure constraints theory

Notwithstanding the successes reported above, seasonal variations in tourism remain a prominent feature of the industry. The 'stubbornness' of these patterns has led to the suggestion that more attention should to be paid to the needs and behaviours of the consumer (Baum & Hagen, 1999). Leisure constraints theory represents one framework that provides additional insight into this area (Hinch *et al.*, 2001; Hinch & Jackson, 2000). This theory considers what prevents non-participants from taking part in the leisure pursuits. In the context of sport tourism seasonality, leisure constraints theory raises the question, 'What is it that inhibits people from travelling for sport at certain times of the year?' The answers to this question would provide a better understanding of sport tourist seasonal behaviour and would identify constraints that can be targeted by managers.

Hudson *et al.* (2010) used a leisure constraints framework to examine the barriers to snowboarding and skiing in Canada. Their framework is positioned in a tourism context and operationalises the hierarchical model of leisure constraints (Crawford *et al.*, 1991; Walker & Virden, 2005) to identify management options designed to increase participation in downhill skiing. For example, one of the constraints that they found was that non-skiers were afraid that they would be cold and uncomfortable on the slopes. A logical management response to this is to raise consumer awareness of technological advances in the manufacture of winter clothing that will allow enhanced comfort.

Figure 9.3 has been modified from the hierarchical model of leisure constraints (Jackson *et al.*, 1993) to emphasise its relevance in the study of sport tourism seasonality.

One of the key characteristics of this model is the order in which seasonal constraints are encountered and negotiated. In the context of sport tourism seasonality, sporting preferences are the starting point. A major consideration at this stage is the centrality of seasonal factors in terms of the motivations for travel. In cases where natural seasonal factors such as climatic conditions are the primary attraction or motivation for the sport tourists (e.g. sunny warm conditions for casual sport tourists and favourable snow conditions for serious skiers), their absence in a destination during a given time of the year will be a major and perhaps insurmountable constraint. Jackson *et al.* (1993) have

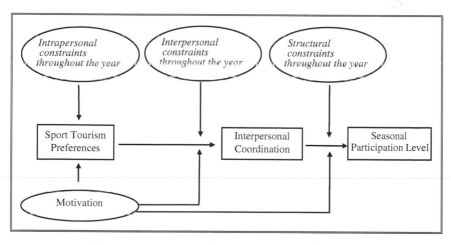

Figure 9.3 Hierarchical model of seasonal sport tourism constraints
Source: Based on Jackson *et al.* (1993)

labelled these as intrapersonal constraints. Where these constraints do not exist, sport tourists proceed to the interpersonal constraint level. Team sports, or those that are enhanced by fellow participants, require the potential sport tourist to coordinate his or her travel plans with others. Potential sport tourists who seek travel and sport companions but cannot find them will fail to participate even though they have the initial motivation. Finally, structural constraints consist of things such as high travel costs, lack of accommodation and school or work commitments. Ways around this last level of constraints may be negotiated by the potential sport tourist, although they too may prove to be insurmountable. Innovative packaging by the host destination can facilitate this negotiation process throughout the year. By understanding this leisure constraint framework, sport tourism destinations can identify appropriate seasonal target markets and help them to negotiate the particular constraints that they face at various times of the year.

Conclusion

This chapter has demonstrated that both tourism and sport are characterised by seasonal variations during the course of a year. Whereas these variations are generally seen as undesirable in a tourism context, there has been relatively little concern about seasonal variation in a sporting context. Somewhat paradoxically, seasonal patterns of tourism tend to be stable despite ongoing attempts to modify them while sporting seasons have undergone extensive change – especially in terms of their extension throughout the year. Various factors influence seasonality in both of these realms, but this chapter highlights the considerable interaction that exists between the seasonal patterns of sport and the seasonal patterns of tourism.

It is clear that sport not only is a factor in tourism seasonality but can potentially be harnessed as a means to modify tourist visitation patterns over the course of a year. Lengthening competition seasons for spectator sports and scheduling sport events during tourism shoulder seasons are direct ways of increasing visitation to a destination during these periods. Active sport tourism also represents an opportunity to consciously influence tourism seasonality in a destination. This is especially true for sport tourists who are members of sport subculture groups. Destinations should consider the resources that they have in their region during the tourism shoulder seasons that may be attractive to specialised sport subcultures. Destinations that offer a unique blend of attributes can adopt a niche marketing strategy that effectively attracts a geographically dispersed but passionate group of visitors during non-peak times of the year. Finally, while nostalgia sport tourists have not been discussed in depth in the chapter, the tourism literature on seasonality highlights the potential for museums and similar types of facilities to attract visitors outside of the summer months (Stevens, 2001).

While tourism managers have long pursued the economic benefits of modifying seasonality, sport managers are increasingly adopting a similar approach. There are financial benefits for sports that can attract sport tourists at non-traditional times of the year. While some of these benefits may be collected directly at the gate of the sporting venue, others can be leveraged through the tourism industry. For example, sport tourists travelling during the off season are likely to enjoy lower rates for accommodation due to higher vacancy rates. These benefits can be maximised if collective action on the part of a particular sport can demonstrate that there are a substantial number of sport-related visitors arriving during this period. Group rates and adjoining travel packages can then be negotiated.

The positive side of tourism seasonality mentioned at the beginning of this chapter should not be lost in the search to solve the 'problem' of seasonality. Sport tourism destinations can benefit from a 'fallow period' that allows for the regeneration of natural and human resources. Notwithstanding the tendency for many sport seasons to expand schedules to the point where they are almost year-round pursuits, there may be a downside to this. Spectators and athletes may 'burn out' if they do not have a chance to re-energise during an off season. Sports offer their most powerful function as tourist attractions when the enthusiasm of participants is at its peak – yet this peak cannot be prolonged indefinitely. In the interest of the sustainability of the sport, sport tourism and the destinations where this activity takes place, it may be strategically prudent to maintain some form of seasonal variation over the course of a year.

Chapter 10
Evolutionary Trends in Sport Tourism

> *In some respects, it was tourists [to France] who thus passed on mountaineering to sports enthusiasts in the 18th and 19th centuries, before the latter, the mountaineers, then offered tourist skiing in return during the 20th century.*
> Bourdeau *et al.*, 2002: 23

Introduction

The relationship between sport and tourism is as dynamic in the long term as it is in the short and medium terms. Sport influences destination life cycles and tourism influences sport life cycles. The first part of the chapter examines these types of interactions. Nostalgia sport tourism, which is motivated by a desire to reconnect to the sporting past, represents a special type of interaction over time in which sport heritage serves as a tourist attraction. Ramshaw's case study of Twickenham Stadium tours illustrates the powerful nature of sport heritage, both in terms of declarative (collective) purpose and personal (visitor) experience. Examples aside from stadium tours include sport halls of fame, sites of past sporting events and imagined pasts played out through fantasy sport camps and programmes. This emerging area of sport tourism is the focus of the second part of this chapter. Neither the interaction between life cycles nor nostalgia sport tourism occurs independently of other forces operating in the broader environment. A dynamic web of local, national and global trends influences these phenomena. The third section of the chapter presents a discussion of these trends.

Cyclical Relationships in Sport and Tourism

Destination and product life cycles are dominant features of tourism (Butler, 2006; Christaller, 1963/64; Doxey, 1975; Plog, 1972; Stansfield, 1978). Butler's (1980) tourist area cycle model epitomises this idea with six stages: exploration, involvement, development, consolidation, stagnation and either rejuvenation or decline. In revisiting Butler's model, Johnston (2001a) suggested that the early part of this cycle could be classified as the pre-tourism era in which some other institutional framework besides tourism dominates the destination. Similarly, the latter stages of stagnation and decline can be described as a post-tourism

190

era, as tourism is replaced as a dominant or important sector of the destination economy. The general pattern of these cycles is one of increasing visitation until the destination's resources are adversely affected at which point visitor numbers begin to decline (Chapter 4). Various implications emerge from these cycles, with the most obvious being that management intervention is needed to sustain tourism resources if the destination's lifespan is to be extended.

Sport attractions play a significant role in the life cycles of many destinations. For example, in his detailed analysis of the destination life cycle of Kona, Hawaii, Johnson (2001b) noted that the original 'Ironman' race was transferred from Honolulu to Kona in the early 1980s. This shift corresponded to the last period of Kona's development phase and served as an image-maker for the destination. It marked a critical point in the development of Kona by replacing the 'way of life' image with a sports theme. Other destinations have used sport as a tourism development strategy in a similar fashion.

The evolutionary dynamics of sport

Sport is increasingly being used as a strategy to rejuvenate tourism destinations. Successful implementation of this approach requires insight into sport life cycles.

> Like tourism products, individual sports, sports disciplines and sport events have their own life cycles. They too go 'out of fashion'. And they increasingly find themselves having to compete against other leisure activities and events. ... In sport too there is a constant need for the adaptation of individual sports and events to the changing requirements of sportsmen and sportswomen, as well as spectators. (Keller, 2001: 4, 5)

Just as a primary measure of the tourism destination life cycle is the number of visitors to a destination, a primary indicator of sport life cycle is the number of participants and spectators involved. Other measures of the status of a sport within its life cycle include the sophistication of rule structures that characterise a sport, the level of skill development and physical performance, and, increasingly, the extent of commodification and professionalisation.

The dynamics of sport have been clearly illustrated in recent years by the slower growth of many highly structured team sports and the ascent of individualised and extreme sports (Breivik, 2010; de Villers, 2001; Murray & Dixon, 2000; Thomson, 2000; Wheaton, 2004). For example, Keller (2001: 13, 14) suggests that

> [t]he membership for organized types of sport is on the decline, as are the proving grounds from which top-level sports traditionally

draw new blood. The new generation is a sliding, gliding and rolling generation. Their sports are freestyle events like 'inline skating', 'street basketball' and 'snowboarding', which in many cases are associated with a youthful subculture. Performance and rankings no longer play any role. What counts are the aesthetic, 'feel-good', atmospheric effects.

Breivik (2010) characterises these emerging sports by risk, participation sites inclusive of demanding natural and constructed environments, loose organisation, distance from the dominant sport culture and individual participation within developing subcultures. Such sport is manifested in the dramatic differentiation found in traditional sports such as mountain climbing (e.g. indoor climbing, bouldering and ice climbing), the emergence of air sports (paragliding, hang gliding and sky diving through to base jumping, sky boarding and acrobatics), new board sports (snow, skate, wake, etc.) and variations of bicycling (trick, mountain, BMX), skating (inline) and luge (street luge). It is safe to assume that innovative forms of sport will continue to surface although the individual popularity and longevity of each of these sports is more difficult to predict.

Three general explanations for the increasing popularity of extreme sports have been offered (Breivik, 2010). The first is one of 'compensation'. As the modern societies become more controlled and safety-oriented, some individuals – especially youth – will look to extreme sport as an antidote or a countermeasure to boredom. Alternatively, this shift may be seen as an extention or 'adaptation' of a modern life that features more sensory stimulation as manifested in areas such as entertainment, cuisine and travel. Seeking variation in sport may be a simple extension of the variation found in these other areas of life. Finally, a third possible explanation is that the variation in modern and postmodern society just described may be seen as superficial and is often virtual (e.g. social networking). Extreme sport provides participants with the opportunity to express themselves in a real way through their bodies – not just their minds.

One of the dilemmas facing extreme sports concerns its evolution. Typically, these sports have emerged for people who wish to get away from someone else's rules and regulations and set up their own renegade groups. Yet even these sports are part of an evolutionary process. As sports institutions, media, equipment and clothing manufactures and the tourism industry interact, extreme sports tend to shift from subculture to mainstream (Breivik, 2010; Hoffer, 1995). Evolution tends to introduce structures and rules that serve to ensure that the activity is managed in a way that facilitates commodification until some group once again breaks away to begin something new.

Snowboarding provides a good illustration of this process. It emerged as a subculture activity in resistance to the dominant culture of alpine skiing which had become mainstream by the 1980s. It was characterised by a non-traditional view of sport. Yet the initial radical nature of snowboarding has been steadily moderated through the pressures of commodification. The development of snowboarding as a commercial television product by ESPN illustrates this point (Focus point 10.1). Another benchmark in the evolution of snowboarding from a subculture to a mainstream sport was the inclusion of snowboarding in the 1998 Winter Olympic Games.

Focus point 10.1

Snowboarding: From Non-competitive Sport to High Entertainment Drama

The consumption of sport through media involves processes of commodification of sport to enhance its entertainment value to the point that sports may become a branch of show business. The popularity of snowboarding as a participation sport is exceeded by the popularity of snowboarding as consumed through media. Capturing spectator markets, those who do not actively engage in a sport, increases the superficiality of consumption because of spectator demand for sensationalism over subtlety (Heino, 2000). This point is recognised by television producers:

> In 1997, ESPN hosted its first Winter X (eXtreme) Games. They invented a new snowboarding competition for these games titled 'Boarder X'. Instead of just one snowboarder racing down the mountain or being judged on his or her tricks in the half pipe, ESPN put six snow boarders on a course at once. The snowboarders raced up 20-foot side embankments, over bumps; and around sharp curves, and launched off a 40-foot jump at the end. The simultaneous action of six snowboarders getting air, doing tricks, and pushing off each other as they race down the course was quite sensational. It was spontaneous and unpredictable rather than rigid and controlled. The moment everyone recalls from that competition was the act of one snowboarder passing another one in the air while doing a back flip off the forty foot jump. The fairly non-competitive sport of snowboarding, with just the rider, his board, and the mountain, was transformed into high-drama entertainment. (Heino, 2000: 186)

Other emerging issues involve the relationship of these activities to nature. While initially seen as eco-friendly, increasing participation in remote areas is causing environmental stress. At the same time that remote natural areas are under pressure, new urban-based extreme sports such as free running or parkour (the physical practice of traversing urban elements) are becoming popular. More generally, extreme sports tend to be dominated by Western male youth and it will be interesting to see whether this changes significantly in the future.

The evolutionary dynamics of tourism

At a global level, tourism is relatively unique in that it has demonstrated continuous growth with the interplay of domestic and international travel. Butler (2009) has characterised this growth in terms of cycles (e.g. life), waves (e.g. successive cycles) and wheels (cycles within waves) at a destination level. While he cautions that chaos theory suggests that prediction is difficult, he also points out that tourism has continued to grow despite major disruptions such as the Gulf War, terrorist attacks, SARS, bird flu and natural disasters. This resilience appears to be rooted in the high value that people place on their leisure and in the diversity of destinations and activities that characterise the tourism system.

In the context of this overall growth, tourism cycles and waves have a significant influence on the development of sport. For example, over the past two decades, golf has been introduced to many warm climate destinations as a tourism development strategy (Bartoluci & Čavlek, 2000; Priestley, 1995). In the process of this development, opportunities to participate in the sport of golf have been extended to and taken up by local residents. A reciprocal relationship also exists in that tourism provides

> an opportunity for leisure activities to be popularised. With increased popularity they have developed into formally organized sporting activities. Some even progressed from leisure activities to Olympic disciplines. Beach volleyball and snowboarding are two good examples of this. (de Villers, 2001: 13)

Tourism not only introduces sport to new areas but also fosters innovation within sport. Figure 10.1 illustrates that change in sport occurs in recreational and competitive settings, the former being more conducive to major innovation than the latter. Both settings are influenced by external trends associated with the economy, politics, society, technology and the natural environment. Sport innovations often originate from the external environments. Recreational sport tends to be more conducive to innovation because experimentation is encouraged in

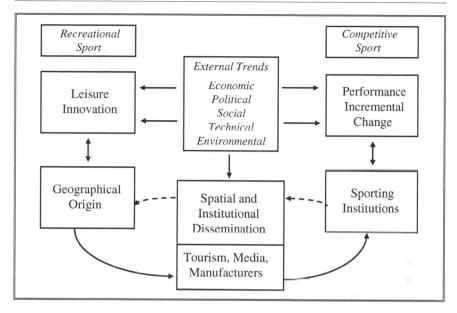

Figure 10.1 Innovation in sport
Source: Adapted from Keller (2001)

most leisure and tourism settings. Keller (2001) argues that the change in location and uninterrupted free time that tourists enjoy while on holiday is conducive to innovation in sport pursuits.

In competitive settings, the focus is on performance in terms of recognised physical skills and rules. These are structured in ways that preclude radical change. Major innovations in recreational sport settings are shaped by leisure patterns that may be unique to specific geographic regions. In contrast to the relatively unconstrained settings in a recreational context, various sporting institutions act as gatekeepers that inhibit change in competitive sport environments. The spatial and institutional dissemination of major innovations and incremental change in sports occurs through the broadcast of entertainment and news programmes by a range of media and by the marketing efforts of sporting goods manufacturers. Tourists also act as significant agents of innovation and dissemination. They introduce new sporting interests to tourist destinations and may, in turn, be exposed to new sports while visiting.

Nostalgia Sport Tourism

Like sport tourism, heritage tourism is recognised as a major category of tourism activity as well as an important realm of academic endeavour

(Timothy & Boyd, 2006). Ramshaw and Gammon (2007) suggest that at the nexus of these realms is the phenomenon of heritage sport tourism. Other authors such as Gibson (1998) have used the somewhat narrower concept of nostalgia-based sport tourism.

Nostalgia sport tourism positions sport heritage as a tourist attraction. It provides tangible evidence of the way that sport life cycles can have a direct impact on tourism in the form of sports halls of fame and museums, high-profile sporting venues and a range of thematic programmes, all of which take on the mantra of tourist attractions in their own right (Delpy, 1998). In general terms, nostalgia '... involves a bittersweet longing for an idealised past which no longer exists' (Goulding, 1999: 2). As such, sport has always been closely associated with nostalgia, perhaps because it connects people to their youth when they were typically more active (Gammon, 2002). Snyder (1991: 229) builds on this idea by suggesting that sport nostalgia can trigger reflections on our own mortality, which often results in an idealisation of the past.

> On the surface it appears that halls and museums attract people because of their fascination with sport, including the idolized figures and memorabilia from the past. But this is only part of the explanation; the attraction may also be based on the contrasts in incongruity between past and present. This juxtaposition of the past with the present creates the context for feelings of nostalgia.

Past sporting experiences may become reference points from which sport-oriented people derive meaning for their lives. This meaning results from both collective and individualised views of the past. In the case of the former, popular media and various sporting institutions celebrate an assortment of sporting victories, events and personalities in a way that impresses them upon the popular consciousness. In the latter case, sport nostalgia is linked to the benchmarks of an individual's sport involvement and identity at different points in his or her life. Fairley and Gammon (2005) point out that this nostalgia is not just focused on sport memorabilia or other tangible manifestations of sport heritage but is, in part, due to the desire to relive a social experience that one may have had related to sport. The combination of collective and individualised nostalgia creates a powerful force that is increasingly being mined by the sport and tourism industries in order to create economic development opportunities.

As could be expected, people of middle age or older are often seen as the primary cohorts for nostalgia-based tourism. Snyder (1991: 238) suggested that for many people sport triggers feelings of longing for the past when they had pleasant experiences associated with sport. This reflection is most evident for the middle-aged and elderly, which have had more sport experiences, but perhaps more important, this is a period of their lives when concern about their own mortality is salient in their self-reflections. Consequently, for those involved in sport, nostalgia may provide a source of consolation and a means of adjustment to the uncertainties of their lives.

Gammon (2002) extends this view by arguing that nostalgia is also of interest to youth as part of a popular culture that draws on the past as a way of establishing 'new' trends.

Sport museums and halls of fame are probably the primary manifestation of nostalgia sport tourism (Redmond, 1991). The first reported example of a sport hall of fame is the National Baseball Hall of Fame located in Cooperstown, NY. It was opened in 1939 and attracts approximately 400,000 visitors per year (Gammon, 2002) with a running total that has surpassed 14 million visitors. The induction of new members is a high profile annual media event in the United States. Clearly, the National Baseball Hall of Fame is a major tourist attraction.

Past, current and, in some cases, future sites (e.g. designated Olympic sites) of sporting events and activities are a second type of nostalgia sport tourism attraction (Bale, 1993b). These sites have an inherent appeal as special places where heroes played and legends were made (Stevens, 2001). Such an aura fosters an emotional nostalgic experience, which focuses on the connection between place and sporting performance. However, tensions between heritage and modernity are common. While modern facilities that enhance the performance of athletes, the spectator experience and revenue opportunities are sought through the development of new facilities, the loss of sporting place identity is recognised as a high price to pay. Elaborate strategies designed to inject the soul of the old facility into its replacement include orchestrated ceremonies involving former athletes who starred in the old facility figuratively or literally, passing the torch to the current generation of athletes in the new facility (Belanger, 2000). Another approach to capturing nostalgia is the inclusion of sport museums and halls of fame in new facilities. For example, the sport museum at FC Barcelona (football stadium) attracts a purported 500,000 visitors a year. Ramshaw's case study of Twickenham Stadium (London) highlights the use of interpretation (including imagery, artefacts, narrative and song) and 'timeless elements' (such as the field of play) as means to projecting continuity between past and present (see Case study 10.1).

Case study 10.1
Coming Home: Twickenham Stadium Tours

Gregory Ramshaw, Clemson University

Background

Notions of home are both powerful and widespread in sport. The birthplace of a particular sport or world-renowned athlete could be considered a type of sporting 'home.' However, the most obvious representation of home is that of the sports stadium or arena. Bale (2000) describes the home stadium as the 'focal point for location pride and awareness and a source of dynamic geographic memories' (p. 92) and, as such, visiting the home venue of a favourite team or the home stadium of a world-renowned franchise can be a powerful tourism experience. While many tourists will plan their holidays to coincide with seeing a match at a particular venue, they often desire a deeper familiarity with a home venue than experienced during an event. They seek to cross the boundary between front and back stages and see parts of the stadium not normally accessible to the general public (Gammon & Fear, 2007; Ramshaw & Gammon, 2010). Fans also face travel constraints and may only be able to 'visit' their teams on non-match days and out of season. From the host franchise perspective, fostering facility-based revenue streams on non-game days is an attractive strategy. Such initiatives include selling souvenirs and tickets year-round, exposing visitors to other consumption opportunities at the venue (such as sections of the stadium available for rental for business meetings and social gatherings) and, more generally, solidifying their fan base. As such, many sports organisations and franchises offer stadium tours.

Stadium tours vary between venues, but normally feature visits to the dressing room area, the luxury suites and media areas, and views from beside (though, rarely on) the playing surface. Certain areas of stadiums may be included on tours, depending on the type of sport played at the stadium or various historical associations or moments that occurred at the venue. Tours are also often combined with other tourism infrastructure, such as a team museum, gift shop and cafe, creating a rich retail experience for the visitor. However, these rather benign elements of the stadium tour will often combine to reveal broader heritage constructions, often with very specific economic or cultural aims. Such is the case with the tours of Twickenham Stadium, home venue for England Rugby, where the venue is constructed as 'home' in three different ways: as the literal home of the English national team, as the spiritual home of the sport both domestically and internationally and as the home of a particular traditional manifestation of England and Englishness.

Home of the National Team

Twickenham Stadium tours emphasise the venue as the home of the national team, not just the current squad but of all England teams for all time. By highlighting continuity, visitors can still enjoy the tour even if they do not have the knowledge of recent team performance or current players. However, should visitors actively follow the current squad, the tour can provide an authentic and intimate sporting experience. Tour narratives emphasise continuity by highlighting the 'timeless' elements of the stadium, in particular the pitch, as tangible legacies between past and present. Guides rarely discuss particular players or matches, allowing visitors to interpret the spaces using their own memories and experiences. Creating a timeless narrative and highlighting continuity, the tours solidify the stadium as the true and authentic home of England Rugby, regardless of era, while also assuring continued economic support (e.g. through tour admissions and gift shop purchases) regardless of the fortunes of the current squad.

Spiritual Home of Rugby

Twickenham Stadium tours construct the venue as the 'keepers of the flame' for rugby, both in England and for the sport internationally. Tour narratives actively dispute the 'Webb Ellis Myth' of rugby's invention and rather describe the formation and role of the Rugby Football Union (who own and operate Twickenham Stadium) in the codification of the sport. Many of the artefacts displayed during the tour, especially the infamous Roses Match painting, further re-enforce Twickenham Stadium as the 'true' home of the sport in England. Tour promotions also recognise that the venue is globally significant as well by enticing fans from around the world to visit the sport's most famous venue. Furthermore, tour narratives explicitly describe the norms and values of rugby spectatorship, especially the camaraderie between fans of all stripes, implying that Twickenham Stadium both maintains and protects these rugby traditions. These tour narratives not only help to establish Twickenham as the authentic home of the sport nationally and internationally but also help to position a venue as significant and, therefore, worthy of visitation.

Home of Traditional 'Englishness'

Twickenham Stadium tours espouse particular forms of English identity. Firstly, they emphasise romanticised notions of Englishness. The tour spends much time in the sections of the stadium that reflect

Part 4: Sport Tourism Development and Time

the sport's public school roots, such as in the wood-panelled Council room and the English Rose-adorned President's Suite. Tour narratives also discuss at length the patronage of the Royal Family, the role of national symbols such as the St. George's Cross and hymns such as *Jerusalem* in English rugby tradition, and the sport's heritage of upper-class amateurism. Secondly, tour narratives also, in a sense, welcome visitors from Britain's former colonies 'home' to England through the description of artefacts, such as a Springbok head from South Africa and a poster from England's 2003 World Cup victory versus Australia that features the title 'The Empire Strikes Back', which help to re-enforce a past colonial relationship. By espousing a traditional 'chocolate-box' forms of Englishness, the tour can compete with other stadium tours in the London area, most notably Wimbledon and Lord's, which also present a similar brand of national identity. Similarly, positioning Twickenham Stadium as focal point for rugby-playing nations may help attract visitors whose relationship to the 'Homeland' is through sport.

A Future for Home?

Stadium tours are an important aspect of the sport tourism landscape (Ramshaw & Gammon, 2007). They offer dedicated fans and curious spectators alike the opportunity to see behind the scenes at a world-famous venue, while also providing sport organisations and franchises a mechanism to use their venue year-round as well as provide a new outlet for sales of tickets, merchandise, corporate hospitality and catering. In this, Twickenham Stadium is no different, as it is clearly an important and unique tourist attraction. Through the construction of various 'home' narratives through the stadium tour, Twickenham also reveals the role these venues play in creating and maintaining identity, particularly in the face of change. Home represents a form of stability, continuity and conservatism, and tours of Twickenham Stadium reassure and reaffirm that the 'Home of Rugby,' and all that it represents, will carry on. However, home narratives can also be inflexible, myopic and hostile to change, and stadium tours must attempt to be both flexible and adaptable in order to address future cultural and economic challenges (Ramshaw & Gammon, 2010).

Literature cited in this case study is included in the list of references at the end of this book.

Fantasy sport programmes are a third and particularly intriguing variation of nostalgia sport tourism. They range from mock training camps to themed cruises, restaurants and bars. However, one of the most exciting variants of this type of programme is the sport fantasy camp where

> for a mere few thousand dollars, fans can spend a week, or a weekend, training with and finally competing against the legends of the game. The allure of being that close to one's heroes is so powerful that these camps have taken off in popularity. (Schlossberg, 1996: 110)

Gammon (2002) suggests that there are five main motivations to travel to these camps as reflected in promotional literature:

(1) the desire to be associated with a famous event;
(2) the opportunity to train in a famous or meaningful facility;
(3) to increase identification with a particular team or club;
(4) to be closely associated with sporting heroes; and
(5) general interest in the sport and in skill development.

For the nostalgia sport tourist, these camps enable participants to escape from the routine of their day-to-day existence. They provide nostalgia sport tourists with the opportunity to relive or recreate their sporting histories (Focus point 10.2).

Focus point 10.2
Wayne Gretzky's Fantasy Camp

Fantasy camps provide sport fans the opportunity to 'take ambrosia with the gods' (Gammon, 2002). For participants of ice hockey legend Wayne Gretzky's Fantasy Camp, this is clearly a big part of the experience. Video testimonials on the official website repeatedly refer to the personal contact that participants have with Gretzky and other hockey greats including numerous Hall-of-Fame inductees. In one testimonial, a camper recounts his first shift on the ice with Gretzky and Russ Courtnall as his line mates. The shift ended with the 'happy camper' scoring a goal set up by his hockey heroes and a highlight reel in which he was one of the stars, indelibly etched in his memory. In addition to the on-ice sessions, a range of off-ice sessions are scheduled including poker nights with the 'boys'. This opportunity to rub shoulders with one's sporting heroes is truly a dream come true for many middle age hockey fanatics who can afford to pay the rather hefty price of admission. At one point the price was US$9999 for the week-long camp, which was a nice play on Gretzky's former jersey number of 99. Inflation has somewhat muted this play on numbers with Fantasy Camp IX in 2001 at the Bellagio Hotel and Resort in Las Vegas priced at US$10,999. Eleven thousand dollars is not cheap, but its good value for many middle age hockey fanatics taking 'ambrosia with the [hockey] gods'.

Source: http:/www.gretzky.com/fantasycamp. Accessed 25 November 2010.

Major Trends Affecting Sport Tourism

Strategic planning is a critical aspect of sport tourism development, albeit one that is fraught with challenge. Few phenomena are more problematic in forecasting than trends in sport and tourism, both of which are ultimately discretionary activities. Trend analysis does, however, provide general insights into probable future scenarios in sport and tourism demand.

Various predictions have been made about sport tourism. Most foresee continued growth in demand for sport and tourism experiences (Delpy, 2001; Getz, 1998; Standeven & de Knop, 1999; Turco *et al.*, 2002). However, this growth is unlikely to take the form of a simple linear extension of existing sport tourist participation patterns. Table 10.1 summarises trends in sport that are currently affecting sport tourism. Bourdeau *et al.* (2002) see the underlying trend in sport as one of diversification with a shift towards individual sports. New sporting opportunities will continue to emerge in urban settings, but peripheral areas will also grow in stature as sport places of uncertainty and risk.

These trends are themselves rooted in more general tendencies in the broader context in which sport and tourism exist. Economic, environmental (Chapter 7), political, societal and technological trends form the context for participation in both sport (Collins, 1991) and tourism (Dwyer *et al.*, 2008; Hall, 1995).

Economic trends

Rising income is the greatest generator of tourist flows and conversely falling income is one of the most powerful retardants to growth (Dwyer *et al.*, 2008). Economic surges and downturns will be reflected in sport tourism activity. Positive economic factors for tourism include deregulation, increased trade, improved information technology and dynamic private sectors, while negative factors include cyclical economic downturns, protectionist trading practices and large disparities in growth and development between countries and regions.

Globalisation is perhaps the most dominant economic trend that has emerged from the latter part of the 20th century (Chapter 4; Higham & Hinch, 2009). It has exerted increased pressure for the commodification

Table 10.1 Key trends in sport

Trend	Description
1. The increasing development of individual sports as opposed to collective sports.	This view is consistent with a societal change in mentality towards 'neo-individualism' and personal development. Participants may gravitate towards other individuals who share their sporting passion, but this will likely be done outside of the traditional sporting institutions.
2. Diversification of sports participation models.	People will generally be willing to try a broader range of sport activities than they have in the past. Similarly, sport disciplines will tend to open up their membership to a wider spectrum of participants.
3. Exaggerated segmentation of sports disciplines.	An increasing variety of sport hybrids and specialisations will emerge as new sporting experiences are sought.
4. Adaptation of sports activities to the constraints of urban life.	The experiences associated with outdoor adventure sports will be simulated in the city where it is accessible to urbanites constrained by time from pursuing these activities in natural settings. A recent example is the emergence of indoor climbing facilities in urban areas.
5. Development of a mythology of adventure in a natural environment.	Natural environments will grow in significance in real and symbolic terms as places where sport tourists confront uncertainty, risk and destiny.

Source: Adapted from Bourdeau *et al.* (2002)

of sport and tourism. Of particular significance is the tendency towards the convergence of tourism, leisure, sport and entertainment. This is especially true of elite organised sport where the trend toward professionalism and 'show business' is already evident (de Villers, 2001; Keller, 2001).

The media plays an important role in this process. Popular media has had a long association with sport inclusive of the golden ages of newspapers, radio and television. It is the last of these forms of media, however, that is perceived as having the greatest impact on elite sport (McKay & Kirk, 1992). From the outset, the television broadcasting of sport generated concern that fans would stop going to the actual competition in favour of viewing sports from the comfort of their homes. At the root of this concern was the belief that sport revenues would shift from traditional sporting institutions to the broadcasters.

> The economics of sport were founded on the principle of persuading large numbers of people to leave their homes, to travel to enclosed sporting venues and to pay for entry in order to view professional performers engage in various forms of structured, physical competition. (Rowe, 1996: 569)

History has shown that broadcasters have indeed enjoyed substantial financial rewards, but they have also generated significant financial benefits for owners and administrators of televised sports as well as the destinations where these sports take place. Television revenues for professional sport now far exceed gate revenues. Despite this changing economic context, there are still concerns that the media has subverted sport for its own purposes, and by doing so, it has eroded the integrity of these sports. For example, Rowe (1996: 573) noted that

> [t]elevision has progressively exerted pressure on sports to be played at times convenient to broadcast schedules and to modify rules in order to guarantee results, to prevent events going too far 'over time', and to overcome any dull passages that might tempt viewers to reach for the dial (later the remote control). The global spread of sports television has created its own severe pressures on sport by, for example, demanding that wherever possible 'live' sports should be transmitted at a time convenient for the largest and most lucrative TV markets.

Interactive technology in the form of pay-per-view television, the Internet and video games presents substantial challenges for sport tourism. Some authors have speculated that the increasingly interactive experience of watching sport from the comfort of home may eventually result in the need to pay spectators to attend televised games in order to create an exciting atmosphere in the sporting venue (Johnson, 1991). The overall benefits of the on-site experience for sport tourists must clearly exceed the costs associated with the trip. It is also important for sport tourism managers to advocate the retention of the things that make sport unique. While pure entertainment can be a very powerful tourist attraction, sport as entertainment is unique. The inherent authenticity of sport provides a competitive advantage to many tourism destinations that may be lost if the nature of the activity shifts to staged entertainment.

The influential role of the media is not limited to mainstream sports. Subculture sports can also be closely tied to the media. In today's postmodern society '... the specialized press ... plays a fundamental role in initiating participants to techniques, equipment, cultural codes and languages which lay the foundations for the identity of the sports "tribes" ' (Bourdeau *et al.*, 2002: 27). This media is, therefore, of particular interest to sport tourism managers as it influences where subculture members travel in pursuit of their sporting passions.

Environmental trends

The long-term interaction of sport and tourism will be strongly influenced by environmental trends. Chapter 7 articulates the fundamental place of the environment and issues of sustainability in the context of sport tourism development. While there are many environmental trends of relevance, climatic change is especially important (Case study 9.1). Climatic change refers to shifts in the long-term patterns of temperature, precipitation and atmospheric conditions. While there remains much political debate about its measurement, causes and implications, there is widespread recognition of its existence and concern for its implications in the scientific realm. Climatic change has received an increasing level of attention by academics working in the area of tourism (Hall & Higham, 2005). The bulk of this work has concentrated in the implications of climatic change on projected visitor flows and the distribution of impacts. More recent consideration has been given to the role of tourism as a causal factor in the process of this change.

Studies of the impact of climatic change on the level and distribution of tourist arrivals and expenditures are generally based on modelling. Projections are made about changing climatic conditions and then translated into maps of shifting distributions of tourist arrivals as tourists seek out their preferred climatic conditions. It has been noted that there will be both winners and losers as a result of this redistribution given that in some locations conditions will improve while in others they will be less attractive (Hein *et al.*, 2009; Iordache & Cebuc, 2009). While tourism in general is subject to these shifts, tourism related to winter- and summer-based sporting activities is seen as being particularly sensitive to these changes (Dodds & Graci, 2009; Nicholls, 2006). This is particularly the case in terms of the ski industry with its dependence on snow. Moen and Fredman (2007) predict a decrease in the number and the expenditures of skiers to existing ski resorts in Sweden as snow accumulations decrease. Scott and McBoyle (2007) recognise similar challenges facing the ski industry elsewhere but note that these impacts can be moderated by strategic responses in terms of demand and supply. On the demand side, the response to changing climatic conditions can be moderated by improved weather forecasting and reporting along with an assortment of constraint negotiation strategies that skiers can implement (e.g. altering the timing of their ski vacations). On the supply side, a suite of technological practices can also be used to moderate the impact of changing natural snow conditions. These include (1) the use of snowmaking equipment, (2) improved ski slope landscaping and operational practices and (3) cloud seeding. Business strategies include (1) the development of ski conglomerates, (2) revenue diversification and (3) modified marketing practices. A more radical but already existing alternative is the construction of indoor ski facilities.

Tourism is also increasingly being recognised as a significant contributing factor to climatic change, with approximately 4%–6% of all of the world's carbon dioxide emissions estimated to accrue from tourism activities (Dodds & Graci, 2009). Approximately 70%–75% of this total is attributed to the transport sector, with the balance coming from the accommodation, food and beverage and the attraction sectors (Iordache & Cebuc, 2009). The tourism industry is, therefore, in a position to reduce carbon dioxide emissions proactively or to be targeted by regulatory agencies, thereby forcing a reactive response. In their exploratory study of the 2010 FIFA World Cup, Otto and Heath (2009) found that hosting a mega event such as the World Cup increased the level of awareness of tourism and sport stakeholders on the impact of their activities on climatic change. This consciousness led to concrete strategies and initiatives designed to reduce carbon dioxide emissions during the event and in subsequent activities.

Political trends

Political stability is a precondition of intensive tourism development (Dwyer _et al._, 2008). The United States and Europe are likely to remain very influential in global politics but face growing competition from China, India and Russia as these economies grow. Non-state actors (e.g. terrorists) pushing their own agendas will become increasingly vigorous, likely leading to spatial and temporal disruptions to sport tourism activity. Increasing disparities between have and have not countries will continue to impact the flow and distribution of sport-based tourism.

Changing balances of power and influence drive political trends. The emergence of free trade agendas highlights changing power configurations throughout the world. The economic benefits of free trade are unlikely to be evenly distributed. Hall (2000b: 88) predicts that there will be

> increased conflict between developing and developed countries over global economic development strategies as it becomes apparent to large numbers of the population in developing countries that they will never be able to have western lifestyles due to population and resource constraints.

The repercussions of such sentiments and other political grievances are already being felt in terms of protest activities that have direct impacts on tourism and sport.

Terrorism is not a new challenge in tourism (Hall, 2000b; Sonmez *et al.*, 1999), nor is it alien to sport (Wedemeyer, 1999). Perhaps the most notable terrorism incident in a sport tourism context was the fatal attack on Israeli athletes at the Munich (1972) Olympic Village (Wedemeyer, 1999). Yet despite the high profile of sporting events as terrorist targets, there have been surprisingly few politically motivated attacks on sport. Indeed, it has been suggested that sport tourism was one of the more resilient types of tourism in the aftermath of the terrorist attacks in America on 11 September 2001 (World Tourism Organization, 2001).

The most obvious implication of this is that major sporting events are going to require high levels of security. In the case of the Vancouver 2010 Winter Olympics, these security cost rose from an estimated $150 million in 2003 to $900 million by the end of the games (Reuters, 2010). Not only will such high costs make hosting some of these events prohibitive for many cities, it may also lead to an increase in preference for off-site spectatorship over on-site consumption if spectators feel at risk. Active sports characterised by dispersed spatial patterns of participation may increase in popularity relative to major event sport tourism. Similarly, nostalgic tourism may increase as traditional patterns of event sport tourism consumption are altered.

Socio-demographic trends

Socio-demographic trends are also likely to exert considerable influence over the future of sport tourism (Delpy Neirotti, 2001). Dwyer *et al.* (2008: viii) suggest that '[t]ourists are increasingly interested in discovering, experiencing, participating in, learning about and more intimately being included in the everyday life of the destinations that they visit'. Sport offers a mechanism for meeting this desire. In terms of specific demographic trends, immigration has resulted in changing sport activity patterns. This has presented a challenge to sport tourism activities such as ski industry in Canada where Asian immigrants are much less likely to patronise ski resorts than of residents of Anglo Saxon descent (Hudson *et al.*, 2010). Similar challenges exist in terms of ageing populations in North America.

> People born between 1946 and 1964 make up almost a third of the North American population and they started switching to more gentle winter sports such as snowshoeing and cross-country skiing, because their aging bodies could no longer handle the rigours of alpine runs. High-tech computer designed skis and equipment, which make it safer and easier for even aging outdoor lovers to

learn or continue to enjoy the sport, have halted that trend somewhat in recent years. (Loverseed, 2000: 53)

In the face of this trend, sport tourism operators have to adjust their products to match the needs of their markets. This adjustment will involve a shift from hard adventure activities to less physically demanding soft adventure outdoor sport activities. An ageing population will likely become more health conscious and, therefore, seek sport activities that will help them to retain and perhaps regain their health rather than put it at risk.

The shift from a modern to a postmodern society is also mediating the context of sport tourism. At one level, this shift has its economic roots in the rejection of the welfare state and regulated markets in favour of competition, free trade and globalisation (Coalter, 1999; Dwyer *et al.*, 2008; Merkel *et al.*, 1998; Stewart & Smith, 2000). Niche markets, individualism, flexibility, time fragmentation, new technologies, innovative communication networks and commercialisation all characterise today's society. The role of place in postmodern sport is also changing. Local tribal loyalties based on the 'home team' have tended to be replaced by attachments to corporate identities or brands. Table 10.2 summarises the changing face of organised sport from the modern to the postmodern era.

Murray and Dixon (2000) have argued that the emergence of 'instant sports' is the result of the shift from modernity to postmodernity. This is consistent with the emphasis on consumer orientations over citizenship orientations and on unstructured over structured sports in Western society.

Technological trends

Technological innovations have irrevocably changed the face of sport and tourism. They have improved sporting performances and enriched tourism experiences. Moreover, technology has further blurred the line between sport and tourism. For example, the development of the Internet has resulted in the creation of a multitude of sport related websites that vary from the static provision of basic information about a sport to interactive sport sites that can form the basis of a leisure experience in their own right (Jackson, 1999). Dwyer *et al.* (2008) identify advances in information and communication technology as having the most important implications for tourism. Fundamentally, they argue that advances in this realm 'provide businesses with the tools to respond to individual preferences and to stimulate tourism purchases' (p. x). A good example of the power of this new technology is the growing role of social networking in the decision-making of travellers (Xiang & Gretzel, 2010).

Table 10.2 A comparison of modern and postmodern sport

Dimension/ component	Modern sport	Postmodern sport
Game structure	Rules are sacred	Rule modification and experimentation
Team leadership	Conservative	Adventurous
Values and customs	Amateurism, respect for authority, character building	Professionalism, innovation
Organisation and management	Central control	Diffusion of authority
Financial structure	Gate receipts	Sponsorship, television rights, gate receipts, sport as business
Venues and facilities	Basic seating at stadia	Customised seating, video support
Promotion	Limited	Extensive
Viewing	Live match attendance	TV audiences dominate
Spectator preference	Display of traditional craft	Eclectic blend of entertainment
Fan loyalties	Singular and parochial loyalty	Multiple loyalties – all spatial scales
The sports market	Undifferentiated mass market	Fragmented and niche markets
Coaching and training	Rigid, repetitive practices	Blend of science and naturalistic practices – variety

Source: Adapted from Stewart and Smith (2000)

At a more fundamental level, virtual reality and cyberspace technology is having direct impacts on the way people experience leisure (Basset & Wilbert, 1999). The extent to which sport experiences in cyberspace can substitute for sport experience in real space remains a matter of speculation. Current examples of sport experiences that take place in cyberspace include live online sports commentaries, sports gambling online, real-time viewer surveys during sport broadcasts, and instant progress updates and live digital video images of sports contests. On another level, many computer games conform closely to definitions of sport (Chapter 2) inclusive of a physical activity component. For example, the Wii video game console released by Nintendo in 2006 incorporated a hand-held pointing device that detected movement in three directions, thereby facilitating the development of a range of physically interactive video games. While the physical activity component of these games is relatively basic at this point, there is no doubt that it will become increasingly more sophisticated as the virtual reality aspect of computer technology advance. Similarly, advances in broadcast technology have seen the emergence of off-site 'fan fests' where big screen broadcasts of the sporting events may actually rival spectator numbers at the site of the competition. This trend has led Weed (2010) to question whether basic assumptions that have been traditionally held related to sport travel motivations are still valid.

Past technological advances in transportation have played a key role in tourism development and they are likely to continue to do so. The anticipated introduction of a new generation long haul, wide bodied and multiple level jet aircraft will increase access and reinforce 'hub and spoke' transportation patterns (Hall, 2000b). Continued advances in space travel will result in increased access to weightless environments, which may spawn a whole new generation of sport activities (Focus point 10.3). Similar developments in marine environments are likely to present dramatic new opportunities for sport tourism in that realm.

Focus point 10.3
Sky Diving Wind Tunnel

Have you ever had the superman dream of independent flight? Outside of a small elite who have had the privilege of experiencing weightlessness in outer space, few of us have ever had these independent flight fantasies come to realisation. Increasingly, however adventurous souls are participating in the extreme sport trends ranging from hang gliding through to base jumping. A novel variation of these activities has recently emerged in the form of vertical wind tunnel flying.

> Extreme Sports Cafe's partner Wind Tunnel is located just outside Kuala Lumpur in Malaysia and is the one and only wind tunnel in Asia! It is a state of the art skydiving wind tunnel that gives ordinary people the chance to feel the thrill and sensation of jumping out of an airplane and freefalling through the sky just like a skydiver. Only 15km northeast of KL and easily accessible by road. It takes roughly 45min to get there from KL. The Wind Tunnel is an attraction ride that is part of an indoor 'future' theme park; so there is plenty to do for friends or family members who may accompany you on the trip … that is if they don't fancy some body flight!

> Is this sport or is it a new variation of an amusement ride? Opinion may be divided but the argument for sport is strengthened by the fact that these facilities are used by skydivers as training sites. It is not difficult to see them following the trend of indoor climbing walls which were initially viewed as training grounds for 'real' rock climbing in the outdoors. It did not take long for these indoor climbing facilities to take on a life of their own with unique sport subcultures and competitions soon emerging. A similar potential exists in terms of vertical wind tunnels and the sport of 'body flight'.
>
> *Source*: http://www.extremesportscafe.com/brochure/content/skydiving-wind-tunnel. Accessed 17 April 2011.

Recently, various environmentally controlled sport facilities have been built like the Skydome in Toronto with its retractable roof. This trend goes beyond major spectator sports to sporting activities that were once the exclusive domain of the outdoors and wilderness areas.

Sports-oriented theme parks are all the rage with free climbing, water slides, hydrospeeding, golf training or skateboarding. In the United Kingdom and the Netherlands there are ski domes where beginners can test their ability at skiing and experienced skiers can get into shape before the season starts. ... Generally speaking leisure parks and theme parks do not rely on any [natural] landscape. They are in fact genuine industrial zones for sport-related enjoyment. (Keller, 2001: 15)

These facilities tend to be constructed in urban areas where participants have easy access in terms of time (i.e. they can ski after work on a week day) and in terms of space (i.e. they can participate in their preferred sporting activity close to home) (Chapter 5). If these urban-based artificial sporting environments were perfect substitutes for the same activities in natural settings, then it is logical to predict that there would be fewer visits to peripheral areas. In reality, these artificial environments are not exact substitutes. They may in fact serve as demand shifters in that more people will be introduced to the sport and may eventually seek out traditional activity sites. In the foreseeable future, the original natural settings are likely to remain the preferred location for the vast majority of participants.

Conclusion

The long-term time horizon is characterised by the interaction of the respective life cycles found in sport and tourism. It is evident that sport can influence the nature and pace of tourism destination life cycles and that tourism can have similar impacts on sport life cycles. The conscious manipulation of these forces offers a powerful tool for pursuing sustainable development strategies.

Sport and tourism are very dynamic in the long term. A significant manifestation of this dynamic is nostalgia sport tourism in which tourists seek out the past by visiting places infused with sport heritage and participating in programmes that bring the past to life. The sport tourism industry has only recently started to appreciate the breadth of products that are of interest to these tourists. Sport tourism nostalgia offers the opportunity for sport tourists to become time travellers if only in their imaginations.

Finally, sport tourism does not operate in a vacuum. There are various trends in the economic, environmental, political, socio-demographic and technological realms that may have a direct and, in some cases, an overbearing influence on sport tourism. By studying trends that exist within the external environment, sport tourism managers will be in a better position to set sustainable sport tourism development goals and objectives and to develop effective plans of action.

Part 5

Conclusions

Chapter 11
Reflections and Conclusions

Introduction

The study of sport tourism development provides varied and important insights into the ways in which sport tourism has changed, and continues to change, across space and time. In this book, Chapters 1 through 10 may be read as a series of purposely positioned essays on related themes of sport tourism development. Each one attempts to contribute to an understanding of the particular theme or topic that it addresses. Chapter 1 raises three basic questions: 'What makes sport unique as a focus for tourism development?' 'How is sport tourism manifest in space?' and 'How do these manifestations change over time?' In addressing these questions, the objective of this book is to build understandings of sport tourism development. This chapter revisits these questions and reflects upon the relationship between sport and tourism development.

Foundations for Sport Tourism Development

The study of sport tourism development requires a foundation that includes (1) an underlying framework highlighting the relationship between sport and tourism, (2) an appreciation of sport tourism markets and (3) an understanding of fundamental development concepts and issues. In this book, sport tourism is conceptualised as sport-based travel away from the home environment for a limited time where sport is characterised by unique rule sets, competition related to physical prowess and a playful nature. From this perspective, sport is viewed as a tourist attraction. By consciously treating sport as a unique type of tourist attraction, readers are able to better understand the nature of sport as it relates specifically to tourism development. This perspective is based on a substantive body of literature. Case study 2.1 outlines the development over the last five years of the *Journal of Sport & Tourism* as one manifestation of significant academic progress in this field of scholarship. The nature of sport tourism markets must also be appreciated. Sport tourism not only is a specialised segment of the tourism market but is, in fact, also composed of highly specialised and fragmented niche markets. The nature of these niche markets varies in terms of intensity, types of involvement in sports (e.g. event, active and nostalgia) and types of sport. Not only do the motivations, needs and

215

general socio-demographic characteristics differ for each niche but so too do travel behaviours and destination impacts. The emergence of dragon boat festivals presents an insightful example (Case study 3.1) of the development of new sport tourism markets in North America.

Three key development issues are explored in this book. The first relates to commodification and authenticity. Tourism is just one of the forces that are commodifying sport, but it is an important one. A key advantage of sport as a tourist attraction is its propensity for authenticity. This is found in its uncertain outcomes, display as part of performance, its physical basis and all-sensory nature, self-making and the construction of identity, and its tendency to develop community. Sport provides visitors with access to the 'back stage' of a destination.

Globalisation is a second key issue in the context of sport tourism development. Sport is a high-profile manifestation of globalisation, featuring professional leagues that increasingly cross borders and recruit players from a global pool. Sports such as football (soccer) are global phenomena, yet there remain important distinctions in the way the game is played in different parts of the world. These differences represent opportunities for sport tourism development. In such cases, sport contributes to the unique regional character of a place, thereby providing a competitive tourism advantage. Major sport events such as the Beijing Olympics (Case study 4.1) are increasingly being used to position host cities and countries in a global marketplace.

Strategic alliances and partnerships in sport tourism address the third development issue – that of fragmentation. Attempts to overcome the problem of fragmentation through the creation of sport tourism alliances have been encouraging. Continued articulation of the benefits of cooperation is required. If these benefits cannot be demonstrated, it is unlikely that the various stakeholders in sport tourism, including sport event organisers and promoters, sport associations, managers of sporting venues, destination managers and tourism marketers, will work in a cooperative fashion.

Sport Tourism Development and Space

The study of the locations and travel flows associated with sports, the way sport infuses space with meaning to create unique tourism places and the resource requirements and impacts of sport tourism are all key themes within the spatial analysis of sport tourism development. Central place theory is a particularly useful tool to explain the locational tendencies of urban sport facilities, events and professional sport teams. Sports that require the construction of major indoor facilities or that depend upon high numbers of spectators or participants will gravitate towards the larger centres. This is especially true of commercial sports. The challenge for sport and tourism managers in these locations is to maximise the synergies that are inherent in existing transportation networks, accommodation, food and beverage facilities, and other elements of urban infrastructure. The redevelopment of Melbourne Park (Case study 5.1) offers an excellent example of an investment strategy designed to protect Melbourne's advantage as a globally prominent centre for sport and sport events.

Sport tourism in peripheral areas is characterised by quite different spatial dynamics. Rather than development being driven by the location of the market, it tends to be driven by the location of the resource. The distinguishing feature in most cases is that the sporting activity is dependent on natural resources that are not normally found in or adjacent to urban areas. The planning and development of peripheral sport locations present the challenges of relative isolation and much lower levels of available infrastructure. Significant competitive advantages can be achieved where sport tourism developments in peripheral areas are clustered so as to allow the concentrated development of tourism infrastructure and services.

Place is described in this book as space with meaning. It is especially attractive to tourism marketers who use sport to sell destinations. Hosts and visitors develop attachment to these places based on a combination of their dependence on the attributes found at the place and the extent to which place contributes to their identity. Case study 6.1 demonstrates that place attachment occurs across the spectrum of outdoor and indoor climbing sites. The spectre of homogenised sportscapes threatens tourism, as it contributes to a breakdown of distinctive regional place meaning based on sport. It is, therefore, important to be proactive in the retention of unique regional meanings and identities associated with sporting facilities and activities. Tourism interests should support the efforts of sport managers who defend the 'integrity' of their sports. There should also be consistency between the images used to promote a sport tourism destination and the images that residents have of their home. Conflicting views of place may result in conflicting attitudes and behaviours.

The environment and, more particularly, regional landscapes and resources are important elements of sport tourism development. Urban-based sport tourism is often connected to the cultural landscape while sport tourism activity in the periphery tends to be connected to natural landscapes. Large-scale sport events are typical of the urban context, and it is usually the scale of urban sport events that determines the range and extent of the associated impacts. Sport tourism in peripheral areas often requires substantial alteration of the physical landscape. Case study 7.1 provided an example of this with the development of Sipadan Island, Malaysia, as a globally recognised scuba diving site. In the initial enthusiasm to develop this diving site, the very resource on which the attraction was based was severely compromised in the short-term interests of development. Development controls have since been implemented with initial indicators suggesting that the resource and the industry are recovering.

The requirement that Olympic organising committees articulate and implement an environmental protection policy represents a significant shift in the approach to planning large-scale events. With the continued pressure of environmental and social advocacy groups, it is likely that this shift will be echoed in social and cultural environments. Sport tourism developers not only have an ethical obligation to be proactive in this regard but also have an economic and professional interest. Tourism revenues depend on the maintenance of the resources upon which the attraction is built and upon the hospitality of the hosts.

Sport Tourism Development and Time

The temporal dimensions of sport tourism include the experience of sport tourists during their travels, seasonal variations in sport and tourism activities, and long-term evolutionary dynamics. The sport tourism experience takes place in several phases including anticipation, travel to the destination, on-site experience, return travel and recollection. Generalisations about on-site experiences are difficult as it is clear that these experiences vary substantially between specific market segments. Nevertheless, Case study 8.1 examines the British and Irish Lions rugby union tour of South Africa in terms of the large groups of fans following the tour from the United Kingdom. In addition to the growing popularity of such tours, there appears to be a trend to independent travel along with the more common group travel options which currently dominate. The extent to which sport tourists engage in other types of tourist activities in the destination is influenced by two key factors: The first is the travel profile of the tourist, including the distance travelled, mode of transportation and length of stay. The nature of the sporting activity, including scheduling, sporting role (e.g. athlete and spectator), performance, level of competition and the outcome of the competition also influence the propensity of sport tourists to engage in other tourist activities. Essentially, these types of characteristics determine or reflect the extent to which the sport tourist is interested and, indeed, able to partake in other types of tourism activities. Sport tourism developers should, therefore, develop detailed profiles of market segments rather than generalise about the motivations and behaviours of sport tourists as a whole.

Seasonal patterns in sport and tourism represent a distinct temporal dimension of sport tourism development. Tourism managers have typically seen seasonal variation in visitor numbers as a problem due to underutilised capacity and decreased revenue flows during the low season. From a tourism management perspective, sport has been used as a strategy to influence seasonality with considerable success. The scheduling of sporting events during the shoulder tourism seasons is an increasingly prominent aspect of event production and planning. In terms of active sport tourism, destinations that are characterised by specialised resources available during the off-season can be particularly attractive to sport subculture groups. Similarly, nostalgia sport tourism attractions remain functional outside the main tourism seasons. If properly promoted, they too offer the opportunity to alter seasonal patterns of visitation to a destination. Climate change is having a significant impact on the seasonality of sport tourism. Despite evidence to confirm changing seasonal patterns, Case study 9.1 suggests that ski resort managers in Scotland have been optimistic about the future and have been slow to develop strategies to address likely changes in seasonality.

Tourism destination cycles as well as sport life cycles offer valuable theoretical insight into the long-term evolution of sport and tourism. As sports progress through their life cycles, they impact the destinations where they take place. For example, evolving trends in alpine skiing have a direct impact on alpine resort developments. Fortunately for these resorts, declining participation in downhill skiing has been offset by the emergence of snowboarding and other new alpine sports. Sport life cycles are also influenced by tourism. Leisure-based activities such as windsurfing are popular tourist activities, which have become serious competitive sports that have been disseminated throughout the world.

Nostalgia sport tourism demonstrates how the evolution of sport can have a direct impact on tourism. Sport nostalgia is, in part, a reaction to a rapidly changing society. It is not only a chance for tourists to revisit their youth but an opportunity to escape back into what is often considered a simpler time. These temporal journeys are facilitated by spatial journeys as tourist seek out sports halls of fame, sites of historic sporting moments and fantasy programmes that enable participants to recreate or relive history. Case study 10.1 provides specific insights into one such journey for Rugby Union enthusiasts who are able to visit the 'home' of rugby via tours of Twickenham Stadium.

More generally, there are various macro-level trends that will influence the future of sport tourism. Globalisation processes appear to underlie the majority of these trends. Dynamic economic, environmental, political, socio-demographic and technological realms present opportunities as well as challenges for sport tourism development. Not only is each of these realms characterised by changing characteristics, but these characteristics interact with those found in the other realms, making cause–effect relationships difficult to identify, let alone predict. As challenging as this exercise may be, the ability to influence sport tourism development depends on an understanding of the cause–effect relationships that characterise this activity.

Sport Tourism Development Principles

At a basic level, the contribution of the second edition of *Sport Tourism Development* is best considered in the context of two closely related areas: research and practice. In terms of research, the underlying argument presented is that understanding why sport and tourism interact in the way that they do is a prerequisite for influencing development in a controlled manner. Such understanding requires the support of theory and empirical evidence.

While it is beneficial to know what has happened in the context of sport tourism development, it is much more useful to know how and why it happened. Research in sport tourism has begun to move beyond description to the realms of explanation and prediction as facilitated by theory. At this stage in the evolution of the study of sport tourism, theoretical insight has tended to come from more advanced fields of study. Theoretical insights that have been referenced in this book have been drawn primarily from geography such as central place theory touched on in Chapter 7 and place attachment in Chapter 8. To the extent that these theories provide additional insight into sport tourism development, they should be adopted, applied and further developed in their application to the study of sport tourism. The driving forces behind such theory building not only should include the obvious need to solve real and potential problems related to the practice of sport tourism but should also be curiosity driven with the potential of providing more general insight into the phenomenon. Basic research into the complex spatial and temporal relationships between sport and tourism will be the foundation upon which both profound and more mundane but practical advances can be made in the field.

Theory building requires accurate measurement of many aspects of the sport tourism phenomenon. The various costs associated with the development of partnerships, policy and planning in sport tourism should form one part of the measurement process. To a large extent, the need to demonstrate the return on investment explains the prevalence of economic impact studies associated with major sporting events. These impact studies should continue, albeit with rigorous and standardised methodologies that allow for accurate and comparable findings. However, this type of assessment research must move beyond a narrow economic focus to a triple bottom line assessment as well as the broader concept of leveraging. Just as there are a multitude of research questions being asked in both tourism and sport contexts, there are a multitude of useful questions that can be asked in relation to sport tourism. A research ethic needs to be adopted on the assumption that good evidence will lead to good theory and subsequently to good practice. Empirical research should be characterised by rigorous data collection, analysis and interpretation. It must also be paired with appropriate dissemination outlets that include translational research that is accessible to practitioners. While alternative interpretations and perspectives should be welcomed, rigorous scientific standards should be upheld. Research must be driven by a genuine search for insight rather than an advocacy or booster orientation as has sometimes been the case with this field in the past.

The environment in which sport tourism exists is complex, dynamic and, as argued throughout this book, contingent on the spatial and temporal context of a given situation. This second edition focuses on exploring, understanding and explaining the dynamic sport tourism nexus. It is this dynamism that underpins the following principles of sport tourism theory and practice.

Critical engagement in the study of sport and tourism

The academic study of sport and tourism seeks to build edifices of knowledge that inform both theory and practice. Descriptive analyses and specialised academic and professional programmes designed to provide students with an understanding of this phenomenon are helpful but not sufficient. Students with interests in sport tourism, whose study programmes are primarily based on tourism or sport management, must develop a balanced knowledge of the varied disciplinary perspectives of this field of scholarship. The development of teaching and research links between the fields of sport and tourism may also foster synergies within and between disciplines of scholarship. Influential scholars and practitioners in this field will remain students of relevant theory and explanatory research. Rapidly changing environments and advances in the understanding of complex associations and causal relationships underscore the need for timely and critical research to inform theory and practice. Ethical considerations must be part of this research agenda. The sometimes conflicting interests of multiple stakeholders along with issues of sustainability in the cultural and physical environments in which sport tourism development occurs are fundamental to critical engagement in the study of sport and tourism.

Policy development

While day-to-day operating decisions are the things that ultimately determine the nature of sport tourism, it is necessary to have policy direction so that daily operating decisions are made systematically rather than on an ad hoc basis. It is incumbent upon policy-makers to consciously and publicly set directions for sport tourism. The logical starting point is to recognise the mutual relationship of sport and tourism within public and private organisational structures. This does not mean that existing sport and tourism ministries should necessarily combine, although there are numerous present and past examples where this has been the case. Unfortunately, the divisions within sport and tourism organisations can be just as rigid as they are between organisations. Effective sport tourism development policy requires real commitment. As in the case of alliance and partnership, the mutual benefit of cooperation must be evident. Policy initiatives must then be articulated and operationalised in a way that captures these benefits in a measurable manner. The guiding rule of such initiatives should be sustainable development, which requires a long-term rather than a short-term perspective.

Active planning interventions

Policy is implemented through planning. Planning, in turn, occurs at various levels from strategic through to operational. Various spatial levels of planning ranging from global through to local site plans need to be considered. A full array of public and private sector stakeholders must be involved as sport tourism plans require popular support if they are to be successful. As in any planning exercise, the probability of success is enhanced as a better understanding of the dynamic nature of sport tourism development emerges.

Coordination and leadership through alliance and partnership

The need for coordinated efforts within and between sport and tourism agencies emerges consistently throughout the pages of this book. Weak alliances and partnerships will undermine the effectiveness of sport tourism development initiatives. The establishment and main-tenance of strong alliances and partnerships is critical, although such initiatives may seem to be secondary to the core functions of sport and tourism managers. An enduring commitment requires that the purpose and benefits of such alliances be clearly articulated and demonstrated from the outset.

Conclusion

Sport provides a unique focus for the study of tourism. The significant, and in some cases overwhelming, profile of sports in a broad range of local, regional, national and global media offers considerable advantages and opportunities in terms of the way sport is harnessed to foster tourism development interests. Perhaps more important, the fundamental rule structures, competitive dimensions and ludic qualities of sport present a complex array of opportunities and challenges associated with tourism development. Thus, sport is characterised by markets that are distinguishable from those associated with other forms of tourism and development issues that warrant dedicated research and publication.

This book explores the functions of sport as a distinctive and potentially powerful type of tourist attraction. The defining qualities of sport provide an exceptional and unique attraction nucleus that offers tourism industry interests and sport tourism researchers fertile grounds to explore. The human element of sport as a tourist attraction is notable for its diversity. Among the many dimensions or continua upon which sport tourists may be conceptualised, elite athletes and recreational participants, event competitors and sport spectators, sports teams and individual contestants, and sports junkies and casual sport tourists are just a few. The diverse forms of sport tourism that exist within these continua may be explored in terms of the diverse market niches that they represent. Finally, media coverage of sport makes a significant contribution to the marking and the marketing of sport tourist attractions and the destination in which they are located.

In treating sport as a peculiar and distinctive type of tourist attraction, this book demonstrates that sport tourism has real manifestations in space and time. Sport tourism influences travel patterns, the meaning ascribed to tourism destinations and landscapes. It also influences the nature of travel experiences, seasonal visitation patterns and the evolution of sport, tourism and host destinations. An appreciation of these dynamics supports continuing engagement in theory building and empirical research. These activities will further contribute to an understanding of the dynamic relationship between sport and tourism in the development process.

References

Ajzen, I. and Driver, B.L. (1992) Application of the theory of planned behavior to leisure choice. *Journal of Leisure Research* 24 (3), 207–225.

Alin, J.M., Primus, D.D. and Razli, I.A. (2006) The roles of eco-entrepreneurs in conserving common pool resources: Wildlife and natural areas in Sipadan Island. Paper presented at the Survival of the Commons: Mounting Challenges and New Realities, the Eleventh Conference of the International Association for the Study of Common Property Location, Bali, Indonesia, 19–23 June 2006. On WWW at http://hdl.handle.net/10535/627. Accessed 2.7.10.

Allcock, J.B. (1989) Seasonality. In S.F. Witt and L. Moutinho (eds) *Tourism Marketing and Management Handbook* (pp. 387–392). Englewood Cliffs, NJ: Prentice-Hall.

Allen, G., Dunlop, S. and Swales, K. (2007) The economic impact of regular season sporting competitions: The Glasgow Old Firm football spectators as sports tourists. *Journal of Sport & Tourism* 12 (2), 63–97.

Amelung, B., Nicholls, S. and Viner, D. (2007) Implications of global climate change for tourism flows and seasonality. *Journal of Travel Research* 45, 285–296.

Ames, C. (1984) Competitive, co-operative, and individualistic goal structures: A motivational analysis. In R. Ames and C. Ames (eds) *Research on Motivation in Education* (Vol. 1, pp. 177–207). New York: Academic Press.

Andrews, D. (2006) *Sports–Commerce–Culture: Essays on Sport in Late Capitalist America*. New York: Peter Lang.

Archer, B. and Cooper, C. (1994) The positive and negative impacts of tourism. In W. Theobald (ed.) *Global Tourism: The Next Decade* (pp. 73–91). Oxford: Butterworth-Heinemann.

Atkisson, A. (2000) *Believing Cassandra: An Optimist Looks at a Pessimist's World*. New York: Scribe Publishers.

Attarian, A. (1999) Artificial climbing environments. In J.C. Miles and S. Priest (eds) *Adventure Programming* (pp. 341–345). State College, PA: Venture Publishing, Inc.

Attarian, A. (2003) Managing groups at climbing sites. In R. Poff, S. Guthrie, J. Kafsky-DeGarmo, T. Stenger and W. Taylor (eds) *Proceedings of the 16th International Conference on Outdoor Recreation and Education* (pp. 20–26). Bloomington, IL: Association of Outdoor Recreation and Education. On WWW at www.aore.org/ICOREProceedings2002.pdf. Accessed 6.6.08.

Attfield, P. (2010) Infrastructure gets a tune-up. *The Globe and Mail*, National Edition, Toronto, A12 and A13, 3 December.

Bagheri, A. and Hjorth, P. (2007) Planning for sustainable development: A paradigm shift towards a process-based approach. *Sustainable Development* 16, 83–96.

Bailey, R. (2006) Science, normal science and science education – Thomas Kuhn and education. *Learning for Democracy* 2 (2), 7–20.

Bale, J. (1982) *Sport and Place: A Geography of Sport in England, Scotland and Wales*. London: C. Hurst and Co. Ltd.

Bale, J. (1989) *Sports Geography*. London: E and FN Spon.

Bale, J. (1993a) *Sport, Space and the City.* London: Routledge.

Bale, J. (1993b) The spatial development of the modern stadium. *International Review for the Sociology of Sport* 28 (2/3), 121–134.

Bale, J. (1994) *Landscapes of Modern Sport.* Leicester: Leicester University Press.

Bale, J. (2000) The changing face of football: Stadiums and community. *Soccer & Society* 1 (1), 91–101.

Ball, R.M. (1988) Seasonality: A problem for workers in the tourism labour market? *The Services Industries Journal* 8 (4), 501–513.

Ball, R.M. (1989) Some aspects of tourism, seasonality, and local labour markets. *Area* 21 (1), 35–45.

Baloglu, S. and McCleary, K.W. (1999) A model of destination image formation. *Annals of Tourism Research* 26 (4), 868–897.

BarOn, R.R.V. (1975) *Seasonality in Tourism: A Guide to the Analysis of Seasonality and Trends for Policy Making.* London: Economist Intelligence Unit.

Bartoluci, M. and Cavlek, N. (2000) The economic basis of the development of golf in Croatian tourism: Prospects and misconceptions. *Acta Turistica* 12 (2), 105–138.

Basset, C. and Wilbert, C. (1999) Where you want to go today (like it or not) In D. Crouch (ed.) *Leisure/Tourism Geographies* (pp. 181–194). London: Routledge.

Baum, T. and Hagen, L. (1999) Responses to seasonality: The experiences of peripheral destinations. *International Journal of Tourism Research* 1, 299–312.

Beezer, A. and Hebdige, D. (1992) Subculture: The meaning of style. In M. Barker and A. Beezer (eds), *Reading into Cultural Studies* (pp. 101–117). London: Routledge.

Belanger, A. (2000) Sport venues and the spectacularization of urban spaces in North America. *International Review for the Sociology of Sport* 35 (3), 278–397.

Bellan, G.L. and Bellan-Santini, D.R. (2001) A review of littoral tourism, sport and leisure activities: Consequences on marine flora and fauna. *Aquatic Conservation: Marine and Freshwater Ecosystems* 11 (4), 325–333.

Berger, I.E. and Greenspan, I. (2008) High (on) technology: Producing tourist identities through technologized adventure. *Journal of Sport & Tourism* 13 (2), 89–114.

Bernstein, A. (2000) Things you can see from there you can't see from here: Globalization, media, and the Olympics. *Journal of Sport and Social Issues* 24 (4), 351–369.

Bickerstaff, K. (2004) Risk perception research: Socio-cultural perspectives on the public experience of air pollution. *Environment International* 30, 827–840.

Bicknell, S. and McManus, P. (2006) The Canary in the coalmine: Australian ski resorts and their response to climate change. *Geographical Research* 44 (4), 386–400.

Binns, T. (1995) Geography in development: Development in geography. *Geography* 80, 303–322.

Black, D. (2008) Dreaming big: The pursuit of 'second order' games as a strategic response to globalization. *Sport in Society* 11 (4), 467–480.

Bleda, M. and Shackley, S. (2008) The dynamics of belief in climate change and its risks in business organisations. *Ecological Economics* 66, 517–532.

Boniface, B.G. and Cooper, C. (1994) *The geography of Travel and Tourism* (2nd edn). Oxford: Butterworth-Heinemann.

Boorstin, D.J. (1975) *The Image: A Guide to Pseudo-Events in America.* New York: Atheum.

Booth, D. and Loy, J.W. (1999) Sport, status, and style. *Sport History Review* 30, 1–26.

Bourdeau, P., Corneloup, J. and Mao, P. (2002) Adventure sports and tourism in the French mountains: Dynamics of change and challenges for sustainable development. *Current Issues in Tourism* 5 (1), 22–32.

Breivik, G. (2010) Trends in adventure sports in a post-modern society. *Sport in Society* 13 (2), 260–273.

British Tourist Authority (2000) *Sporting Britain: Play It, Love It, Watch It, Live It, Visit.* London: Haymarket Magazines Ltd.

Brown, G., Chalip, L., Jago, L. and Mules, T. (2002) The Sydney Olympics and brand Australia. In N. Morgan, A. Pritchard and R. Pride (eds) *Destination Branding: Creating the Unique Destination Proposition.* Oxford: Butterworth-Heinemann.

Brown, G. and Raymond, C. (2007) The relationship between place attachment and landscape values: Toward mapping place attachment. *Applied Geography* 27 (1), 89–111.

Brymer, E. Downey, G. and Gray, T. (2009) Extreme sports as a precursor to environmental sustainability. Journal of Sport & Tourism 14 (2/3), 193–204.

Bull, C. and Weed, M.E. (1999) Niche markets and small island tourism: The development of sports tourism in Malta. *Managing Leisure* 4 (3), 142–155.

Burgan, B. and Mules, T. (1992) Economic impact of sporting events. *Annals of Tourism Research* 19 (4), 700–710.

Burki, R. (2000) *Climatic Change and Adjustment Processes in Tourism: Represented by the Example of the Winter Tourism.* Publication of the East Swiss Geographical Society, Gallen.

Burton, R. (1995) *Travel Geography* (2nd edn). London: Pitman Publishing.

Butler, R.W. (1980) The concept of the tourist area lifecycle of evolution: Implications for the management of resources. *Canadian Geographer* 24 (1), 5–12.

Butler, R.W. (1993) Tourism: An evolutionary perspective. In J.G. Nelson, R.W. Butler and G. Wall (eds) *Tourism and Sustainable Development: Monitoring, Planning, Managing* (Series No. 37, pp. 27–43). Waterloo, Canada: Department of Geography, University of Waterloo.

Butler, R.W. (1994) Seasonality in tourism: Issues and problems. In A.V. Seaton (ed.) *Tourism: The State of the Art* (pp. 332–339). Chichester: John Wiley & Sons.

Butler, R.W. (1996) The role of tourism in cultural transformation in developing countries. In W. Nuryanti (ed.) *Tourism and Culture: Global Civilization in Change* (pp. 91–101). Yogyakarta, Indonesia: Gadjah Mada University Press.

Butler, R.W. (2001) Seasonality in tourism: Issues and implications. In T. Baum and S. Lundtorp (eds) *Seasonality in Tourism* (pp. 5–23). London: Pergamon.

Butler, R.W. (ed.) (2006) *The Tourist Area Life Cycle, Vol. 1: Applications and Modifications* (pp. 250–268). Clevedon: Channel View Publications.

Butler, R.W. (2009) Tourism in the future: Cycles, waves or wheels. *Futures* 41 (6), 346–352.

Butler, R.W. and Mayo, B. (1996) Seasonality in tourism: Problems and measurement. In P.E. Murphy (ed.) *Quality Management in Urban Tourism* (pp. 9–23). Chichester: John Wiley & Sons.

Canadian Sport Tourism Alliance (2010) 2009 Canada summer games: Economic impact assessment. Ottawa, Canada. On WWW at http://www.canadiansporttourism.com/app/DocRepository/1/reports_en/2009_CSG_EIAssess_May2010.pdf. Accessed 26.11.10.

Canadian Tourism Commission and Coopers and Lybrand (1996) *Domestic Tourism Market Research Study.* Ottawa, Canada: Canadian Tourism Commission.

Cantelon, H. and Letters, M. (2000) The making of the IOC environmental policy as the third dimension of the Olympic movement. *International Review for the Sociology of Sport* 35 (3), 294–308.

Capo Parrilla, J., Riera Font, A. and Rossello Nadal, J. (2007) Accommodation determinants of seasonal patterns. *Annals of Tourism Research* 34 (2), 422–436.

Carmichael, B. and Murphy, P.E. (1996) Tourism economic impact of a rotating sports event: The case of the British Columbia Games. *Festival Management and Event Tourism* 4, 127–138.

Carter, J., Dyer, P. and Sharma, B. (2007) Dis-placed voices: Sense of place and place-identity on the Sunshine Coast. *Social and Cultural Geography* 8, 755–773.

Chadwick, G. (1971) *A Systems View of Planning*. Oxford: Pergamon Press.

Chalip, L. (2001) Sport tourism: Capitalising on the linkage. In D. Kluka and G. Schilling (eds) *Perspectives: The Business of Sport* (pp. 77–89). Oxford: Meyer and Meyer.

Chalip, L. (2004) Case study 3.1: Olympic teams as market segments. In T.D. Hinch and J.E.S. Higham (eds) *Sport Tourism Development* (pp. 52–54). Clevedon: Chanel View Publications.

Chalip, L. (2005) Marketing, media, and place promotion. In J.E.S. Higham (ed.) *Sport Tourism Destinations: Issues, Opportunities and Analysis* (pp. 162–176). Oxford: Elsevier Butterworth-Heinemann.

Chalip, L. (2006) Towards social leverage of sport events. *Journal of Sport & Tourism* 11 (2), 109–127.

Chalip, L. (2010) Guest editorial: The cogency of culture in sport tourism research. *Journal of Sport & Tourism* 15 (1), 3–5.

Chalip, L., Green, C. and Vander Velden, L. (1998) Sources of interest in travel to the Olympic Games. *Journal of Vacation Marketing* 4 (1), 7–22.

Chalip, L. and Mcguirty, J. (2004) Bundling sport events with the host destination. *Journal of Sport & Tourism* 9 (3), 267–282.

Chernushenko, D. (1996) Sports tourism goes sustainable – The Lillehammer experience. *Visions in Leisure and Business* 15 (1), 65–73.

Chogahara, M. and Yamaguchi, Y. (1998) Resocialization and continuity of involvement in physical activity among elderly Japanese. *International Review for the Sociology of Sport* 33 (3), 277–289.

Christaller, W. (1963/64) Some considerations of tourism location in Europe: The peripheral regions–underdeveloped countries–recreation areas. *Papers, Regional Science Association* 12, 95–105.

Clawson, M. and Knetsch, J. (1966) *The Economics of Outdoor Recreation*. Baltimore: Johns Hopkins Press.

Coalter, F. (1999) Sport and recreation in the United Kingdom: Flow with the flow or buck with the trends? *Managing Leisure* 4 (1), 24–39.

Cohen, E. (1988) Authenticity and the commoditization of tourism. *Annals of Tourism Research* 15, 371–386.

Cohen, E. (1996) A phenomenology of tourist experiences. In Y. Apostolopoulos, S. Leivadi and A. Yiannakis (eds) *The Sociology of Tourism* (pp. 90–111). London: Routledge.

Cole, S. (2007) Beyond authenticity and commodification. *Annals of Tourism Research* 34, 943–960.

Collier, A. (1999) *Principles of Tourism: A New Zealand Perspective* (5th edn). Auckland, New Zealand: Longman.

Collins, A., Jones, C. and Munday, M. (2009) Assessing the environmental impacts of mega sporting events: Two options? *Tourism Management* 30 (6), 828–837.

Collins, H.M. and Evans, R. (2002) The third wave of social science studies: Studies of expertise and experience. *Social Studies of Science* 32 (2), 235–296.

Collins, M.F. (1991) The economics of sport and sports in the economy: Some international comparisons. In C.P. Cooper (ed.) *Progress in Tourism, Recreation and Hospitality Management* (pp. 184–214). London: Belhaven Press.

Collins, M.F. and Jackson, G. (2001) Evidence for a sports tourism continuum. Paper presented at the Journeys in Leisure: Current and Future Alliances Conference, Luton, England, 17–19 July 2001.

Commonwealth Department of Industry, Science and Resources (2000) *Towards a National Sport Tourism Strategy*. Draft Report. Canberra, Australia: Commonwealth Department of Industry, Science and Resources.

Cooper, C., Fletcher, J., Gilbert, D. and Wanhill, S. (1993) *Tourism: Principles and Practice*. Harlow, England: Longman Group Limited.

Cornelissen, S. (2010) Football's tsars: Proprietorship, corporatism and politics in the 2010 FIFA World Cup. *Soccer and Society* 11 (1/2), 131–143.

Cowell, R. (1997) Stretching the limits: Environmental compensation, habitat creation and sustainable development. *Transactions of the Institute of British Geographers* 22 (3), 292–306.

Crawford, D.W., Jackson, E.L. and Godbey, G. (1991) A hierarchical model of leisure constraints. *Leisure Sciences* 13, 309–320.

Crouch, D. (2000) Places around us: Embodied lay geographies in leisure and tourism. *Leisure Studies* 19 (2), 63–76.

Cuthbertson, B., Heine, M. and Whitson, D. (1997) Producing meaning through movement: An alternative view of sense of place. *Trumpeter* 14 (2), 72–75.

Daniels, M.J. (2007) Central place theory and sport tourism impacts. *Annals of Tourism Research* 34 (2), 332–347.

Dann, G.M.S. (1981) Tourist motivation: An appraisal. *Annals of Tourism Research* 8 (2), 187.

Dauncey, H. and Hare, G. (2000) World Cup France'98: Metaphors, meanings and values. *International Review for the Sociology of Sport* 35 (3), 331–347.

Davies, J. and Williment, J. (2008) Sport tourism – Grey sport tourists, all black and red experiences. *Journal of Sport & Tourism* 13 (3), 221–242.

Dawson, J. and Scott, D. (2007) Climate change vulnerability in the Vermont ski tourism sector. *Annals of Leisure Research* 10 (3/4), 550–571.

de Villers, D.J. (2001) Sport and tourism to stimulate development. *Olympic Review* 27 (38), 11–13.

Del Carme, L. (2009) Cashing in on rugby. *Sunday Times*, Johannesburg. 5 July 2009 p. 10.

Delpy, L. (1997) An overview of sport tourism: Building towards a dimensional framework. *Journal of Vacation Marketing* 4 (1), 23–38.

Delpy, L. (1998) Editorial. *Journal of Vacation Marketing* 4 (1), 4–5.

Delpy, L. (2001) Preparing for the rise in sports tourism. Paper presented at the World Conference on Sport and Tourism, Barcelona, Spain, 22–23 February 2001.

Delpy Neirotti, L., Bosetti, H.A. and Teed, K.C. (2001) Motivation to attend the 1996 Summer Olympic Games. *Journal of Travel Research* 39 (3), 327–331.

Denham, D. (2004) Global and local influences on English Rugby League. *Sociology of Sport Journal* 21 (2), 206–182.

Devine, A. and Devine, F. (2004) The politics of sports tourism in Northern Ireland. *Journal of Sport Tourism* 9 (2), 171–182.

Dietvorst, A.G.J. (1995) Tourist behaviour and the importance of time–space analysis. In G.J. Ashworth and A.G.J. Dietvorst (eds) *Tourism and Spatial*

Transformations: Implications for Policy and Planning. Wallingford, UK: CAB International.

Dietvorst, A.G.J. and Ashworth, G.J. (1995) Tourism transformations: An introduction. In G.J. Ashworth and A.G.J. Dietvorst (eds) *Tourism and Spatial Transformations: Implications for Policy and Planning*. Wallingford, UK: CAB International.

Dodds, R. and Graci, S. (2009) Canada's tourism industry – Mitigating the effects of climate change: A lot of concern but little action. *Tourism and Hospitality Planning and Development* 6 (1), 39–51.

Donnelly, P. and Young, K.M. (1988) The construction and confirmation of identity in sport subcultures. *Sociology of Sport Journal* 5, 223–240.

Doxey, G. (1975) Visitor–resident interaction in tourist destinations: Inferences from empirical research in Barbados, West Indies and Niagara-on-the-Lake, Ontario. Paper presented at the Symposium on the Planning and Development of the Tourist Industry in the ECC Region, Dubrovnik, Yugoslavia, 8–11 September, 1975.

Dunning, E. (1999) *Sport Matters: Sociological Studies of Sport, Violence and Civilisation*. London: Routledge.

Dweck, C. (1986) Motivational processes affecting learning. *American Psychologist* 41, 1040–1048.

Dwyer, L., Edwards, D., Mistilis, N., Roman, C., Scott, N. and Cooper, C. (2008) Megatrends underpinning tourism to 2020: Analysis of key drivers for change. CRC for Sustainable Tourism Pty Ltd website. At http://crctourism.com.au/WMS /Upload/Resources/bookshop/80046%20Dwyer_TourismTrends2020%20WEB.pdf. Accessed 23.4.10.

Echtner, C.M. and Ritchie, J.B.R. (1993) The measurement of destination image: An empirical assessment. *Journal of Travel Research* (Spring), 3–13.

Elsasser, H. and Burki, R. (2002) Climate change as a threat to tourism in the Alps. *Climate Research* 20, 253–257.

Esfahani, N., Goudarzi, M. and Assadi, H. (2009) The analysis of the factors affecting the development of Iran sport tourism and the presentation of a strategic model. *World Journal of Sport Sciences* 2, 136–144.

Ewert, A. and Shultis, J. (1999) Technology and backcountry recreation: Boom to recreation or bust for management. *Journal of Physical Education, Recreation and Dance* 70 (8), 22–31.

Fairley, S. and Gammon, S. (2005) Something lived, something learned: Nostalgia's expanding role in sport tourism. *Sport in Society* 8 (2), 182–197.

Fairley, S. and Tyler, B.D. (2009) Cultural learning through a sport tourism experience: The role of the group. *Journal of Sport Tourism* 14 (4), 273–292.

Faulkner, B., Tideswell, C. and Weston, A.M. (1998) Leveraging tourism benefits from the Sydney 2000 Olympics. Paper presented at the Sport Management Association of Australia and New Zealand, Gold Coast, Australia, 26–28 November 1998.

Flagestad, A. and Hope, C.A. (2001) Strategic success in winter sports destinations: A sustainable value creation perspective. *Tourism Management* 22 (5), 445–461.

Fougere, G. (1989) Sport, culture and identity: The case of rugby football. In D. Novitz and B. Willmott (eds) *Cultural Identity in New Zealand* (pp. 110–122). Wellington, New Zealand: GP Books.

Francis, S. and Murphy, P. E. (2005) Sport Tourism Destinations: The Active Sport Tourist Perspective. In J. E. S. Higham (ed.) Sport Tourism Destinations: Issues, Opportunities and Analysis (pp. 73–92). Oxford: Elsevier.

Frechtling, D.C. (1996) *Practical Tourism Forecasting*. Oxford: Butterworth-Heinemann.

Freidmann, J. (1986) The world city hypothesis. *Development and Change* 17, 69–84.

Funk, D. and Bruun, T. (2007) The role of socio-psychological and culture-education motives in marketing international sport tourism: A cross-cultural perspective. *Tourism Management* 28, 806–819.

Funk, D.C., Toohey, K. and Bruun, T. (2007) International sport event participation: Prior sport involvement; destination image; and travel motives. *European Sport Management Quarterly* 7 (3), 227–248.

Fyall, A. and Jago, L. (2009) Guest editorial: Sustainability in sport & tourism. *Journal of Sport & Tourism* 14 (2/3), 77–81.

Gallarza, M.G., Saura, I. and Garcia, H. (2002) Destination image: Towards a conceptual framework. *Annals of Tourism Research* 29 (1), 56–78.

Gammon, S. (2002) Fantasy, nostalgia and the pursuit of what never was. In S. Gammon and J. Kurtzman (eds) *Sport Tourism: Principles and Practice* (pp. 61–72). Eastbourne, UK: Leisure Studies Association.

Gammon, S. and Fear, V. (2007) Stadia tourism and the power of backstage. In S. Gammon and G. Ramshaw (eds) *Heritage, Sport and Tourism: Sporting Pasts – Tourist Futures* (pp. 23–32). London: Routledge.

Gammon, S. and Kurtzman, J. (eds) (2002) *Sport Tourism: Principles and Practice*. Eastbourne, UK: Leisure Studies Association.

Gammon, S. and Ramshaw, G. (2007) *Heritage, Sport and Tourism: Sporting Pasts – Tourist Futures*. Abington, MA: Taylor & Francis.

Gammon, S. and Robinson, T. (1997) Sport and tourism: A conceptual framework. *Journal of Sport Tourism* 4 (3), 8–24.

Gammon, S. and Robinson, T. (2003) Sport and tourism: A conceptual framework. *Journal of Sport & Tourism* 8, 21–26.

Garmise, M. (1987) *Proceedings of the International Seminar and Workshop on Outdoor Education, Recreation and Sport Tourism*. Netanya, Israel: Emmanuel Gill Publishing.

Getz, D. (1991) *Festivals, Special Events and Tourism*. New York: Van Nostrand Reinhold.

Getz, D. (1997) *Event Management and Event Tourism*. New York: Cognizant Communications Corporation.

Getz, D. (1998) Trends, strategies, and issues in sport-event tourism. *Sport Marketing Quarterly* 7 (2), 8–13.

Getz, D. and Andersson, T.D. (2010) The event-tourist career trajectory: A study of high-involvement amateur distance runners. *Scandinavian Journal of Hospitality and Tourism* 10 (4), 468–491.

Getz, D. and Cheyne, J. (1997) Special event motivations and behaviour. In C. Ryan (ed.) *The Tourist Experience: A New Introduction* (pp. 136–154). London: Cassell.

Gibson, H. and Yiannakis, A. (1992) Tourist roles: Needs and the lifecourse. *Annals of Tourism Research* 29 (2), 358–383.

Gibson, H.J. (1998) Sport tourism: A critical analysis of research. *Sport Management Review* 1 (1), 45–76.

Gibson, H.J. (2002) Sport tourism at a crossroad? Considerations for the future. In S. Gammon and J. Kurtzman (eds) *Sport Tourism: Principles and Practice* (Vol. 76, pp. 111–128). Eastbourne, UK: Leisure Studies Association.

Gibson, H.J. (2005) Towards an understanding of why sport tourists do what they do. In H. J. Gibson (ed.) *Sport Tourism: Theory and Concepts* (pp. 66–85). London: Routledge.

Gibson, H.J. (ed.) (2006) *Sport Tourism: Concepts and Theories*. New York: Routledge.

Gibson, H.J., Attle, S. and Yiannakis, A. (1998) Segmenting the sport tourist market: A lifespan perspective. *Journal of Vacation Marketing* 4, 52–64.

Gibson, H.J., Willming, C. and Holdnak, A. (2002) Small-scale event sport tourism: College sport as a tourist attraction. In S. Gammon and J. Kurtzman (eds) *Sport Tourism: Principles and Practice*. Eastbourne, UK: Leisure Studies Association.

Giddens, A. (1993) *Modernity and Self-Identity. Self and Society in the Late Modern Age*. Cambridge: Polity Press.

Gillett, P. and Kelly, S. (2006) 'Non-local' Masters Games participants: An investigation of competitive active sport tourist motives. *Journal of Sport & Tourism* 11 (3/4), 239–257.

Gilmore, J.H. and Pine, B.J. (2007) *Authenticity: What Consumers Really Want*. Boston: Harvard Business School Press.

Giulianotti, R. (1995) Participant observation and research into football hooliganism: Reflections on the problems of entree and everyday risks. *Sociology of Sport Journal* 12 (1), 1–20.

Giulianotti, R. (1996) Back to the future: An ethnography of Ireland's football fans at the 1994 World Cup Finals in the USA. *International Review for the Sociology of Sport* 31 (3), 323–347.

Glyptis, S.A. (1982) *Sport and Tourism in Western Europe*. London: British Travel Education Trust.

Glyptis, S.A. (1989) Leisure and patterns of time use. *Proceedings of the Leisure Studies Association Annual Conference, Bournemouth, England, 24–26 April 1987*. Eastbourne, UK: Leisure Studies Association.

Glyptis, S.A. (1991) Sport and tourism. In C.P. Cooper (ed.) *Progress in Tourism, Recreation and Hospitality Management* (pp. 165–187). London: Belhaven Press.

Go, F.M. (2004) Tourism in the context of globalization. In S. Williams (ed.) *Tourism: Critical Concepts in the Social Sciences* (pp. 49–80). London: Routledge.

Godbey, G. and Graefe, A. (1991) Repeat tourism, play and monetary spending. *Annals of Tourism Research* 18 (2), 213–225.

Goldman, R. and Papson, S. (1998) *Nike Culture: The Sign of the Swoosh*. London: Sage Publications.

Gomez Martin, M.B. (2005) Weather, climate and tourism: A geographic perspective. *Annals of Tourism Research* 32, 571–591.

Gössling, S. and Hall, C.M. (eds) (2006) *Tourism and Global Environmental Change*. London: Routledge.

Goulding, C. (1999) Heritage, nostalgia, and the 'grey' consumer. *Journal of Marketing Practice: Applied Marketing Science* 5 (6), 177–199.

Graburn, N.H.H. (1989) Tourism: The sacred journey. In V.L. Smith (ed.) *Hosts and Guests: The Anthropology of Tourism* (2nd edn, pp. 21–36). Philadelphia: University of Pennsylvania Press.

Graefe, A.R., Vaske, J.J. and Kuss, F.R. (1984) Social carrying capacity: An integration and synthesis of twenty years of research. *Leisure Sciences* 6 (4), 395–431.

Grant, T. (2010) FIFA gets an oil change. *The Globe and Mail*, National Edition, Toronto, A12 and A13, 3 December.

Gratton, C., Dobson, N. and Shibli, S. (2000) The economic importance of major sports events: A case-study of six events. *Managing Leisure* 5 (1), 17–28.

Gratton, C., Shibli, S. and Coleman, R. (2005) The economics of sport tourism at major sports events. In J.E.S. Higham (ed.) *Sport Tourism Destinations: Issues,*

Opportunities and Analysis (pp. 233–247). Oxford: Elsevier Butterworth-Heinemann.

Green, B.C. (2001) Leveraging subculture and identity to promote sport events. *Sport Management Review* 4 (1), 1–19.

Green, B.C. and Chalip, L. (1998) Sport tourism as the celebration of subculture. *Annals of Tourism Research* 25 (2), 275–291.

Greenwood, D.J. (1989) Culture by the pound: An anthropological perspective on tourism as cultural commodification. In V.L. Smith (ed.) *Hosts and Guests: The Anthropology of Tourism* (pp. 17–31). Philadelphia: University of Pennsylvania Press.

Gu, H. and Ryan, C. (2008) Place attachment, identity and community impacts of tourism – The case of a Beijing hutong. *Tourism Management* 29, 637–647.

Halberstam, D. (1999) *Playing for Keeps: Michael Jordan and the World He Made.* New York: Random House.

Hall, C.M. (1992a) *Hallmark Tourist Events: Impacts, Management and Planning.* London: Belhaven Press.

Hall, C.M. (1992b) Review: Adventure, sport and health tourism. In B. Weiler and C.M. Hall (eds) *Special Interest Tourism* (pp. 186–210). London: Belhaven Press.

Hall, C.M. (1993) The politics of leisure: An analysis of spectacles and mega-events. In A.J. Veal, P. Johnson and G. Cushman (eds) *Leisure and Tourism: Social and Environmental Changes* (pp. 620–629). Sydney: World Leisure and Recreation Association, University of Technology.

Hall, C.M. (1995) *Introduction to Tourism in Australia: Impacts, Planning and Development* (2nd edn). South Melbourne: Addison-Wesley Longman Australia.

Hall, C.M. (1998) Imaging, tourism and sports event fever: The Sydney Olympics and the need for a social charter for mega-events. In C. Gratton and I.P. Henry (eds) *Sport in the City: The Role of Sport in Economic and Social Regeneration* (pp. 166–183). London: Routledge.

Hall, C.M. (2000a) *Tourism Planning: Policies, Processes and Relationships.* Harlow, England: Prentice-Hall.

Hall, C.M. (2000b) The future of tourism: A personal speculation. *Tourism Recreation Research* 25 (1), 85–95.

Hall, C.M. (2004) Sport Tourism and Urban Regeneration. In B. Ritchie and D. Adair (eds) *Sport Tourism: Interrelationships, Impacts and Issues* (pp. 192–205). Clevedon: Channel View Publications.

Hall, C.M. and Higham, J.E.S. (eds) (2005) *Tourism, Recreation and Climate Change: International Perspectives.* Clevedon: Channel View Publications.

Hall, C.M. and Lew, A.A. (eds) (1998) *Sustainable Tourism: A Geographical Perspective.* Harlow, England: Addison-Wesley Longman Ltd.

Hall, C.M. and Page, S.J. (1999) *Geography of Tourism and Recreation: Environment, Place, and Space.* London: Routledge.

Hall, C.M. and Weiler, B. (eds) (1992) *Special Interest Tourism.* London: Belhaven Press.

Harahousou, Y. (1999) Elderly people, leisure and physical recreation in Greece. *World Leisure and Recreation* 41 (3), 20–24.

Harris, J. (2006) The science of research in sport and tourism: Some reflections upon the promise of the sociological imagination. *Journal of Sport & Tourism* 11 (2), 153–171.

Harrison, S.J., Winterbottom, S.J. and Johnson, R.C. (2001) A preliminary assessment of the socio-economic and environmental impacts of recent changes in winter snow cover in Scotland. *Scottish Geographical Journal* 117 (4), 297–312.

Harrison, S.J., Winterbottom, W.J. and Shepard, C. (1999) The potential effects of climate change on the Scottish tourism industry. *Tourism Management* 20 (2), 25–33.

Hartmann, R. (1986) Tourism, seasonality and social change. *Leisure Studies* 5 (1), 25–33.

Harvey, J. and Houle, F. (1994) Sport, world economy, global culture, and new social movements. *Sociology of Sport Journal* 11 (4), 337–355.

Harvey, J., Rail, G. and Thibault, I. (1996) Globalization and sport: Sketching a theoretical model for empirical analyses. *Journal of Sport and Social Issues* 23 (3), 258–277.

Hawkins, D.E. and Mann, S. (2007) The World Bank's role in tourism development. *Annals of Tourism Research* 34, 348–363.

Hein, L., Metzger, M. and Moren, A. (2009) Potential impacts of climate change on tourism: A case study for Spain. *Current Opinion in Environmental Sustainability* 1, 170–178.

Heino, R. (2000) What is so punk about snowboarding? *Journal of Sport and Social Issues* 24 (1), 176–191.

Hidalgo, M.C. and Hernandez, B. (2001) Place attachment: Conceptual and empirical questions. *Journal of Environmental Psychology* 21, 273–281.

Higham, J.E.S. (2005a) Sport tourism as an attraction for managing tourism. *Sport in Society* 8, 238–262.

Higham, J.E.S. (1999) Sport as an avenue of tourism development: An analysis of the positive and negative impacts of sport tourism. *Current Issues in Tourism* 2 (1), 82–90.

Higham, J.E.S. (ed.) (2005b) *Sport Tourism Destinations: Issues, Opportunities and Analysis*. Oxford: Elsevier.

Higham, J.E.S. and Hinch, T. (2006) Sport and tourism research: A geographic approach. *Journal of Sport & Tourism* 11 (1), 31–50.

Higham, J.E.S. and Hinch, T. (2009) *Sport and Tourism: Globalization, Mobility and Identity*. Oxford: Elsevier Butterworth-Heineman.

Higham, J.E.S. and Hinch, T.D. (2000) Sport tourism and the transition to professional rugby union in New Zealand: The spatial dimension of tourism associated with the Otago Highlanders, Southern New Zealand. In P.L.M. Robinson, N. Evans, R. Sharpley and J. Swarbrooke (eds) *Reflections on International Tourism: Motivations, Behaviour and Tourists Types* (Vol. 4, pp. 145–158). Sunderland, UK: Business Education Publishers Ltd.

Higham, J.E.S. and Hinch, T.D. (2002) Sport, tourism and seasons: The challenges and potential of overcoming seasonality in the sport and tourism sectors. *Tourism Management* 23, 175–185.

Higham, J.E.S. and Hinch, T.D. (2003) Sport, space and time: Effects of the Otago Highlanders franchise on tourism. *Journal of Sports Management* 17 (3), 235–257.

Hiller, H.H. (1998) Assessing the impacts of mega-events: A linkage model. *Current Issues in Tourism* 1 (1), 47–57.

Hinch, T.D., Hickey, G. and Jackson, E.L. (2001) Seasonal visitation at Fort Edmonton Park: An empirical analysis using a leisure constraints framework. In T. Baum and S. Lundtorp (eds) *Seasonality in Tourism* (pp. 173–186). London: Pergamon.

Hinch, T. D and Hickey, G. (1996) Tourism attractions and seasonality: Spatial relationships in Alberta. In K. MacKay and K.R. Boyd (eds) *Tourism for All Seasons: Using Research to Meet the Challenge of Seasonality* (Conference Proceedings of the Travel and Tourism Research Association – Canada

Chapter) (pp. 69–76)., Ottawa, Canada: Travel and Tourism Research Association.

Hinch, T.D. and Higham, J.E.S. (2001) Sport tourism: A framework for research. *The International Journal of Tourism Research* 3 (1), 45–58.

Hinch, T.D. and Higham, J.E.S. (2004) *Sport Tourism Development*. Clevedon: Channel View Publications.

Hinch, T.D. and Higham, J.E.S. (2005) Sport, tourism and authenticity. *European Sports Management Quarterly* 5 (3), 245–258.

Hinch, T.D. and Jackson, E.L. (2000) Leisure constraints research: Its value as a framework for understanding tourism seasonality. *Current Issues in Tourism* 3 (2), 87–106.

Hinch, T.D. and Walker, G. (2006) *Motivations, Travel Behaviours and Socio-Demographic Profiles of Registered Athletes at the 2005 Edmonton World Masters Games*. Edmonton, Canada: University of Alberta.

Hjalager, A. (2007) Stages in the economic globalisation of tourism. *Annals of Tourism Research* 34, 437–457.

Hodge, K. and Hermansson, G. (2007) Psychological preparation of athletes for the Olympic context: The New Zealand Summer and Winter Olympic Teams. *Athletic Insight: The Online Journal of Sport Psychology* 9 (4). On WWW at http://www.athleticinsight.com/. Accessed 26.9.07.

Hodge, K., Lonsdale, C. and Oliver, A. (2009) The elite athlete as a 'Business traveller/tourist'. In J.E.S. Higham and T.D. Hinch (eds) *Sport and Tourism: Globalization, Mobility and Identity* (pp. 88–91). Oxford: Elsevier.

Hodges, J. and Hall, C.M. (1996) The housing and social impact of mega events: Lessons for the Sydney 2000 Olympics. Paper presented at the Proceedings: Towards a More Sustainable Tourism, Dunedin, New Zealand, 3–6 December 1996.

Hoffer, R. (1995) Down and out: On land, sea, air, facing questions about their sanity. *Sports Illustrated* 83 (1), 42–49.

Holden, A. (2000) Winter tourism and the environment in conflict: The case of Cairngorm, Scotland. *International Journal of Tourism Research* 2 (4), 247–260.

Hooper, I. (1998) The value of sport in urban regeneration – A case study of Glasgow. Paper presented at the Sport in the City Conference, Sheffield, UK, 2–4 July 1998.

Hopwood, B., Mellor, M. and O'Brien, G. (2005) Sustainable development: Mapping different approaches. *Sustainable Development* 13, 38–52.

Hritz, N. and Ross, C. (2010) The perceived impacts of sport tourism: An urban host community perspective. *Journal of Sport Management* 24 (2), 119–138.

Hsu, L.-H. (2005) Revisiting the concept of sport. *Journal of Humanities and Social Sciences* 1 (2), 45–54.

Hudson, S. (1999) *Snow Business: A Study of the International Ski Industry*. London: Cassell.

Hudson, S. (ed.) (2003) Sport and adventure tourism. Binghampton: The Haworth Press.

Hudson, S., Hinch, T., Walker, G.J. and Simpson, B. (2010) Constraints to sport tourism: A cross-cultural analysis. *Journal of Sport & Tourism* 15 (1), 71–88.

Hudson, S. and Hudson, L. (2010) *Golf Tourism*. Oxford: Goodfellow Publishing.

Hunter, C. (1995) Key concepts for tourism and the environment. In C. Hunter and H. Green (eds) *Tourism and the Environment: A Sustainable Relationship?* (pp. 52–92). London: Routledge.

Inskeep, E. (1991) *Tourism Planning: An Integrated and Sustainable Development Approach*. New York: Van Nostrand Reinhold.

International Olympic Committee and World Tourism Organization (2001) *Conclusions of the World Conference on Sport and Tourism.* Barcelona: International Olympic Committee and World Tourism Organization.

Iordache, M.C. and Cebuc, I. (2009) Analysis of the impact of climate change on some European countries. *Analele Stiintifice ale Universitatii 'Alexandru Ioan Cuza' din Iasi* 56, 270–286. . On WWW at http://anale.feaa.uaic.ro/anale/resurse/22_M03_Iordache_sa.pdf. Accessed 24.4.10.

Isle of Man Sports Challenge Website (2010) On WWW at http://www.iomsportschallenge.com/index.html. Accessed 6.12.10.

Jackson, E.L. (1989) Environmental attitudes, values and recreation. In E.L. Jackson and T.L. Burton (eds) *Understanding Leisure and Recreation: Mapping the Past, Charting the Future* (pp. 357–384). State College, PA: Venture Publishing.

Jackson, E.L. (1999) Leisure and the Internet. *Journal of Physical Education, Recreation and Dance* 70 (9), 18–22.

Jackson, E.L., Crawford, D.W. and Godbey, G. (1993) Negotiation of leisure constraints. *Leisure Sciences* 15 (1), 1–11.

Jackson, G. and Reeves, M. (1997) Evidencing the sport tourism relationship. In M.F. Collins and I.S. Cooper (eds) *Leisure Management: Issues and Applications.* Wallingford, UK: CAB International.

Jackson, S.J. (1994) Gretzky, crisis, and Canadian identity in 1988: Rearticulating the Americanization of culture debate. *Sociology of Sport Journal* 11 (4), 428–450.

Jackson, S.J. (1997) Sport, violence and advertising: A case study of global/local disjuncture in New Zealand. Paper presented at the North American Society for the Sociology of Sport Conference, Toronto, Canada, 5–8 November 1997.

Jackson, S.J. and Andrews, D.L. (1999) Between and beyond the global and local: American popular sporting culture in New Zealand. In A. Yiannakis and M. Melnik (eds) *Sport Sociology: Contemporary Themes* (5th edn, pp. 467–474). Champaign, IL: Human Kinetics.

Jackson, S.J., Batty, R. and Scherer, J. (2001) Transnational sport marketing at the global/local nexus: The adidasification of the New Zealand all Blacks. *International Journal of Sports Marketing and Sponsorship* 3 (2), 185–201.

Jamal, T.B. and Getz, D. (1994) Collaboration theory and community tourism planning. *Annals of Tourism Research* 22, 186–204.

Jang, S. (2004) Mitigating tourism seasonality: A quantitative approach. *Annals of Tourism Research* 31, 819–836.

Jeffrey, D. and Barden, R.D. (2001) An analysis of the nature, causes and marketing implications of seasonality in the occupancy performance of English hotels. In T. Baum and S. Lundtorp (eds) *Seasonality and Tourism* (pp. 119 140). London: Pergamon.

Johnson, W.O. (1991) Sport in the Year 2001: A fan's world. Watching sport in the 21st century. *Sports Illustrated* 75 (4), 40–48.

Johnston, C.S. (2001a) Shoring the foundations of the destination life cycle model. Part 1: Ontological and epistemological considerations. *Tourism Geographies* 3 (1), 2–28.

Johnston, C.S. (2001b) Shoring the foundations of the destination life cycle model. Part 2: A case study of Kona, Hawai'i Island. *Tourism Geographies* 3 (2), 135–164.

Jones, C. (2001) Mega-events and host-region impacts: Determining the true worth of the 1999 Rugby World Cup. *International Journal of Tourism Research* 3, 241–251.

Jones, I. (2000) A model of serious leisure identification: The case of football fandom. *Leisure Studies* 19 (4), 283–298.

Jones, I. and Green, B.C. (2005) Serious leisure, social identity and sport tourism in sport. *Sport in Society* 8 (2), 164–181.

Jones, I. and Green, B. C. (2006) Serious Leisure, Social Identity and Sport Tourism. In H. Gibson (ed.) Sport Tourism: Concepts and Theories (pp. 32–49). London: Routledge.

Judd, D.R. (ed.) (2003) *The Infrastructure of Play*. Armonk, NY: M.E. Sharpe.

Kane, M.J. and Zink, R. (2004) Package adventure tours: Markets in serious leisure careers. *Leisure Studies* 23 (4), 329–35.

Kang, Y.S. and Perdue, R. (1994) Long-term impacts of a mega-event on international tourism to the host country: A conceptual model and the case of the 1988 Seoul Olympics. *Journal of International Consumer Marketing* 6 (3/4), 205–226.

Kaplanidou, K. (2009) Relationships among behavioral intentions, cognitive event and destination images among different geographic regions of Olympic Games spectators. *Journal of Sport & Tourism* 14 (4), 249–272.

Kaspar, R. (1998) Sport, environment and culture. *Olympic Review* 20 (April/May), 1–5.

Keller, P. (2001) Sport and tourism: Introductory report. *Proceedings of the World Conference on Sport and Tourism, Barcelona, Spain, 22–23 February 2001*. Madrid: World Tourism Organization.

Kennedy, E. and Deegan, J. (2001) Seasonality in Irish tourism, 1973–1995. In T. Baum and S. Lundtorp (eds) *Seasonality and Tourism* (pp. 119–140). London: Pergamon.

Kerstetter, D. and Bricker, K. (2009) Exploring Fijian's sense of place after exposure to tourism development. *Journal of Sustainable Tourism* 17, 691–708.

Klemm, M. and Rawel, J. (2001) Extending the school holiday season: The case of Europcamp. In T. Baum and S. Lundtorp (eds) *Seasonality in Tourism* (pp. 141–152). London: Pergamon.

Klenosky, D., Gengler, C. and Mulvey, M. (1993) Understanding the factors influencing ski destination choice: A means-end analytic approach. *Journal of Leisure Research* 25, 362–379.

Koenig-Lewis, N. and Bischoff, E. (2005) Seasonality research: The state of the art. *International Journal of Tourism Research* 7, 201–219.

Kotler, P., Haider, D.H. and Rein, I. (1993) *Marketing Places: Attracting Investment, Industry, and Tourism to Cities, States and Nations*. New York: The Free Press.

Kreutzwiser, R. (1989) Supply. In G. Wall (ed.) *Outdoor Recreation in Canada* (pp. 19–42). Toronto: John Wiley & Sons.

Krippendorf, J. (1986) *The Holidaymakers: Understanding the Impact of Leisure and Travel*. London: Heinemann.

Krippendorf, J. (1995) Towards new tourism policies. In S. Medlik (ed.) *Managing Tourism*. Oxford: Butterworth-Heinemann.

Kulczycki, C. and Hyatt, C. (2005) Expanding the conceptualization of nostalgia sport tourism: Lessons learned from fans left behind after sport franchise relocation. *Journal of Sport Tourism* 10 (4), 273–294.

Kurtzman, J. and Zauhar, J. (1995) Tourism Sport International Council. *Annals of Tourism Research* 22 (3), 707–708.

Kyle, G., Bricker, K., Graefe, A. and Wickham, T. (2004a) An examination of recreationists' relationships with activities and settings. *Leisure Sciences* 26, 123–142.

Kyle, G. and Chick, G. (2007) The social construction of a sense of place. *Leisure Sciences* 29, 209–225.

Kyle, G., Graefe, A. and Manning, R. (2004b) Attached recreationists . . . Who are they? *Journal of Park and Recreation Administration* 22 (2), 65–84.

L'Etang, J. (2006) Public relations and sport in promotional culture. *Public Relations Review* 32, 386–394.

Laidlaw, C. (2010) *Somebody Stole My Game*. Auckland, New Zealand: Hodder Moa.

Law, A. (2001) Surfing the safety net: 'Dole bludging', 'surfies' and governmentality in Australia. *International Review for the Sociology of Sport* 36 (1), 25–40.

Law, C.M. (2002) *Urban Tourism: The Visitor Economy and the Growth of Large Cities.* London: Continuum.

Lawrence, C. (2010) 'How parkour works'. On WWW at http://adventure. howstuffworks.com/outdoor-activities/urban-sports/parkour.htm. Accessed 14.9.10.

Laws, E. (1991) *Tourism Marketing: Service and Quality Management Perspectives.* Cheltenham, England: Stanley Thornes Publishers.

Lawson, R., Thyne, M. and Young, T. (1997) *New Zealand Holidays: A Travel Lifestyles Study.* Dunedin, New Zealand: The Marketing Department, University of Otago.

Lee, C., Bergin-Seers, S., Galloway, G., O'Mahony, B. and McMurray, A. (2008) Seasonality in the tourism industry: Impacts and strategies. The CRC for Sustainable Tourism Pty Ltd. website. At http://www.crctourism.com.au/ WMS/Upload/ Resources/bookshop/80085% 20Lee_TourismIndustSeasonality% 20WEB.pdf. Accessed 21.3.10.

Leiper, N. (1981) Towards a cohesive curriculum for tourism: The case for a distinct discipline. *Annals of Tourism Research* 8 (1), 69–74.

Leiper, N. (1990) Tourist attraction systems. *Annals of Tourism Research* 17 (3), 367–384.

Leisure Time (2002) *Norway Cup* (Publication 44). Bekkelagshogda, Oslo, Norway.

Lesjø, J.H. (2000) Lillehammer 1994: Planning, figurations and the 'green' Winter Games. *International Review for the Sociology of Sport* 35 (3), 282–293.

Lew, A.A. (1987) A framework of tourist attraction research. *Annals of Tourism Research* 14 (3), 553–575.

Lew, A.A. (2001) Tourism and geography space. *Tourism Geographies* 3 (1), 1.

Lions Rugby (2005) History of the Lions. http://www.lionsrugby.com/. Accessed 16.5.05.

Liu, Z. (2003) Sustainable tourism development: A critique. *Journal of Sustainable Tourism* 11, 459–475.

Lockwood, A. and Guerrier, Y. (1990) Labour shortages in the international hotel industry. *Travel and Tourism Analyst* 6, 17–35.

Lopez Bonilla, J.M., Lopez Bonilla, L.M. and Sanz Altamira, B. (2006) Patterns of tourist seasonality in Spanish regions. *Tourism Planning & Development* 3 (3), 241–256.

Lorenzoni, I., Nicholson-Cole, S. and Whitmarsh, L. (2007) Barriers perceived to engaging with climate change among the UK Public and their policy implications. *Global Environmental Change* 17, 445–459.

Loverseed, H. (2000) Winter sports in North America. *Travel and Tourism Analyst* 6, 45–62.

Loverseed, H. (2001) Sports tourism in North America. *Travel and Tourism Analyst* 3, 25–41.

Low, S.M. and Altman, I. (1992) Place attachment: A conceptual inquiry. In I. Altman and S.M. Low (eds) *Place Attachment* (pp. 1–12). New York: Plenum Press.

Loy, J.W., McPherson, B.D. and Kenyon, G. (1978a) *Sport and Social Systems: A Guide to the Analysis of Problems and Literature*. Reading, MA: Addison-Wesley.

Loy, J.W., McPherson, B.D. and Kenyon, G. (1978b) Sport as a social phenomenon. In J.W. Loy, B.D. McPherson and G. Kenyon (eds) *Sport and Social Systems: A Guide to the Analysis of Problems and Literature* (pp. 3–26). Reading, MA: Addison-Wesley.

Lundtorp, S., Rassing, C.R. and Wanhill, S.R.C. (1999) The off-season is 'no season': The case of the Danish island of Bornholm. *Tourism Economic* 5 (1), 49–68.

MacCannell, D. (1973) Staged authenticity – Arrangements of social space in tourist settings. *American Journal of Sociology* 79 (3), 589–603.

MacCannell, D. (1976) *The Tourists: New Theory of the Leisure Class*. New York: Schoken.

Maguire, J. (1994) Sport, identity politics, and globalization: Diminishing contrasts and increasing varieties. *Sociology of Sport Journal* 11 (4), 398–427.

Maguire, J. (1999) *Global Sport: Identities, Societies and Civilisations*. Cambridge: Polity Press.

Maguire, J. (2002) *Sport Worlds: A Sociological Perspective*. Champaign, IL: Human Kinetics.

Maier, J. and Weber, W. (1993) Sport tourism in local and regional planning. *Tourism Recreation Research* 18 (2), 33–43.

Manfredo, M.J. and Driver, B.L. (1983) A test of concepts inherent in experience-based setting management for outdoor recreation areas. *Journal of Leisure Research* 15 (3), 263–283.

Mansfield, L. (2007) Involved-detachment: A balance of passion and reason in feminisms and gender-related research in sport, tourism and sports tourism. *Journal of Sport & Tourism* 12 (2), 115–141.

March, R. and Wilkinson, I. (2009) Conceptual tools for evaluating tourism partnerships. *Tourism Management* 30, 455–462.

Mason, D., Ramshaw, G. and Hinch, T. (2008) Sports facilities and transnational corporations: Anchors of urban tourism development. In C.M. Hall and T. Coles (eds) *International Business and Tourism: Global Issues, Contemporary Interactions* (pp. 220–237). London: Routledge.

Mason, D.S. and Duquette G.H. (2008a) Urban regimes and sport in North American cities: Seeking status through franchises, events and facilities. *International Journal of Sport Management and Marketing* 3 (3), 221–241.

Mason, D.S. and Duquette, G.H. (2008b) Exploring the relationship between local hockey franchises and tourism development. *Tourism Management* 29 (6), 1157–1165.

Mathieson, D. and Wall, G. (1987) *Tourism: Economic, Physical and Social Impacts*. London: Longman.

May, V. (1995) Environmental implications of the 1992 Winter Olympic Games. *Tourism Management* 16 (4), 269–275.

McConnell, R. and Edwards, M. (2000) Sport and identity in New Zealand. In C. Collins (ed.) *Sport and Society in New Zealand* (pp. 115–129). Palmerston North, New Zealand: Dunmore Press.

McEnnif, J. (1992) Seasonality of tourism demand in the European community. *Travel and Tourism Analyst* 3, 67–88.

McFee, G. (2007) Paradigms and possibilities. Or some concerns for the study of sport from the philosophy of science. *Sport, Ethics and Philosophy* 1 (1), 58–77.

McGuirk, P.M. and Rowe, D. (2001) 'Defining moments' and refining myths in the making of place identity: The Newcastle Knights and the Australian Rugby League Grand Final. *Australian Geographical Studies* 39 (1), 52–66.

McIntosh, A.J. and Prentice, R.C. (1999) Affirming authenticity: Consuming cultural heritage. *Annals of Tourism Research* 26, 589–612.

McKay, J. and Kirk, D. (1992) Ronald McDonald meets Baron De Coubertin: Prime time sport and commodification. *Sport and the Media* (Winter), 10–13.

McKercher, B. (1993) Some fundamental truths about tourism: Understanding tourism's social and environmental impacts. *Journal of Sustainable Tourism* 1 (1), 6–16.

McPherson, B.D., Curtis, J.E. and Loy, J.W. (1989) *The Social Significance of Sport: An Introduction to the Sociology of Sport.* Champaign, IL: Human Kinetics Books.

Meinig, D. (1979) The beholding eye. In D. Meinig (ed.) *The Interpretation of Ordinary Landscapes* (pp. 33–48). New York: Oxford University Press.

Melnic, M.J. and Jackson, S.J. (2002) Globalization American-style and reference idol selection: The importance of athlete celebrity others among New Zealand youth. *International Review for the Sociology of Sport* 37 (3/4), 429–448.

Merkel, U., Lines, G. and McDonald, I. (1998) The production and consumption of sport cultures: Introduction. In U. Merkel, G. Lines and I. McDonald (eds) *The Production and Consumption of Sport Cultures: Leisure, Culture and Commerce* (pp. v–xvi). Eastbourne, UK: Leisure Studies Association.

Millington, K., Locke, T. and Locke, A. (2001) Adventure travel. *Travel and Tourism Analyst* 4, 65–97.

Milne, S. and Ateljevic, I. (2004) Tourism economic development and the global–local nexus. In S. Williams (ed.) *Tourism: Critical Concepts in the Social Sciences* (pp. 81–103). London: Routledge.

Mintel (2004) Sports Tourism - International. *Travel and Tourism* Analyst, October 2004. Mintel Group.

Miossec, J.M. (1977) L'image touristique comme introduction ý la gÈographie du tourisme. *Annales de géographie* 86, 473.

Mitchell, L.S. and Murphy, P.E. (1991) Geography and tourism. *Annals of Tourism Research* 18 (1), 57–70.

Mittelstaedt, R. (1997) Indoor climbing walls: The sport of the nineties. *Journal of Physical Education, Recreation & Dance* 69 (9), 26–29.

Moen, J. and Fredman, P. (2007) Effects of climate change on Alpine skiing in Sweden. *Journal of Sustainable Tourism* 15 (4), 418–437.

Moragas Spa, M., Rivenburg, N.K. and Larson, J.F. (1995) *Television in the Olympics.* London: J. Libbey.

Morgan, M. (2007) 'We're not the Barmy Army!': Reflections on the sport tourist experience. *International Journal of Tourism Research* 9 (5), 361–372.

Morgan, M. and Wright R. (2008) Elite sports tours: special events with special challenges. Chapter 13 in Fyall, Robertson, Ali-Knight and Ladkin (eds) *International Perspectives of Festivals and Events*, Oxford: Elsevier

Morse, J. (2001) The Sydney 2000 Olympic Games: How the Australian Tourist Commission leveraged the games for tourism. *Journal of Vacation Marketing* 7 (2), 101–107.

Mortimer, A.J. (1991) *Recommendations for the Management of the Marine Turtle Population and Pulau Sipadan.* Kuala Lumpur, Malaysia: Worldwide Fund for Nature.

Moscardo, G. (2000) Cultural and heritage tourism: The great debates. In B. Faulkner, G. Moscardo and E. Laws (eds) *Tourism in the 21st Century: Lessons from Experience* (pp. 3–17). London: Continuum.

Mourdoukoutas, P.G. (1998) Seasonal employment, seasonal unemployment and unemployment compensation. *American Journal of Economics and Sociology* 47 (3), 315–329.

Moutinho, L., Dionisio, P. and Leal, C. (2007) Surf tribal behaviour: A sports marketing application. *Marketing Intelligence and Planning* 25, 668–690.

Mowforth, M. and Munt, I. (1998) *Tourism and Sustainability: New Tourism in the Third World*. London: Routledge.

Murphy, P.E. (1985) *Tourism: A Community Approach*. New York: Methuen.

Murray, D. and Dixon, L. (2000) Investigating the growth of 'instant' sports: Practical implications for community leisure service providers. *The ACHPER Healthy Lifestyles Journal* 47 (3/4), 27–31.

Murray, J. (1996) How seasonality affects the economic viability of Canadian tourism businesses. In K. MacKay and K.R. Boyd (eds) *Tourism for All Seasons: Using Research to Meet the Challenge of Seasonality* (Conference Proceedings of the Travel and Tourism Research Association – Canada Chapter, Ottawa, Canada) (pp. 135–146). Ottawa, Canada: Travel and Tourism Research Association.

Musa, G. (2002) Sipadan: A SCUBA-diving paradise: An analysis of tourism impact, diver satisfaction and tourism management. *Tourism Geographies* 4 (2), 195–209.

Mykletun, R.J. and Vedø, K. (2002) BASE jumping in Lysefjord, Norway: A sustainable but controversial type of coastal tourism. Paper presented at the Tourism Research 2002, Cardiff, UK, 4–7 September 2002.

Nahrstedt, W. (2004) Wellness: A new perspective for leisure centres, health tourism, and spas in Europe on the global health market. In K. Weiermair and C. Mathies (eds) *The Tourism and Leisure Industry: Shaping the Future* (pp. 181–198). Binghampton, NY: The Haworth Press.

Nash, R. and Johnston, S. (1998) The case of Euro96: Where did the party go? Paper presented at the Sport in the City Conference, Sheffield, UK, 2–4 July 1998.

Nauright, J. (1996) 'A besieged tribe'?: Nostalgia, white cultural identity and the role of rugby in a changing South Africa. *International Review for the Sociology of Sport* 31 (1), 69–89.

Nauright, J. (1997) Masculinity, muscular Islam and popular culture: 'Coloured' rugby's cultural symbolism in working-class Cape Town c. 1930–70. *The International Journal of the History of Sport* 14 (1), 184–190.

New Zealand Tourism Board (1998) All Blacks join forces with McCully, NZTB in South Africa. *Tourism News* 2.

Nicholls, J. (1989) *The Competitive Ethos and Democratic Education*. Cambridge, MA: Harvard University Press.

Nicholls, S. (2006) Climate change, tourism and outdoor recreation in Europe. *Managing Leisure* 11, 151–163.

Nogawa, H., Yamaguchi, Y. and Hagi, Y. (1996) An empirical research study on Japanese sport tourism in sport-for-all events: Case studies of a single-night event and a multiple-night event. *Journal of Travel Research* 35 (2), 46–54.

Nonaka, I. (1994) A dynamic theory of organisational knowledge creation. *Organisational Science* 5 (1), 14–37.

Nowak, J., Petit, S. and Sahli, M. (2009) Tourism and globalization: The international division of tourism production. *Journal of Travel Research* 47, 1–19.

O'Connor, R.E., Bord, R.J. and Fisher, A. (1999) Risk perception, general environmental beliefs, and willingness to address climate change. *Risk Analysis* 19 (3), 461–470.

O'Gorman, K. and Thompson, K. (2007) Tourism and culture in Mongolia: The case of the Ulaanbaatar Naadam. In R. Butler and T. Hinch (eds) *Tourism and Indigenous Peoples*. London: Elsevier Butterworth-Heinemann.

Olds, K. (1998) Urban mega-events, evictions and housing rights: The Canadian case. *Current Issues in Tourism* 1 (1), 2–46.

Olympic Co-ordination Authority (1997) *State of Play: A Report on Sydney 2000 Olympics Planning and Construction*. Sydney: Olympic Co-ordination Authority, New South Wales Government.

Orams, M. (1999) *Marine Tourism: Development, Impacts and Management*. London: Routledge.

Otto, I. and Heath, E.T. (2009) The potential contribution of the 2010 Soccer World Cup to climate change: An exploratory study among tourism industry stakeholders in the Tshwane Metropole of South Africa. *Journal of Sport Tourism* 14 (2/3), 169–191.

Page, S.J., Brunt, P., Busby, G. and Connell, J. (2001) *Tourism: A Modern Synthesis*. London: Thomson Learning.

Page, S.J. and Hall, C.M. (2003) *Managing Urban Tourism*. Harlow, England: Pearson Education Ltd.

Page, S.J., Steele, W. and Connell, J. (2006) Analysing the promotion of adventure tourism: A case study of Scotland. *Journal of Sport & Tourism* 11 (1), 51–76.

Pawlowski, A. (2008) How many dimensions does sustainable development have? *Sustainable Development* 16, 81–90.

Pearce, D.G. (1987) *Tourism Today: A Geographical Analysis*. Harlow, England: Longman Scientific and Technical.

Pearce, D.G. (1989) *Tourism Development* (2nd edn). Harlow, England: Longman Scientific and Technical.

Pearce, P. (1988) *The Ulysses Factor: Evaluating Visitors in Tourist Settings*. New York: Springer-Verlag.

Pelling, M., High, C., Dearing, J. and Smith, D. (2008) Shadow spaces for social learning: A relational understanding of adaptive capacity to climate change within organisations. *Environment and Planning* 40, 867–884.

Pesqueux, Y. (2009) Sustainable development: A vague and ambiguous 'theory'. *Society and Business Review* 4, 231–245.

Pettersson, R. and Getz, D. (2009) Event experiences in time and space: A study of visitors to the 2007 World Alpine Ski Championships in Åre, Sweden. *Scandinavian Journal of Hospitality and Tourism* 9 (2/3), 308–326.

Pigeassou, C. (2002) Sport tourism as a growth sector: The French perspective. In S. Gammon and J. Kurtzman (eds) *Sport Tourism: Principles and Practice* (Vol. 76, pp. 129–140). Eastbourne, UK: Leisure Studies Association.

Pigram, J.J. and Wahab, S. (1997) Sustainable tourism in a changing world. In S. Wahab and J.J. Pigram (eds) *Tourism, Development and Growth* (pp. 17–32). London: Routledge.

Pillay, U. and Bass, O. (2008) Mega-events as a Response to Poverty Reduction: The 2010 FIFA World Cup and its Urban Development Implications. Urban Forum 19, 329–346.

Pitts, B.G. (1997) Sports tourism and niche markets: Identification and analysis of the growing lesbian and gay sports tourism industry. *Journal of Vacation Marketing* 5 (1), 31–50.

Plog, S. (1972) Why destination areas rise and fall in popularity. Paper presented at the Southern California Chapter of the Travel Research Bureau, San Diego, CA, 10 October 1972.

Poon, A. (1993) All-inclusive resorts. *Travel and Tourism Analyst* 2, 54–68.

Porteous, B. (2000) Sports development: Glasgow. *Leisure Manager* 18 (11), 18–21.

Priestley, G.K. (1995) Sports tourism: The case of golf. In G.J. Ashworth and A.G.J. Dietvorst (eds) *Tourism and Spatial Transformations: Implications for Policy and Planning* (pp. 205–223). Wallingford, UK: CAB International.

Preuss, H. (2007) The conceptualisation and measurement of mega sport event legacies. *Journal of Sport & Tourism* 12 (3/4), 207–227.

Proshansky, H.M., Fabian, A.K. and Kaminoff, R. (1983) Place-identity: Physical world socialization of the self. *Journal of Environmental Psychology* 3, 57–83.

Pyo, S., Cook, R. and Howell, R.L. (1991) Summer Olympic tourist market. In S. Medlik (ed.) *Managing Tourism* (pp. 191–198). Oxford: Butterworth-Heinemann.

Pyo, S., Uysal, M. and Howell, R. (1988) Seoul Olympics visitor preferences. *Tourism Management* 9 (1), 68–72.

Ramshaw, G. and Gammon, S. (2007) 'More than just Nostalgia? Exploring the heritage/sport tourism nexus'. In S. Gammon and G. Ramshaw (eds) *Heritage, Sport and Tourism: Sporting Pasts – Tourist Futures* (pp. 9–22). London: Routledge.

Ramshaw, G. and Gammon, S. (2010) On home ground? Twickenham stadium tours and the construction of sport heritage. *Journal of Heritage Tourism* 5 (2), 87–102.

Randles, S. and Mander, S. (2009) Practice(s) and ratchet(s): A sociological examination of frequent flying. In S. Gössling and P. Upham (eds) *Climate Change and Aviation: Issues, Challenges and Solutions* (pp. 245–271). London: Earthscan.

Redmond, G. (1990) Points of increasing contact: Sport and tourism in the modern world. In A. Tomlinson (ed.) *Sport in Society: Policy, Politics and Culture* (pp. 158–167). Eastbourne, UK: Leisure Studies Association.

Redmond, G. (1991) Changing styles of sports tourism: Industry/consumer interactions in Canada, the USA and Europe. In M.T. Sinclair and M.J. Stabler (eds) *The Tourism Industry: An International Analysis* (pp. 107–120). Wallingford, UK: CAB International.

Reeves, M.R. (2000) Evidencing the sport–tourism relationship: A case study approach. Unpublished PhD thesis, Loughborough University.

Reisinger, Y. and Steiner, C.J. (2005) Reconceptualising object authenticity. *Annals of Tourism Research* 33, 65–86.

Relph, E. (1976) *Place and Placelessness*. London: Pion Limited.

Relph, E. (1985) Geographical experiences and being-in-the-world: The phenomenological origins of geography. In D. Seamon and R. Mugerauer (eds) *Dwelling, Place and Environment* (pp. 15–38). Dordrecht, The Netherlands: Nijhoff.

Reuters (2010) Vancouver's 2010 security costs rise sharply. On WWW at http://ca.reuters.com/article/sportsNews/idCATRE51J06W20090220. Accessed 31.5.11.

Richards, G. (1996) Skilled consumption and UK ski holidays. *Tourism Management* 17, 25–34.

Ritchie, J.B.R. (1984) Assessing the impact of hallmark events: Conceptual and research issues. *Journal of Travel Research* 13 (1), 2–11.

Robinson, H. (1979) *A Geography of Tourism*. London: MacDonald and Evans.

Robinson, J.S. (2010) The place of the stadium: English football beyond the fans. *Sport in Society* 13 (6), 1012–1026.

Robinson, T. and Gammon, S. (2004) A question of primary and secondary motives: Revisiting and applying the sport tourism framework. *Journal of Sport Tourism* 9, 1–11.

Roche, M. (1994) Mega-events and urban policy. *Annals of Tourism Research* 21, 1–19.

Roehl, W., Ditton, R., Holland, S. and Perdue, R. (1993) Developing new tourism products: Sport fishing in the south-east United States. *Tourism Management* 14, 279–288.

Rooney, J.F. (1988) Mega sports events as tourist attractions: A geographical analysis. Paper presented at the Tourism Research: Expanding the Boundaries, Nineteenth Annual Conference of the Travel and Tourism Research Association, Montreal, Canada.

Rooney, J.F. (1992) *Atlas of American Sport*. New York: Macmillan Publishing Co.

Rooney, J.F. and Pillsbury, R. (1992) Sports regions of America. *American Demographics* 14 (10), 1–10.

Roselló Nadel, J., Riera Font, A. and Sanso Roselló, A. (2004) The economic determinants of seasonal patterns. *Annals of Tourism Research* 31 (3), 697–711.

Rowe, D. (1996) The global love-match: Sport and television. *Media, Culture and Society* 18, 565–582.

Rowe, D. and Lawrence, G. (1996) Beyond national sport: Sociology, history and postmodernity. *Sporting Traditions* 12 (2), 3–16.

Rowe, D., Lawrence, G., Miller, T. and McKay, J. (1994) Global sport? Core concern and peripheral vision. *Media, Culture and Society* 16, 661–675.

Ruskin, H. (1987) Selected views of socio-economic aspects of outdoor recreation, outdoor education and sport tourism. In M. Garmise (ed.) *Proceedings of the International Seminar and Workshop on Outdoor Education, Recreation and Sport Tourism* (pp. 18–37). Israel: Emmanuel Gill Publishing.

Ryan, C. (1995) *Researching Tourist Satisfaction: Issues, Concepts, Problems*. London: Routledge.

Ryan, C., Smee, A. and Murphy, S. (1996) Creating a database of events in New Zealand: Early results. *Festival Management and Event Tourism* 4 (3/4), 151–156.

Saarinen, J. (2006) Traditions of sustainability in tourism studies. *Annals of Tourism Research* 33, 1121–1140.

Schaffer, W. and Davidson, L. (1985) *Economic Impact of the Falcons on Atlanta: 1984*. Suwanee, GA: The Atlanta Falcons.

Schlossberg, H. (1996) *Sports Marketing*. Oxford: Blakewell.

Schollmann, A., Perkins, H.C. and Moore, K. (2001) Rhetoric, claims making and conflict in touristic place promotion: The case of central Christchurch, New Zealand. *Tourism Geographies* 3 (3), 300–325.

Schreyer, R., Lime, D.W. and Williams, D.R. (1984) Characterizing the influence of past experience on recreation behaviour. *Journal of Leisure Research* 16 (1), 34–50.

Schulenkorf, N. (2009) An ex ante framework for the strategic study of social utility of sport events. *Tourism and Hospitality Research* 9 (2), 120–131.

Scott, D. (2006) US ski industry adaption to climate change. In S. Gossling and C.M. Hall (eds) *Tourism and Global Environmental Change*. London: Routledge.

Scott, D., Jones, B., Lemieux, C., McBoyle, G., Mills, B., Svenson, S. and Wall, G. (2002) *The Vulnerability of Winter Recreation to Climatic Change in Ontario's Lakelands Tourism Region* (Occasional Paper 18). Waterloo, ON: Department of Geography, University of Waterloo.

Scott, D. and McBoyle, G. (2007) Climate change adaptation in the ski industry. *Mitigation and Adaption Strategies for Global Change* 12, 1411–1431.

Scott, D., McBoyle, G. and Minogue, A. (2007) Climate change and Quebec's ski industry. *Global Environmental Change* 17 (2), 181–190.

Selin, S. and Chavez, D. (1995) Developing an evolutionary tourism partnership model. *Annals of Tourism Research* 22 (4), 844–856.

Shapcott, M. (1998) Commentary on 'Urban mega-events, evictions and housing rights: The Canadian case' by Chris Olds. *Current Issues in Tourism* 1 (2), 195–196.

Sherlock, K. (2001) Revisiting the concept of hosts and guests. *Tourist Studies* 1 (3), 271–295.

Shipway, R. and Jones, I. (2007) Running away from home: Understanding visitor experiences and behaviour at sport tourism events. *International Journal of Tourism Research* 9, 373–383.

Silk, M. and Andrews, D.L. (2001) Beyond a boundary? Sport, transnational adverstising, and the reimaging of national culture. *Journal of Sport and Social Issues* 25 (2), 180–201.

Silk, M. and Jackson, S.J. (2000) Globalisation and sport in New Zealand. In C. Collins (ed.) *Sport in New Zealand Society* (pp. 99–113). Palmerston North, New Zealand: Dunmore Press.

Simpson, J.A. and Weiner, E.S.C. (eds) (1989) *The Oxford English Dictionary* (Vol. XVII, 2nd edn). Oxford: Clarendon Press.

Sipadan (2010) Why Sipadan? On WWW at http://www.sipadan.com/sipadan.php. Accessed 14.5.10.

Sjoberg, L. (2000) Factors in risk perception. *Risk Analysis* 20 (1), 11–25.

Smith, A. (2005) Reimaging the city: The value of sport initiatives. *Annals of Tourism Research* 32, 217–236.

Smith, A. (2009) Theorising the relationship between major sport events and social sustainability. *Journal of Sport Tourism* 14 (2/3), 109–120.

Smith, A. (2010) The development of 'sports-city' zones and their potential value as tourism resources for urban areas. *European Planning Studies* 18 (3), 385–410.

Smith, B. and Weed, M. (2007) The potential of narrative research in sports tourism. *Journal of Sport & Tourism* 12 (3/4), 249–269.

Snelgrove, R., Taks, M., Chalip, C. and Green, B.C. (2008) How visitors and locals at a sport event differ in motives and identity. *Journal of Sport & Tourism* 13 (3), 165–180.

Snyder, E. (1991) Sociology of nostalgia: Halls of fame and museums in America. *Sociology of Sport Journal* 8, 228–238.

Sonmez, S.F., Apolstolopoulos, Y. and Talow, P. (1999) Tourism in crisis: Managing the effects of terrorism. *Journal of Travel Research* 38, 13–18.

Spivack, S.E. (1998) Health spa development in the US: A burgeoning component of sport tourism. *Journal of Vacation Marketing* 4, 65–77.

Standeven, J. and De Knop, P. (1999) *Sport Tourism.* Champaign, IL: Human Kinetics.

Stanley, D. and Moore, S. (1997) Counting the leaves: The dimensions of seasonality in Canadian tourism. Paper presented at the Proceedings of the Travel and Tourism Research Association, Canadian Chapter, University of Manitoba, Winnipeg, MB.

Stansfield, C.J. (1978) The development of modern seaside resorts. *Parks and Recreation* 5 (10), 14–46.

Stebbins, R.A. (2007) *Serious Leisure.* London: Transaction Publishers.

Stevens, T. (2001) Stadia and tourism related facilities. *Travel and Tourism Analyst* 2, 59–73.

Stevens, T. and Wooton, G. (1997) Sports stadia and arena: Realising their full potential. *Tourism Recreation Research* 22 (2), 49–56.

Stevenson, D. (1997) Olympic arts: Sydney 2000 and the Cultural Olympiad. *International Review for the Sociology of Sport* 32 (3), 227–238.

Stewart, B. (2001) Fab club. *Australian Leisure Management* (October/November), 16–19.

Stewart, B. and Smith, A. (2000) Australian sport in a postmodern age. *International Journal of the History of Sport* 17 (2/3), 278–304.

Stewart, J.J. (1987) The commodification of sport. *International Review for the Sociology of Sport* 22, 171–190.

Sugden, J. and Tomlinson, A. (1996) What's left when the circus leaves town? An evaluation of World Cup USA 1994. *Sociology of Sport Journal* 13 (3), 238–258.

Swarbrooke, J. and Horner, S. (1999) *Consumer Behaviour in Tourism*. Oxford: Butterworth-Heinemann.

Tabata, R. (1992) Scuba diving holidays. In B. Weiler and C.M. Hall (eds) *Special Interest Tourism* (pp. 171–184). London: Belhaven Press.

Taks, M., Chalip, L., Green, C.B., Kesenne, S. and Martyn, S. (2009) Factors affecting repeat visitation and flow-on tourism as sources of event strategy sustainability. *Journal of Sport Tourism* 14 (2/3), 121–142.

Tassiopoulos, D. and Haydam, N. (2008) Golf tourists in South Africa: A demand-side study of a niche market in sports tourism. *Tourism Management* 29 (5), 870–882.

Teigland, J. (1999) Mega-events and impacts on tourism: The predictions and realities of the Lillehammer Olympics. *Impact Assessment and Project Appraisal* 17 (4), 305–317.

Thamnopoulos, Y. and Gargalianos, D. (2002) Ticketing the large scale events: The case of Sydney 2000 Olympic Games. *Facilities* 20 (1/2), 22–33.

The Outspan Group Inc. in association with Research Resolutions and Consulting Ltd. (2009) The economic impacts of cultural and sport tourism in Canada. Report prepared for Canadian Heritage, Government of Canada, Ottawa, Canada. On WWW at http://www.pch.gc.ca/pc-ch/org/sectr/inter/econ_impct2007/106-eng.cfm. Accessed 31.5.11.

Thibault, L. (2009) Globalization of sport: An inconvenient truth. *Journal of Sport Management* 2, 1–20.

Thompson, S.M. (1985) Women in sport: Some participation patterns in New Zealand. *Leisure Studies* 4 (3), 321–331.

Thomson, R. (2000) Physical activity through sport and leisure: Traditional versus non-competitive activities. *Journal of Physical Education New Zealand* 33 (1), 34–39.

Timothy, D. and Boyd, S. (2006) Heritage tourism in the 21st century: Valued traditions and new perspectives. *Journal of Heritage Tourism* 1 (1), 1–16.

Timothy, D. and Boyd, S.W. (2002) *Heritage Tourism*. London: Prentice-Hall.

Tokarski, W. (1993) Leisure, sports and tourism: The role of sports in and outside holiday clubs. In A.J. Veal, P. Jonson and G. Cushman (eds) *Leisure and Tourism: Social and Environmental Change* (pp. 684–686). Sydney: World Leisure and Recreation Association, University of Technology.

Tomlinson, A. and Young, C. (eds) (2006) *National Identity and Global Sports Events: Culture, Politics and Spectacle in the Olympics and the Football World Cup*. Albany, NY: State University of New York Press.

Tourist Authorities of Göteborg (2002) Gothia Cup. On WWW at http://www.gothiacup.se. Accessed 3.10.02.

Travel News (2010) Sport tourism – Britain's great cash cow. On WWW at http://www.breakingtravelnews.com/news/article/sport-tourists-flock-to-britain/. Accessed 31.5.11.

Tuan, Y. (1974) *Topophilia: A Study of Environmental Perception, Attitudes, and Values*. Englewood Cliffs, NJ: Prentice-Hall.

Tuck, J. (2003) Making sense of emerald commotion: rugby union, national identity and Ireland. *Identities: Global Studies in Culture and Power* 10 (4), 495–515.

Tuppen, J. (2000) The restructuring of winter sports resorts in the French Alps: Problems, processes and policies. *International Journal of Tourism Research* 2 (5), 227–344.

Turco, D.M., Riley, R. and Swart, K. (2002) *Sport Tourism*. Morgantown, WV: Fitness Information Technology.

Twigger-Ross, C.L. and Uzzell, D.L. (1996) Place identity processes. *Journal of Environmental Psychology* 16, 205–220.

Universiti Kebangsaan Malaysia (UKM) (1990) *Assessment of Development Impacts on Pulau Sipadan, Kampus Sabah, Kota Kinabalu, Malaysia*. Kuala Lumpur, Malaysia: UKM.

Urry, J. (1990) *The Tourist Gaze*. London: Sage Publications.

Van Wynsberghe, R. and Ritchie, I. (1998) *(Ir)Relevant Ring: The Symbolic Consumption of the Olympic Logo in Postmodern Media Culture*. Albany, NY: State University of New York Press.

Voumard, S. (1995) Jonah's big date. *The Sydney Morning Herald*, 25 November, 14.

Vuletich, S. (2005) *The Economic Impact of the 2005 DHL Lions Series on New Zealand*. Report prepared by Covec Limited. Auckland: October 2005.

Wahab, S. and Cooper, C. (2001) *Tourism in the Age of Globalisation*. London: Routledge.

Walker, G., Hinch, T.D. and Higham, J.E.S. (2010) Athletes as tourists: Mode of experience and achievement orientation. *Journal of Sport & Tourism* 15 (4), 287–305.

Walker, G.J. and Virden, R.J. (2005) Constraints on outdoor recreation. In E. Jackson (ed.) *Constraints to Leisure* (201–219). State College, PA: Venture Publishing.

Walker, S. (2001) Sport mad nation? *Australian Leisure Management* (October/November), 32–35.

Wall, G. (1997) Sustainable tourism – Unsustainable development. In S. Wahab and J.J. Pigram (eds) *Tourism, Development and Growth* (pp. 33–49). London: Routledge.

Wang, N. (1999) Rethinking authenticity in tourism experience. *Annals of Tourism Research* 26 (2), 349–370.

Washington, R.E. and Karen, D. (2001) Sport and Society. *Annual Review of Sociology* 27, 187–212.

Watson, A.E. and Roggenbuck, J.W. (1991) The influence of past experience on wilderness choice. *Journal of Leisure Research* 23 (1), 21–36.

Weaver, D. and Oppermann, M. (2000) *Tourism Management*. Brisbane, Australia: John Wiley & Sons.

Webb, S. (2005) Strategic partnerships for sport tourism destinations. In J.E.S. Higham (ed.) *Sport Tourism Destinations: Issues, Opportunities and Analysis* (pp. 136–150). Elsevier: Oxford.

Webb, S. and Magnussen, B. (2002) Evaluating major sports events as cultural icons and economic drivers: A case study of Rugby World Cup 1999. Paper presented at the Tourism Research Conference 2002, Cardiff.

Wedemeyer, B. (1999) Sport and terrorism. In J. Riordan and A. Kruger (eds) *The International Politics of Sport in the 20th Century* (pp. 217–233). London: E and FN Spon.

Weed, M.E. (1999) 'More than sports holidays': An overview of the sport-tourism link. In M. Scarrott (ed.) *Exploring Sports Tourism: Proceedings of a SPRIG*

Seminar, *University of Sheffield, 15 April 1999* (pp. 6–28). Sheffield, UK: Sheffield Hallam University.

Weed, M.E. (2002) Football hooligans as undesirable sports tourists: Some meta-analytical speculations. In S. Gammon and J. Kurtzman (eds) *Sport Tourism: Principles and Practice* (pp. 35–52). Eastbourne, UK: Leisure Studies Association.

Weed, M.E. (2006) Sports tourism research 2000–2004: A systematic review of knowledge and a meta-evaluation of method. *Journal of Sport & Tourism* 11, 5–30.

Weed, M.E. (2008a) *Sport & Tourism: A Reader*. London: Routledge.

Weed, M.E. (2008b) *Olympic Tourism*. Elsevier: Oxford.

Weed, M.E. (2009a) Global trends and sports tourism. *Journal of Sport Tourism* 14, 1–4.

Weed, M.E. (2009b) Progress in sports tourism research? A meta-review and exploration of futures. *Tourism Management* 30, 615–628.

Weed, M.E. (2010) Sport fans and travel – Is 'being there' always important. *Journal of Sport & Tourism* 15, 103–109.

Weed, M.E. and Bull, C. (1997a) Integrating sport and tourism: A review of regional policies in England. *Progress in Tourism and Hospitality Research* 3 (2), 129–148.

Weed, M.E. and Bull, C. (1997b) Influences on sport tourism relations in Britain: The effects of government policy. *Tourism Recreation Research* 22 (2), 5–12.

Weed, M.E. and Bull, C. (2009) *Sports Tourism: Participants, Policy and Providers* (2nd edn). Oxford: Butterworth-Heinemann.

Weed, M.E. and Bull, C.J. (2003) *Sports Tourism: Participants, Policy and Providers*. Oxford: Butterworth-Heinemann.

Weed, M.W. (2005) Sports tourism theory and method – Concepts, issues and epistemologies. *Sport Management Quarterly* 5 (3), 229–242.

Weighill, A.J. (2002) Canadian domestic sport travel in 2001. Report prepared for Statistics Canada and the Canadian Tourism Commission, Ottawa, Canada.

Wheaton, B. (2000) 'Just do it?': Consumption, commitment, and identity in the windsurfing subculture. *Sociology of Sport Journal* 17 (3), 254–274.

Wheaton, B. (2004) *Understanding Lifestyle Sports*. New York: Routledge.

Wheaton, B. (2007) After sport culture: Rethinking sport and post-subcultural theory. *Journal of Sport and Social Issues* 31, 283–307.

Wheeller, B. (1991) Tourism's troubled times: Responsible tourism is not the answer. *Tourism Management* (June), 91–96.

White, P. and Wilson, B. (1999) Distinctions in the stands. An investigation of Bourdieu's 'habitus', socioeconomic status and sport spectatorship in Canada. *International Review for the Sociology of Sport* 34 (3), 245–264.

Whitson, D. (2004) Bringing the world to Canada: 'The periphery of the centre'. *Third World Quarterly* 25 (7), 1215–1232.

Whitson, D. and Macintosh, D. (1996) The global circus: International sport, tourism and the marketing of cities. *Journal of Sport and Social Issues* 23, 278–295.

Wilbanks, T.J. (2003) Integrating climate change and sustainable development in a place-based context. *Climate Policy* 3 (1), 147–154.

Wiley, C.E., Shaw, S.M. and Havitz, M.E. (2000) Men's and women's involvement in sports: An examination of the gendered aspects of leisure involvement. *Leisure Sciences* 22 (1), 19–31.

Williams, A.M. and Shaw, G. (eds) (1988) *Tourism and Economic Development: Western European Experiences*. London: Belhaven.

Williams, D. (1988) Measuring perceived similarity among outdoor recreation activities: A comparison of visual and verbal stimulus presentations. *Leisure Sciences* 10, 153–166.

Williams, D., Patterson, M., Roggenbuck, J. and Watson, A. (1992) Beyond the commodity metaphor: Examining emotional and symbolic attachment to place. *Leisure Sciences* 14, 29–46.

Williams, J. (1994) The local and the global in English soccer and the rise of satellite television. *Sociology of Sport Journal* 11 (4), 376–397.

Wolfsegger, C., Gossling, S. and Scott, D. (2008) Climate change risk appraisal in the Austrian ski industry. *Tourism Review International* 12, 13–23.

Wood, E. (1981) *Semporna Marine Park Survey: Expedition Report and Recommendations* (Project MAL 134). Kuala Lumpur, Malaysia: Worldwide Fund for Nature.

Wood, E., George, D., Dipper, F., Lane, D. and Wood, C. (1993) *Pulau Sipadan: Meeting the Challenge of Conservation* (Project MYS 233/9). Kuala Lumpur, Malaysia: Worldwide Fund for Nature.Wood, E., Wood, C., George, D., Dipper, F. and Lane, D. (1995) *Pulau Sipadan: Survey and Monitoring* (Project MYS 319/95). Kuala Lumpur, Malaysia: Worldwide Fund for Nature.

World Commission on Environment and Development (1987) *Our Common Future (The Bruntland Report)*. London: Oxford University Press.

World Tourism Organization (1981) *Technical Handbook on the Collection and Presentation of Domestic and International Tourism Statistics*. Madrid: World Tourism Organization.

World Tourism Organization (1994) *National and Regional Tourism Planning: Methodologies and Case Studies*. London: Routledge.

World Tourism Organization (2001) *Tourism After 11 September 2001: Analysis, Remedial Actions and Prospects* (Special Report, Number 18, Market Intelligence and Promositon Section). Madrid: World Tourism Organization.

World Tourism Organization and International Olympic Committee (2001) *Sport and Tourism: Sport Activities During the Outbound Holidays of the Germans, the Dutch and the French*. Madrid: The World Tourism Organization and International Olympic Committee.

Xiang, Z. and Gretzel, U. (2010) Role of social media in online travel information search. *Tourism Management*, 31 (2).

Yang, L. and Wall, G. (2009) Ethnic tourism: A framework and an application. *Tourism Management* 30, 559–570.

Yeoman, I., Brass, D. and McMahon-Beattie, U. (2007) Current issue in tourism: The authentic tourist. *Tourism Management* 28, 1128–1138.

Yiannakis, A. (1975) A theory of sport stratification. *Sport Sociology Bulletin* 4, 22–32.

Yusof, A. and Douvis, J. (2001) An examination of sport tourist profiles. *Journal of Sport Tourism* 6 (3), 1–10.

Zhu, P. (2009) Studies on sustainable development of ecological sports tour resources and its industry. *Journal of Sustainable Development* 2, 80–83.

Index

Women's British Open Golf Championship 162
World Badminton Championship 162
World Commission on Environment and Development (WCED) 62

World Heli Challenge (*see also* Wanaka) 128
World Tourism Organization (WTO) 19-20, 36, 42, 44, 45, 65, 99-100, 182, 207

Yachting 141, 180